CAPTAIN MARVEL

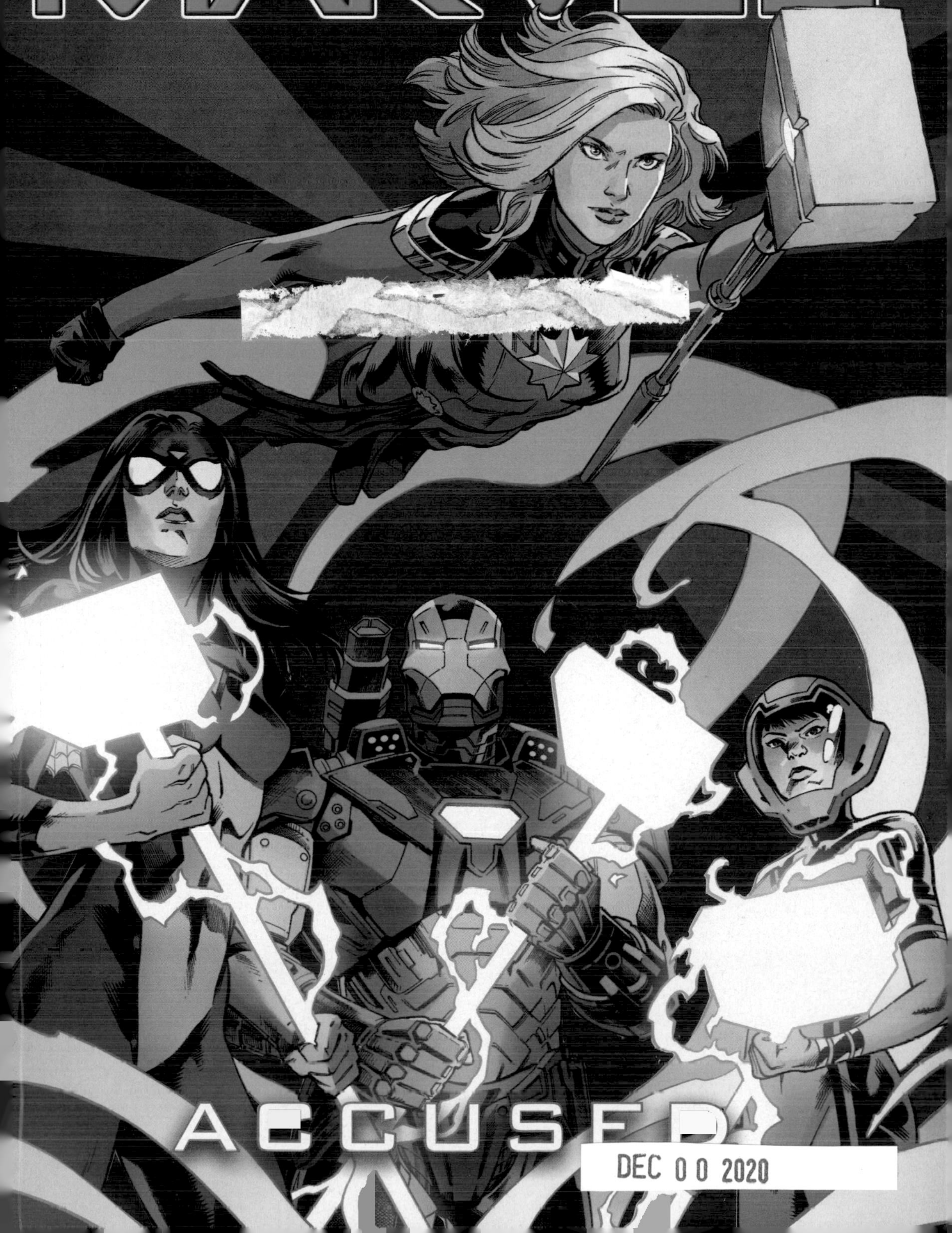

ACCUSED

Born to a Kree mother and a human father, former U.S. Air Force pilot **CAROL DANVERS** became a super hero when a Kree device activated her latent powers. Since then she's become an Avenger and Earth's Mightiest Hero.

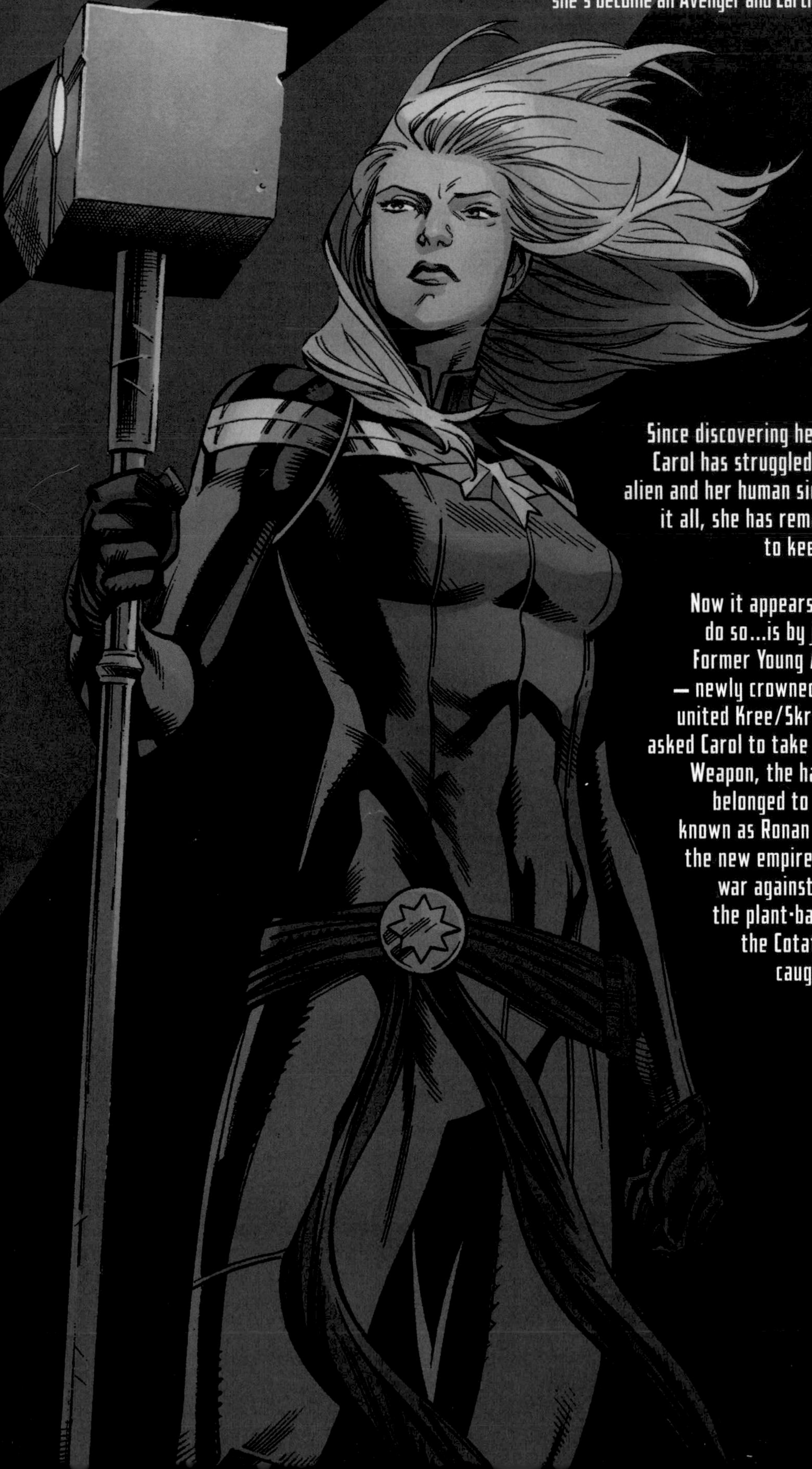

Since discovering her Kree heritage, Carol has struggled to reconcile her alien and her human sides, but through it all, she has remained committed to keeping Earth safe.

Now it appears the only way to do so...is by joining the Kree. Former Young Avenger Hulkling — newly crowned emperor of the united Kree/Skrull Empire — has asked Carol to take up the Universal Weapon, the hammer that once belonged to the Kree Soldier known as Ronan the Accuser. For the new empire is preparing for war against an old enemy — the plant-based aliens called the Cotati — and Earth is caught in the middle.

CAPTAIN MARVEL

ACCUSED

KELLY THOMPSON
Writer

CORY SMITH
Penciler

ADRIANO DI BENEDETTO
Inker

TAMRA BONVILLAIN
Color Artist

VC's CLAYTON COWLES
Letterer

JORGE MOLINA
Cover Art

SARAH BRUNSTAD
Editor

WIL MOSS
Senior Editor

Collection Editor JENNIFER GRÜNWALD
Assistant Managing Editor MAIA LOY
Assistant Managing Editor LISA MONTALBANO
Editor, Special Projects MARK D. BEAZLEY
VP Production & Special Projects JEFF YOUNGQUIST

Book Designers STACIE ZUCKER & ADAM DEL RE with
CLAYTON COWLES & NICK RUSSELL
SVP Print, Sales & Marketing DAVID GABRIEL
Editor in Chief C.B. CEBULSKI

CAPTAIN MARVEL VOL. 4: ACCUSED. Contains material originally published in magazine form as CAPTAIN MARVEL (2019) #18-21 and EMPYRE (2020) #2. First printing 2020. ISBN 978-1-302-92562-8. Published by MARVEL WORLDWIDE, INC., a subsidiary of MARVEL ENTERTAINMENT, LLC. OFFICE OF PUBLICATION: 1290 Avenue of the Americas, New York, NY 10104. © 2020 MARVEL No similarity between any of the names, characters, persons, and/or institutions in this magazine with those of any living or dead person or institution is intended, and any such similarity which may exist is purely coincidental. **Printed in Canada.** KEVIN FEIGE, Chief Creative Officer; DAN BUCKLEY, President, Marvel Entertainment; JOHN NEE, Publisher; JOE QUESADA, EVP & Creative Director; TOM BREVOORT, SVP of Publishing; DAVID BOGART, Associate Publisher & SVP of Talent Affairs; Publishing & Partnership; DAVID GABRIEL, VP of Print & Digital Publishing; JEFF YOUNGQUIST, VP of Production & Special Projects; DAN CARR, Executive Director of Publishing Technology; ALEX MORALES, Director of Publishing Operations, DAN EDINGTON, Managing Editor; RICKEY PURDIN, Director of Talent Relations; SUSAN CRESPI, Production Manager; STAN LEE, Chairman Emeritus. For information regarding advertising in Marvel Comics or on Marvel.com, please contact Vit DeBellis, Custom Solutions & Integrated Advertising Manager, at vdebellis@marvel.com. For Marvel subscription inquiries, please call 888-511-5480. **Manufactured between 10/2/2020 and 11/3/2020 by SOLISCO PRINTERS, SCOTT, QC, CANADA.**

10 9 8 7 6 5 4 3 2 1

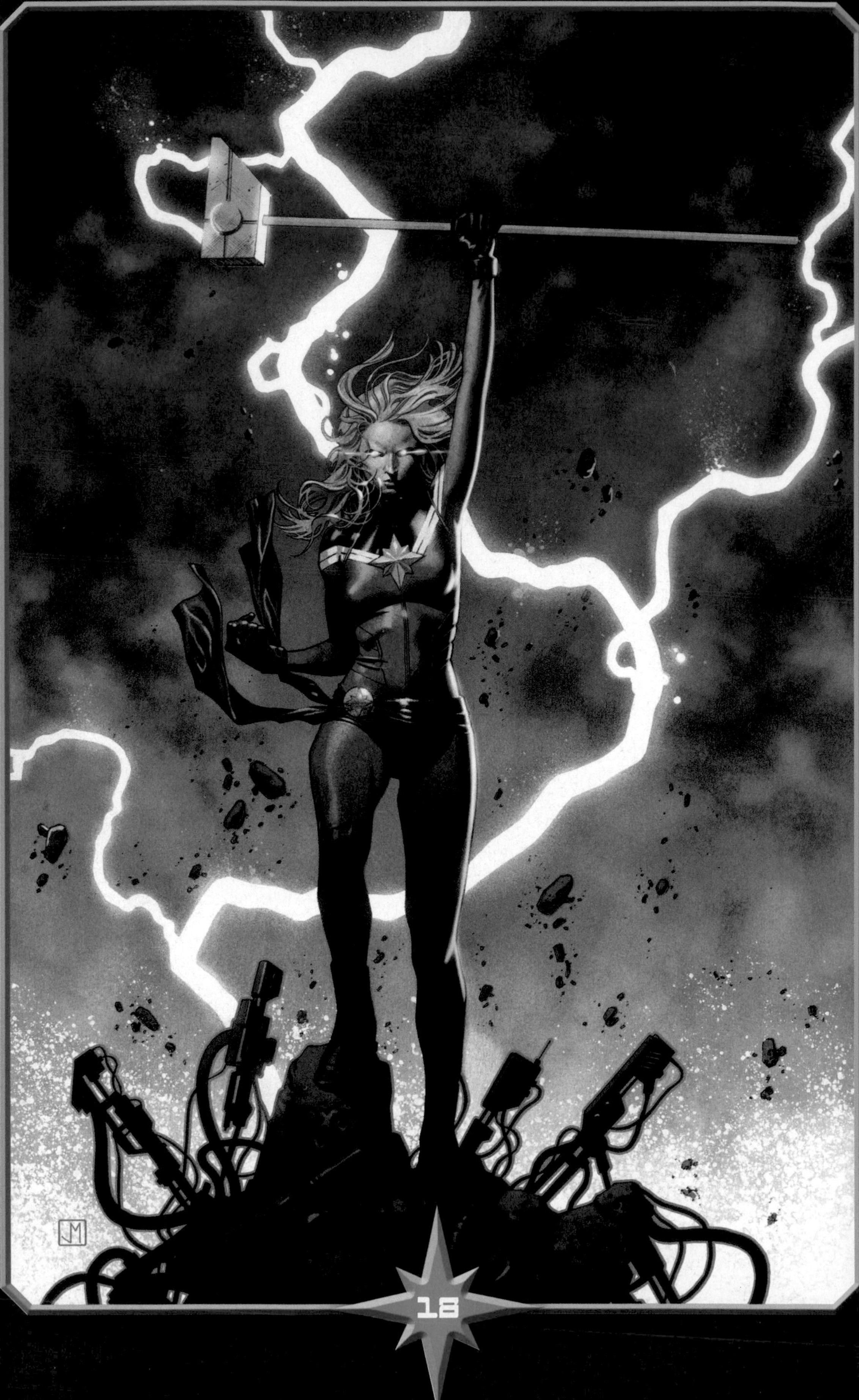
18

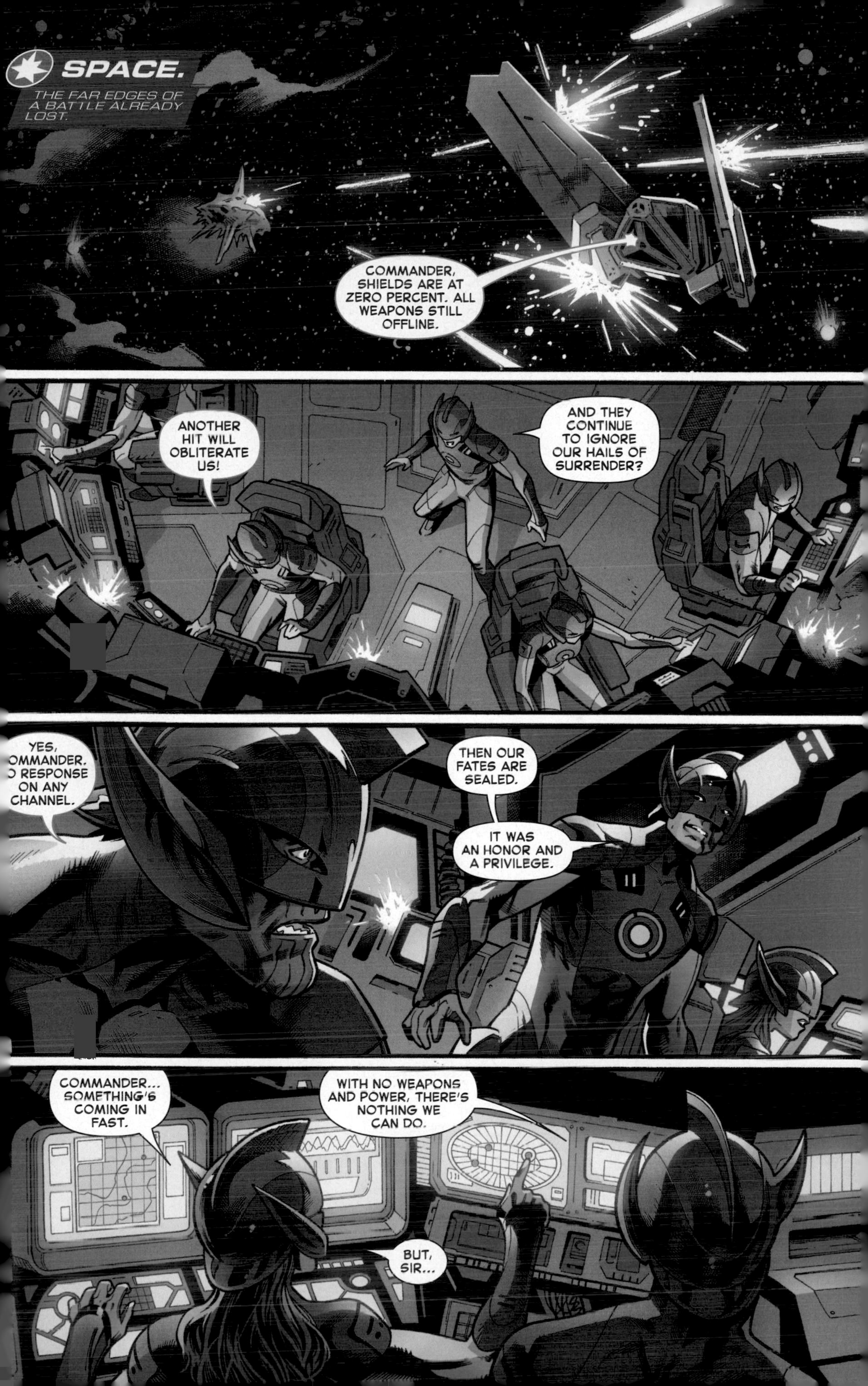
SPACE.
THE FAR EDGES OF A BATTLE ALREADY LOST.
COMMANDER, SHIELDS ARE AT ZERO PERCENT. ALL WEAPONS STILL OFFLINE.
ANOTHER HIT WILL OBLITERATE US!
AND THEY CONTINUE TO IGNORE OUR HAILS OF SURRENDER?
YES, OMMANDER. O RESPONSE ON ANY CHANNEL.
THEN OUR FATES ARE SEALED.
IT WAS AN HONOR AND A PRIVILEGE.
COMMANDER... SOMETHING'S COMING IN FAST.
WITH NO WEAPONS AND POWER, THERE'S NOTHING WE CAN DO.
BUT, SIR...

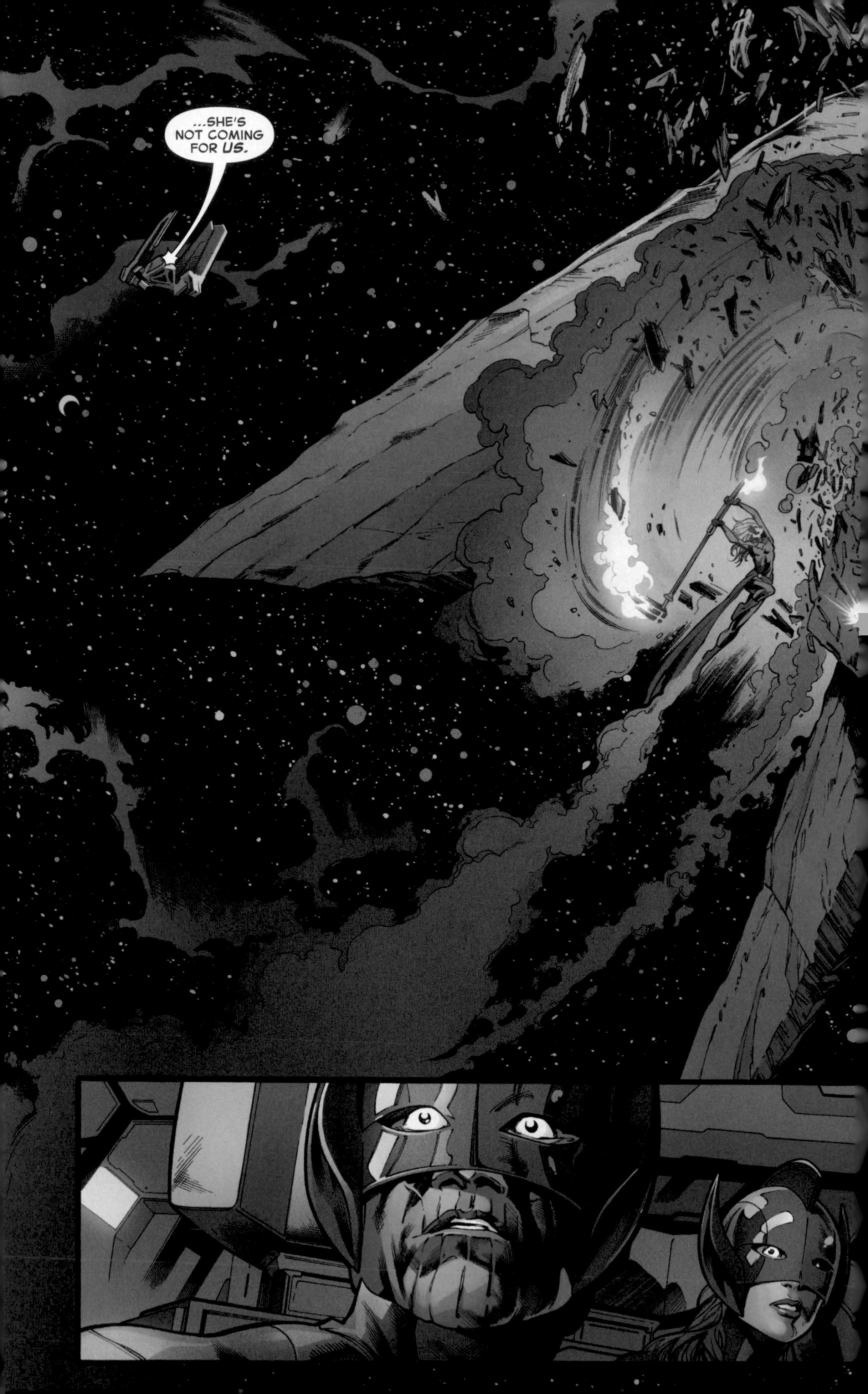
...SHE'S NOT COMING FOR US.

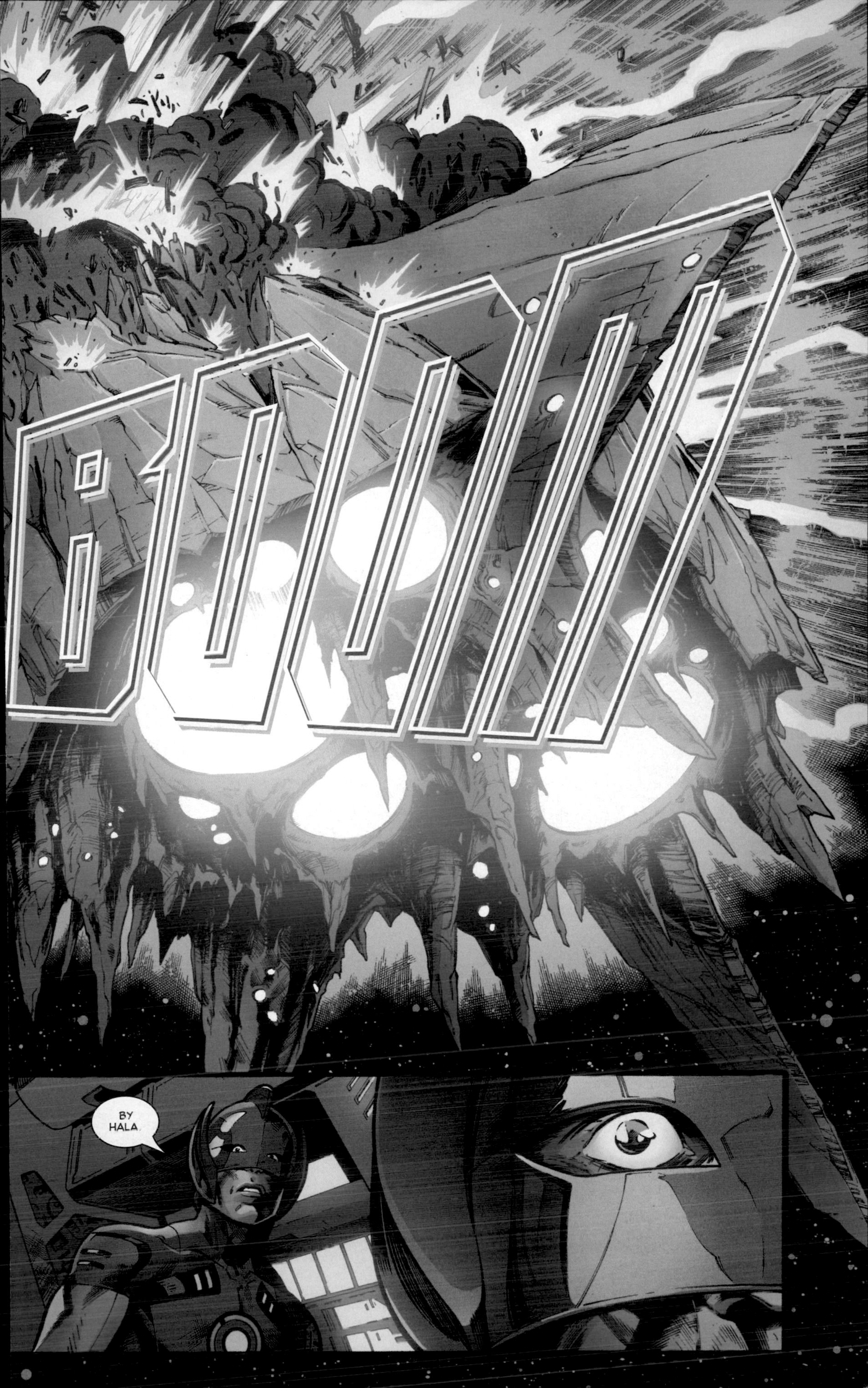
BY HALA.

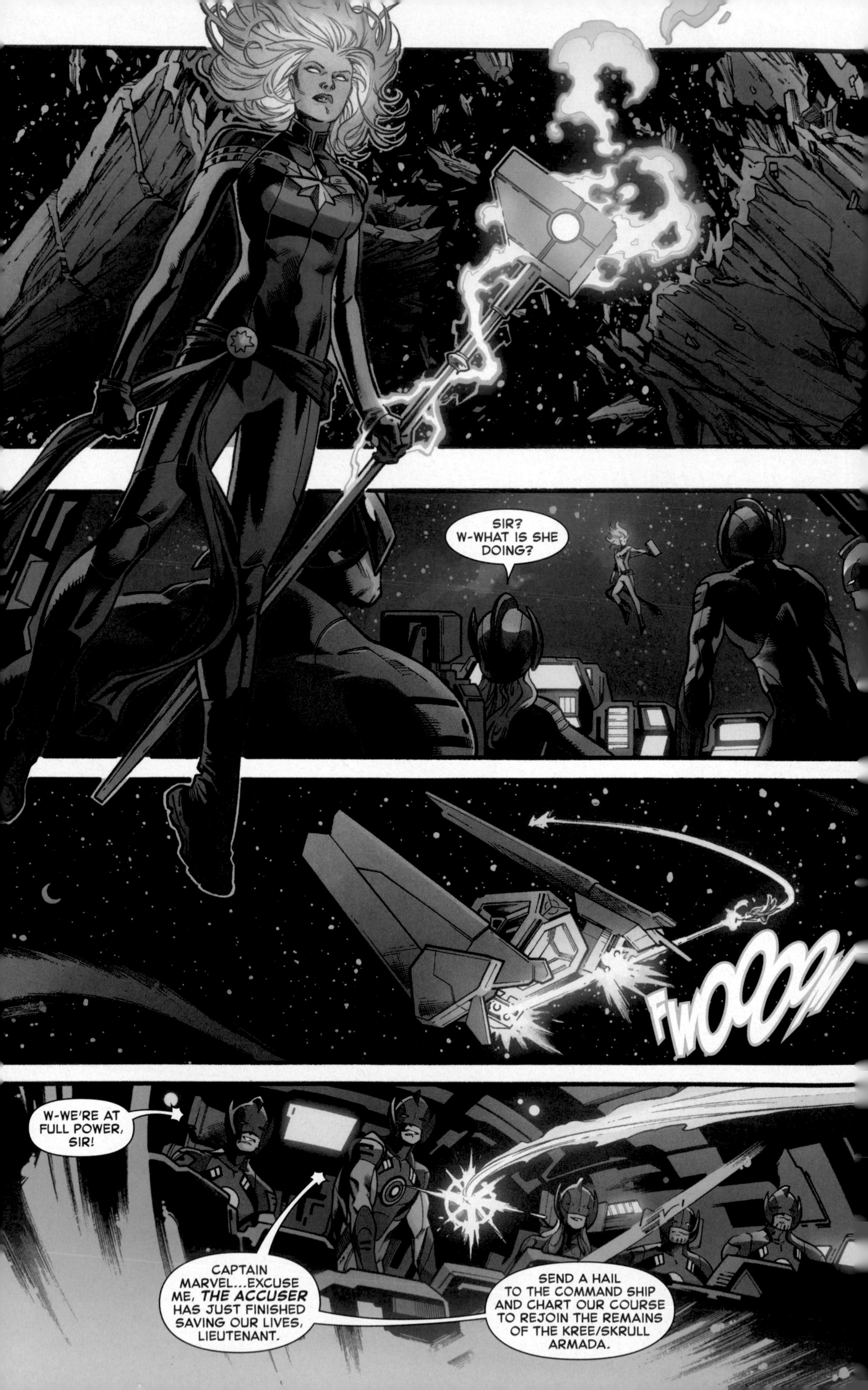
SIR? W-WHAT IS SHE DOING?
FWOOOM
W-WE'RE AT FULL POWER, SIR!
CAPTAIN MARVEL...EXCUSE ME, ***THE ACCUSER*** HAS JUST FINISHED SAVING OUR LIVES, LIEUTENANT.
SEND A HAIL TO THE COMMAND SHIP AND CHART OUR COURSE TO REJOIN THE REMAINS OF THE KREE/SKRULL ARMADA.

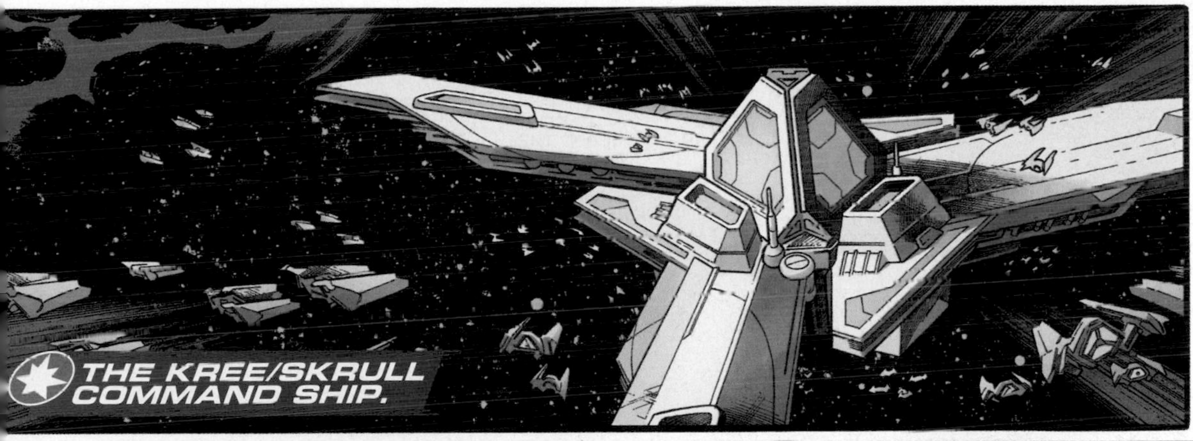
THE KREE/SKRULL COMMAND SHIP.

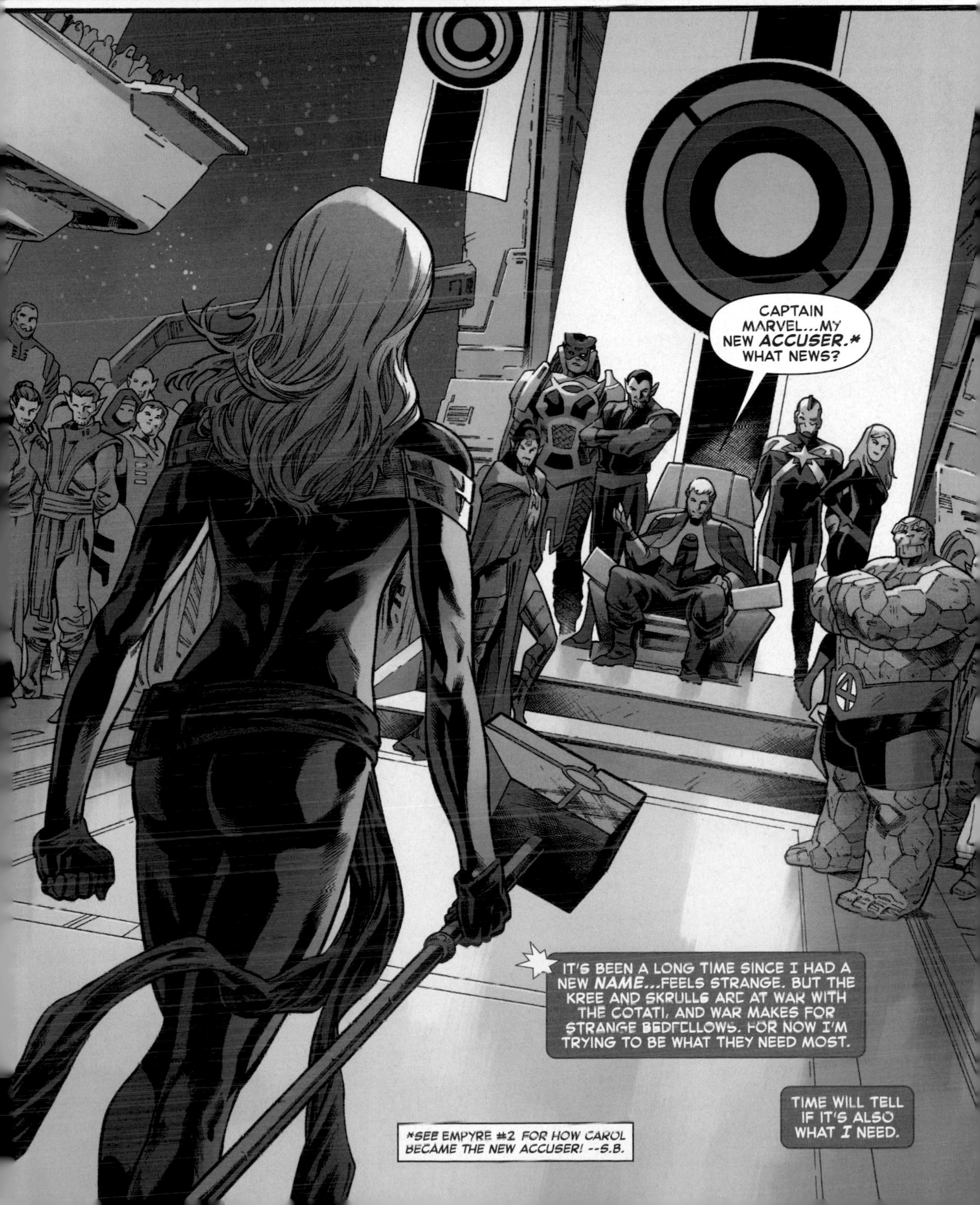
CAPTAIN MARVEL...MY NEW ACCUSER.* WHAT NEWS?
IT'S BEEN A LONG TIME SINCE I HAD A NEW NAME...FEELS STRANGE. BUT THE KREE AND SKRULLS ARE AT WAR WITH THE COTATI, AND WAR MAKES FOR STRANGE BEDFELLOWS. FOR NOW I'M TRYING TO BE WHAT THEY NEED MOST.
TIME WILL TELL IF IT'S ALSO WHAT I NEED.
*SEE EMPYRE #2 FOR HOW CAROL BECAME THE NEW ACCUSER! --S.B.

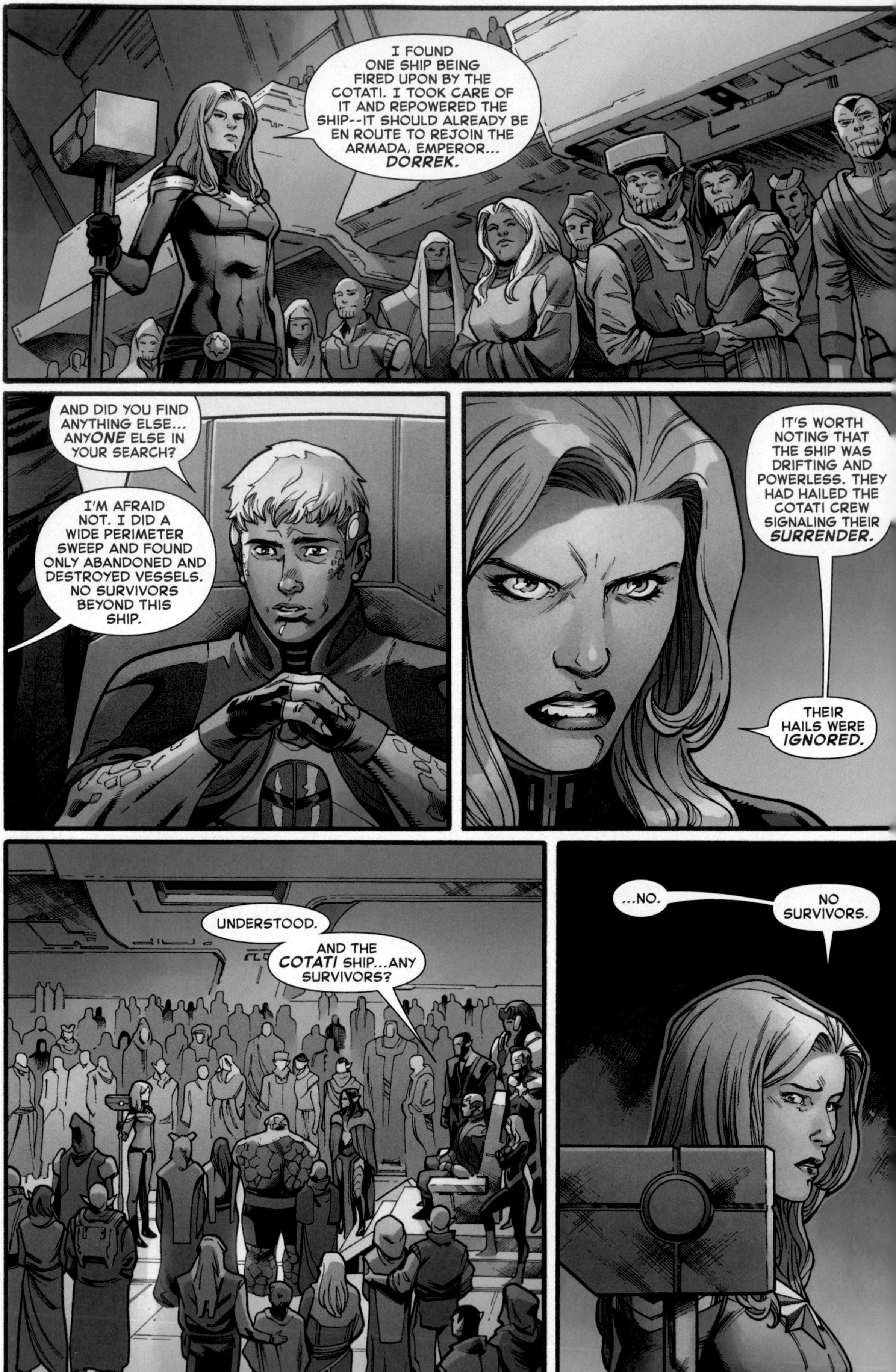
I FOUND ONE SHIP BEING FIRED UPON BY THE COTATI. I TOOK CARE OF IT AND REPOWERED THE SHIP--IT SHOULD ALREADY BE EN ROUTE TO REJOIN THE ARMADA, EMPEROR... DORREK.
AND DID YOU FIND ANYTHING ELSE... ANYONE ELSE IN YOUR SEARCH?
I'M AFRAID NOT. I DID A WIDE PERIMETER SWEEP AND FOUND ONLY ABANDONED AND DESTROYED VESSELS. NO SURVIVORS BEYOND THIS SHIP.
IT'S WORTH NOTING THAT THE SHIP WAS DRIFTING AND POWERLESS. THEY HAD HAILED THE COTATI CREW SIGNALING THEIR SURRENDER.
THEIR HAILS WERE IGNORED.
UNDERSTOOD.
AND THE COTATI SHIP...ANY SURVIVORS?
...NO.
NO SURVIVORS.

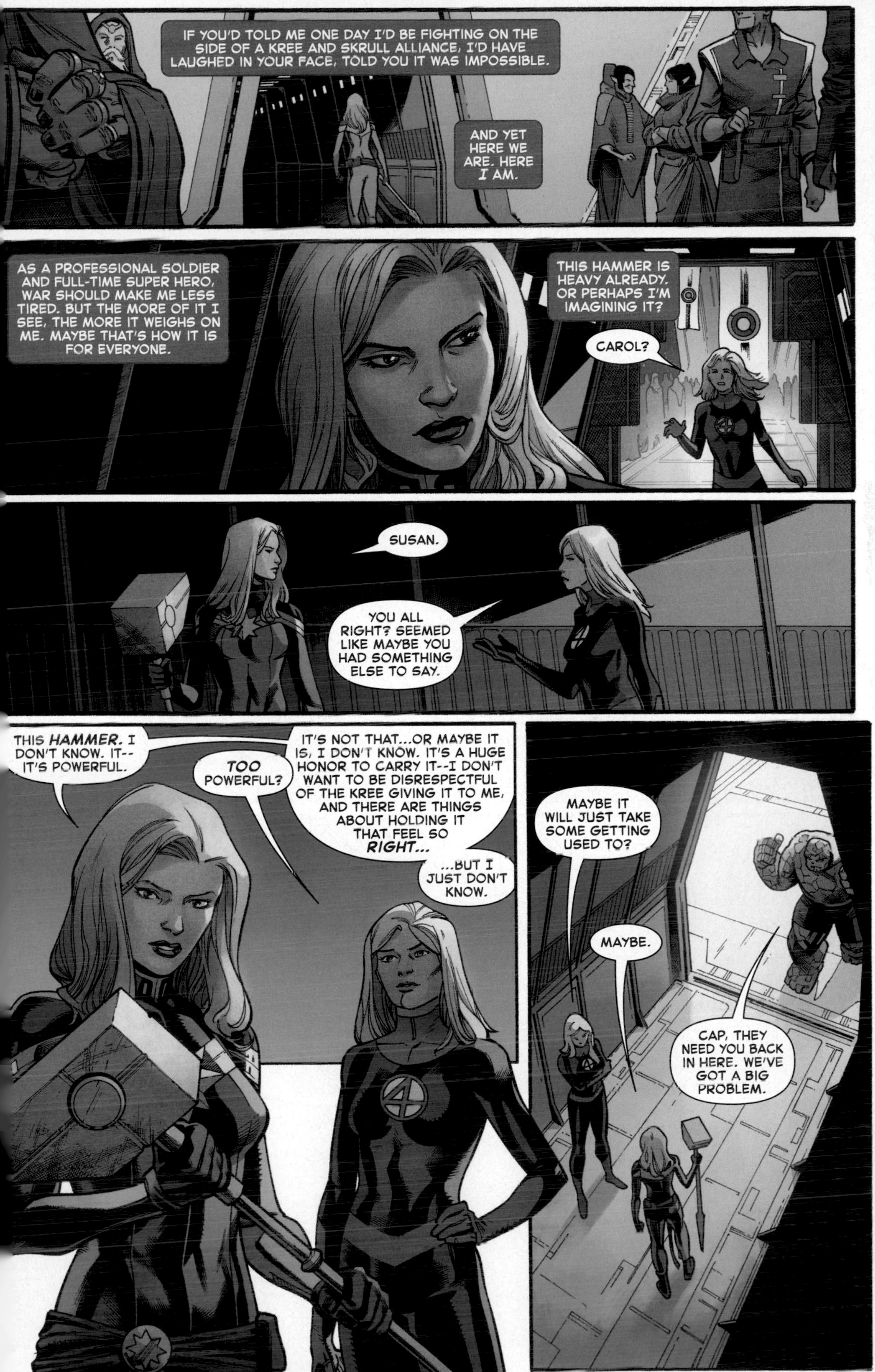
IF YOU'D TOLD ME ONE DAY I'D BE FIGHTING ON THE SIDE OF A KREE AND SKRULL ALLIANCE, I'D HAVE LAUGHED IN YOUR FACE, TOLD YOU IT WAS IMPOSSIBLE.
AND YET HERE WE ARE. HERE I AM.
AS A PROFESSIONAL SOLDIER AND FULL-TIME SUPER HERO, WAR SHOULD MAKE ME LESS TIRED. BUT THE MORE OF IT I SEE, THE MORE IT WEIGHS ON ME. MAYBE THAT'S HOW IT IS FOR EVERYONE.
THIS HAMMER IS HEAVY ALREADY. OR PERHAPS I'M IMAGINING IT?
CAROL?
SUSAN.
YOU ALL RIGHT? SEEMED LIKE MAYBE YOU HAD SOMETHING ELSE TO SAY.
THIS HAMMER. I DON'T KNOW. IT-- IT'S POWERFUL.
TOO POWERFUL?
IT'S NOT THAT...OR MAYBE IT IS, I DON'T KNOW. IT'S A HUGE HONOR TO CARRY IT--I DON'T WANT TO BE DISRESPECTFUL OF THE KREE GIVING IT TO ME, AND THERE ARE THINGS ABOUT HOLDING IT THAT FEEL SO RIGHT...
...BUT I JUST DON'T KNOW.
MAYBE IT WILL JUST TAKE SOME GETTING USED TO?
MAYBE.
CAP, THEY NEED YOU BACK IN HERE. WE'VE GOT A BIG PROBLEM.

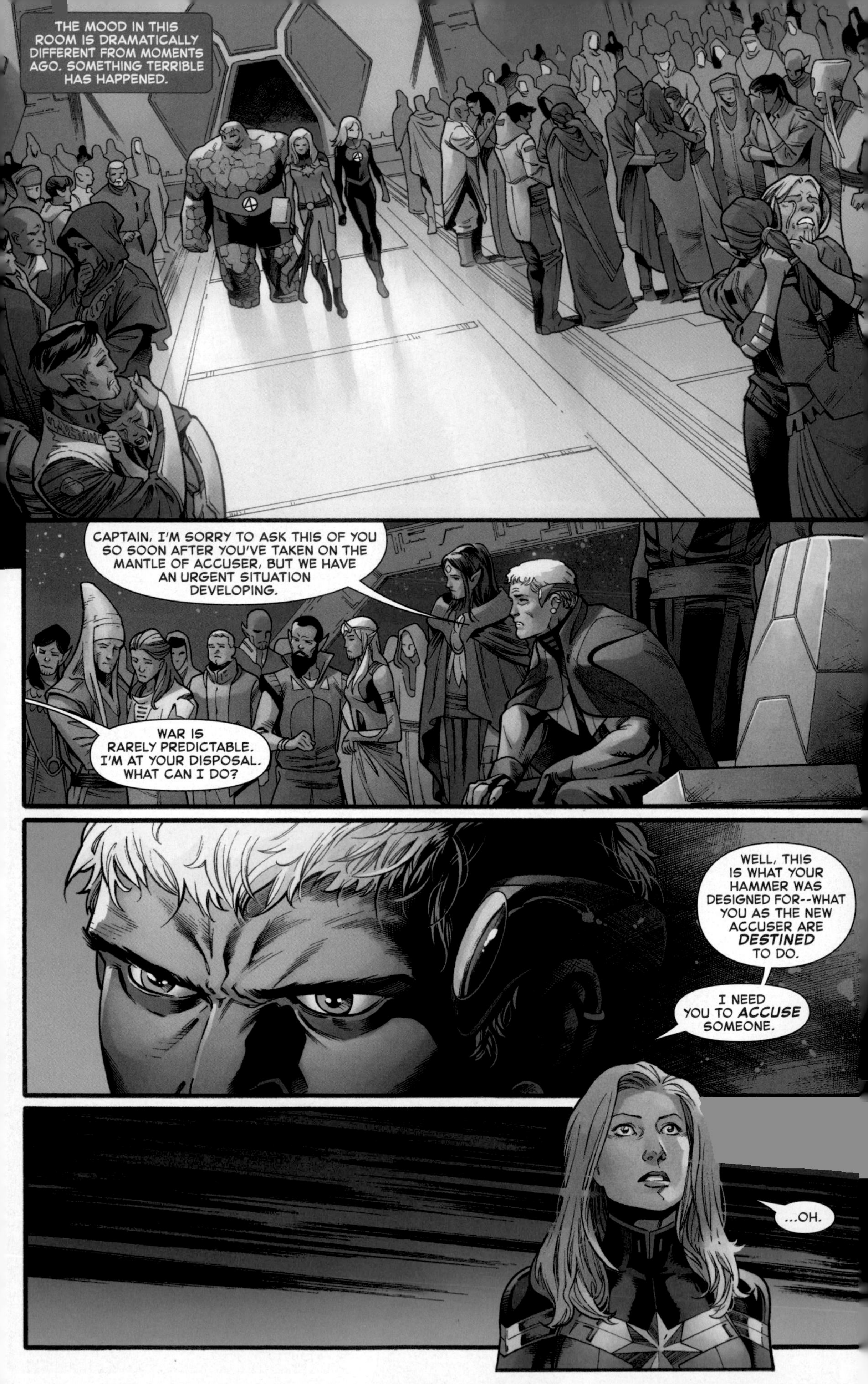
THE MOOD IN THIS ROOM IS DRAMATICALLY DIFFERENT FROM MOMENTS AGO. SOMETHING TERRIBLE HAS HAPPENED.
CAPTAIN, I'M SORRY TO ASK THIS OF YOU SO SOON AFTER YOU'VE TAKEN ON THE MANTLE OF ACCUSER, BUT WE HAVE AN URGENT SITUATION DEVELOPING.
WAR IS RARELY PREDICTABLE. I'M AT YOUR DISPOSAL. WHAT CAN I DO?
WELL, THIS IS WHAT YOUR HAMMER WAS DESIGNED FOR--WHAT YOU AS THE NEW ACCUSER ARE ***DESTINED*** TO DO.
I NEED YOU TO ***ACCUSE*** SOMEONE.
...OH.

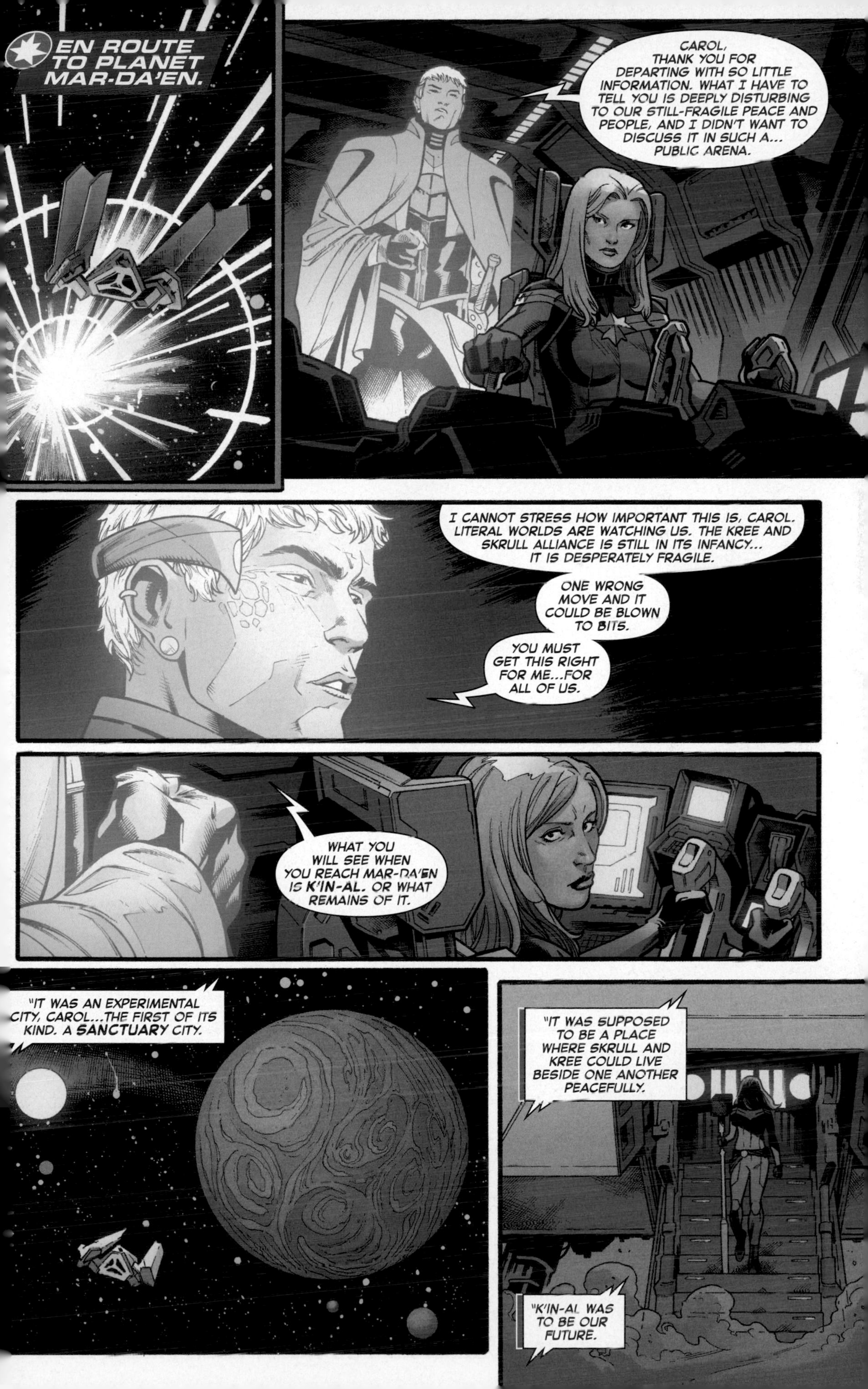
EN ROUTE TO PLANET MAR-DA'EN.
CAROL, THANK YOU FOR DEPARTING WITH SO LITTLE INFORMATION. WHAT I HAVE TO TELL YOU IS DEEPLY DISTURBING TO OUR STILL-FRAGILE PEACE AND PEOPLE, AND I DIDN'T WANT TO DISCUSS IT IN SUCH A... PUBLIC ARENA.
I CANNOT STRESS HOW IMPORTANT THIS IS, CAROL. LITERAL WORLDS ARE WATCHING US. THE KREE AND SKRULL ALLIANCE IS STILL IN ITS INFANCY... IT IS DESPERATELY FRAGILE.
ONE WRONG MOVE AND IT COULD BE BLOWN TO BITS.
YOU MUST GET THIS RIGHT FOR ME...FOR ALL OF US.
WHAT YOU WILL SEE WHEN YOU REACH MAR-DA'EN IS K'IN-AL. OR WHAT REMAINS OF IT.
"IT WAS AN EXPERIMENTAL CITY, CAROL...THE FIRST OF ITS KIND. A SANCTUARY CITY.
"IT WAS SUPPOSED TO BE A PLACE WHERE SKRULL AND KREE COULD LIVE BESIDE ONE ANOTHER PEACEFULLY.
"K'IN-AL WAS TO BE OUR FUTURE.

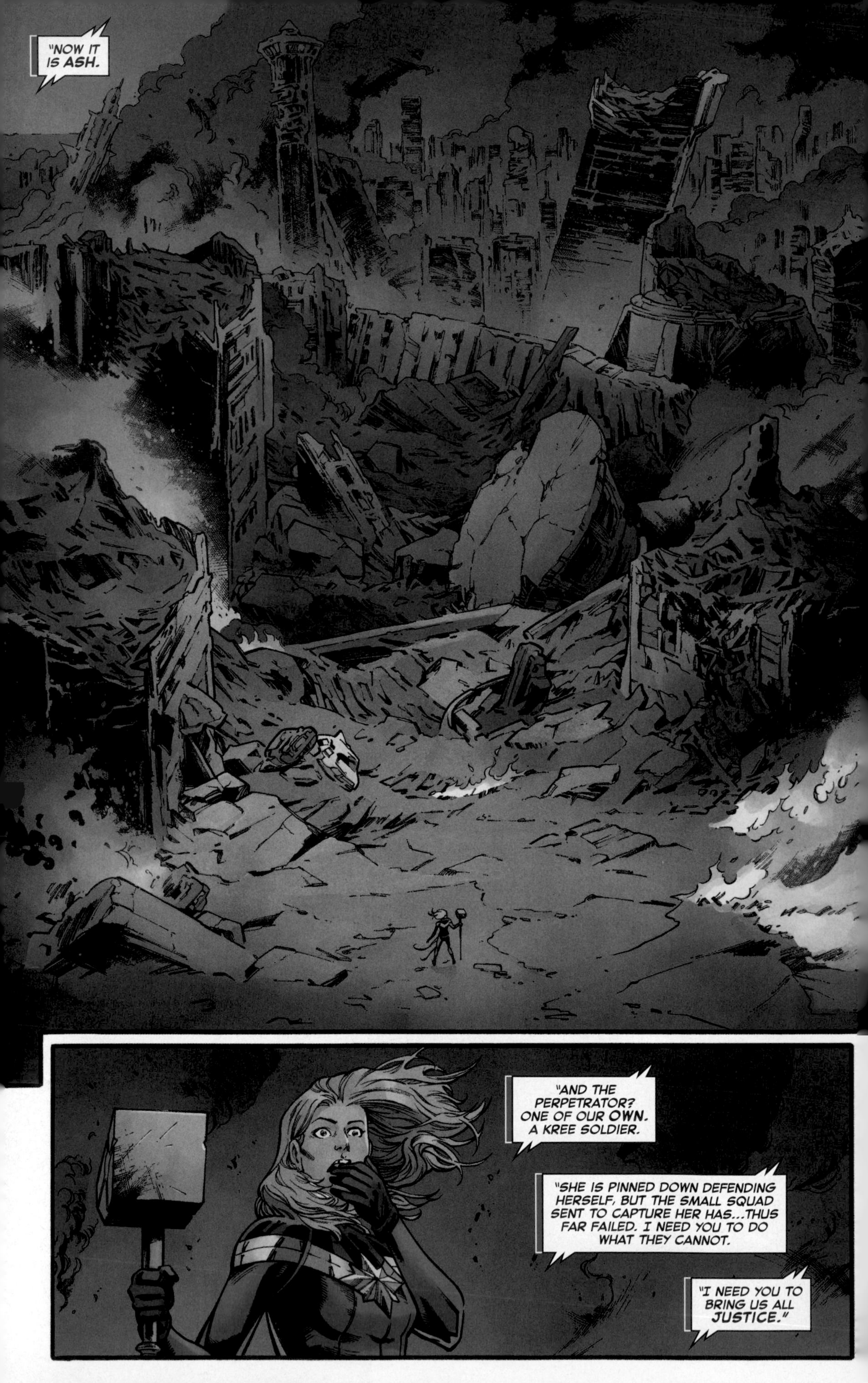
"NOW IT IS ASH.
"AND THE PERPETRATOR? ONE OF OUR OWN. A KREE SOLDIER.
"SHE IS PINNED DOWN DEFENDING HERSELF, BUT THE SMALL SQUAD SENT TO CAPTURE HER HAS...THUS FAR FAILED. I NEED YOU TO DO WHAT THEY CANNOT.
"I NEED YOU TO BRING US ALL JUSTICE."

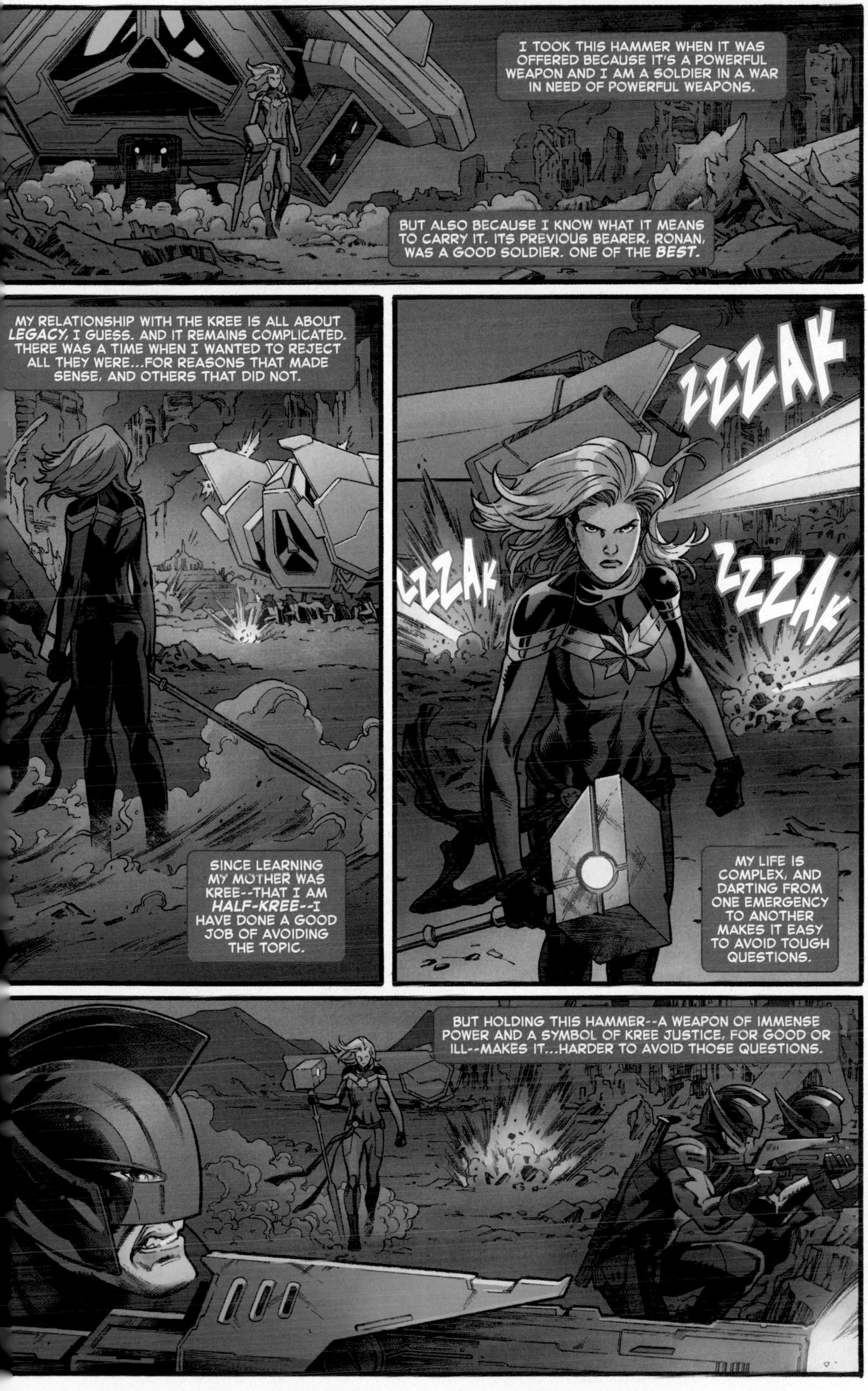

I TOOK THIS HAMMER WHEN IT WAS OFFERED BECAUSE IT'S A POWERFUL WEAPON AND I AM A SOLDIER IN A WAR IN NEED OF POWERFUL WEAPONS.
BUT ALSO BECAUSE I KNOW WHAT IT MEANS TO CARRY IT. ITS PREVIOUS BEARER, RONAN, WAS A GOOD SOLDIER. ONE OF THE *BEST.*
MY RELATIONSHIP WITH THE KREE IS ALL ABOUT *LEGACY,* I GUESS. AND IT REMAINS COMPLICATED. THERE WAS A TIME WHEN I WANTED TO REJECT ALL THEY WERE...FOR REASONS THAT MADE SENSE, AND OTHERS THAT DID NOT.
SINCE LEARNING MY MOTHER WAS KREE--THAT I AM *HALF-KREE*--I HAVE DONE A GOOD JOB OF AVOIDING THE TOPIC.
ZZZAK
ZZZAK
ZZZAK
MY LIFE IS COMPLEX, AND DARTING FROM ONE EMERGENCY TO ANOTHER MAKES IT EASY TO AVOID TOUGH QUESTIONS.
BUT HOLDING THIS HAMMER--A WEAPON OF IMMENSE POWER AND A SYMBOL OF KREE JUSTICE, FOR GOOD OR ILL--MAKES IT...HARDER TO AVOID THOSE QUESTIONS.

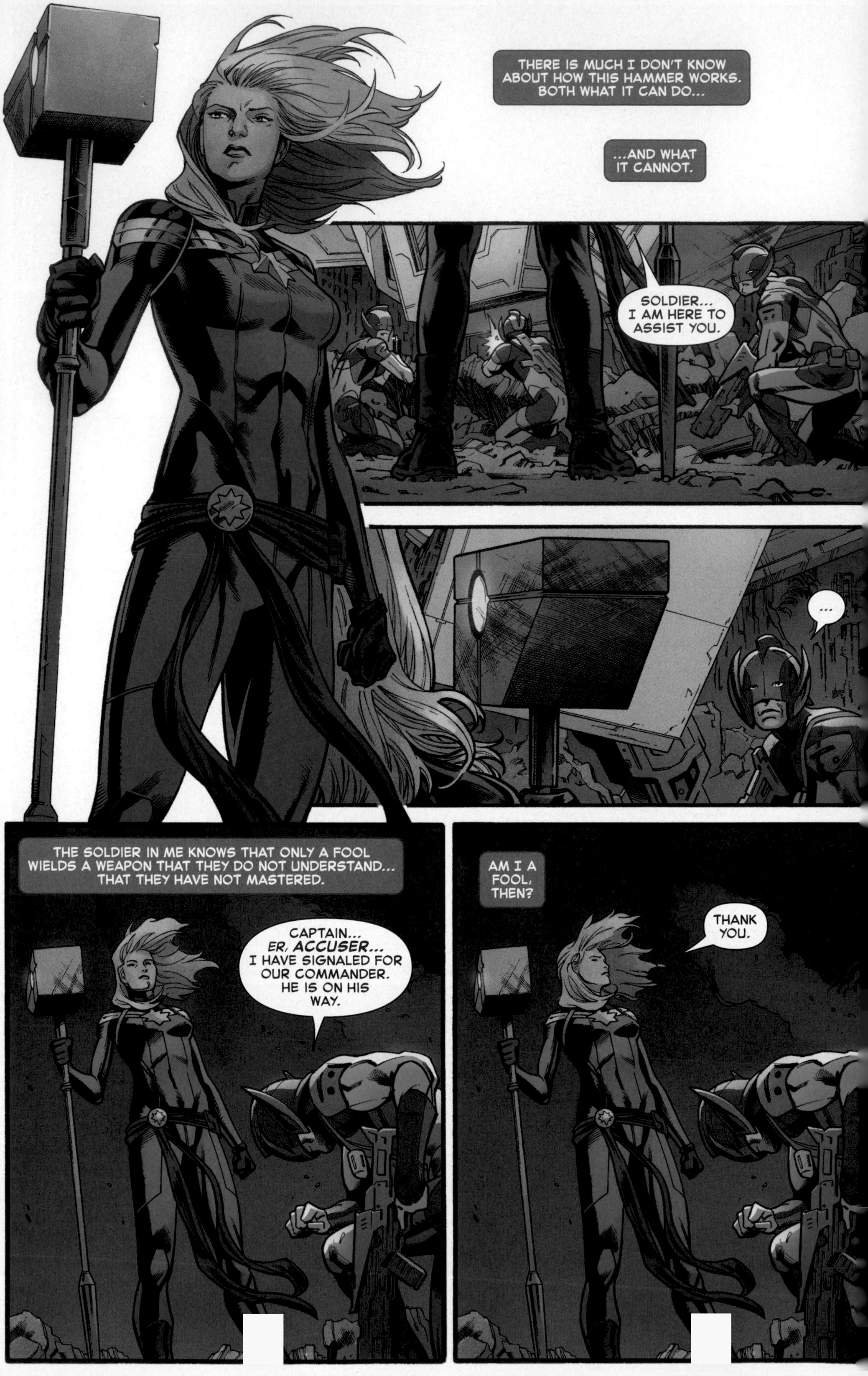
THERE IS MUCH I DON'T KNOW ABOUT HOW THIS HAMMER WORKS. BOTH WHAT IT CAN DO...
...AND WHAT IT CANNOT.
SOLDIER... I AM HERE TO ASSIST YOU.
...
THE SOLDIER IN ME KNOWS THAT ONLY A FOOL WIELDS A WEAPON THAT THEY DO NOT UNDERSTAND... THAT THEY HAVE NOT MASTERED.
CAPTAIN... ER, ACCUSER... I HAVE SIGNALED FOR OUR COMMANDER. HE IS ON HIS WAY.
AM I A FOOL, THEN?
THANK YOU.

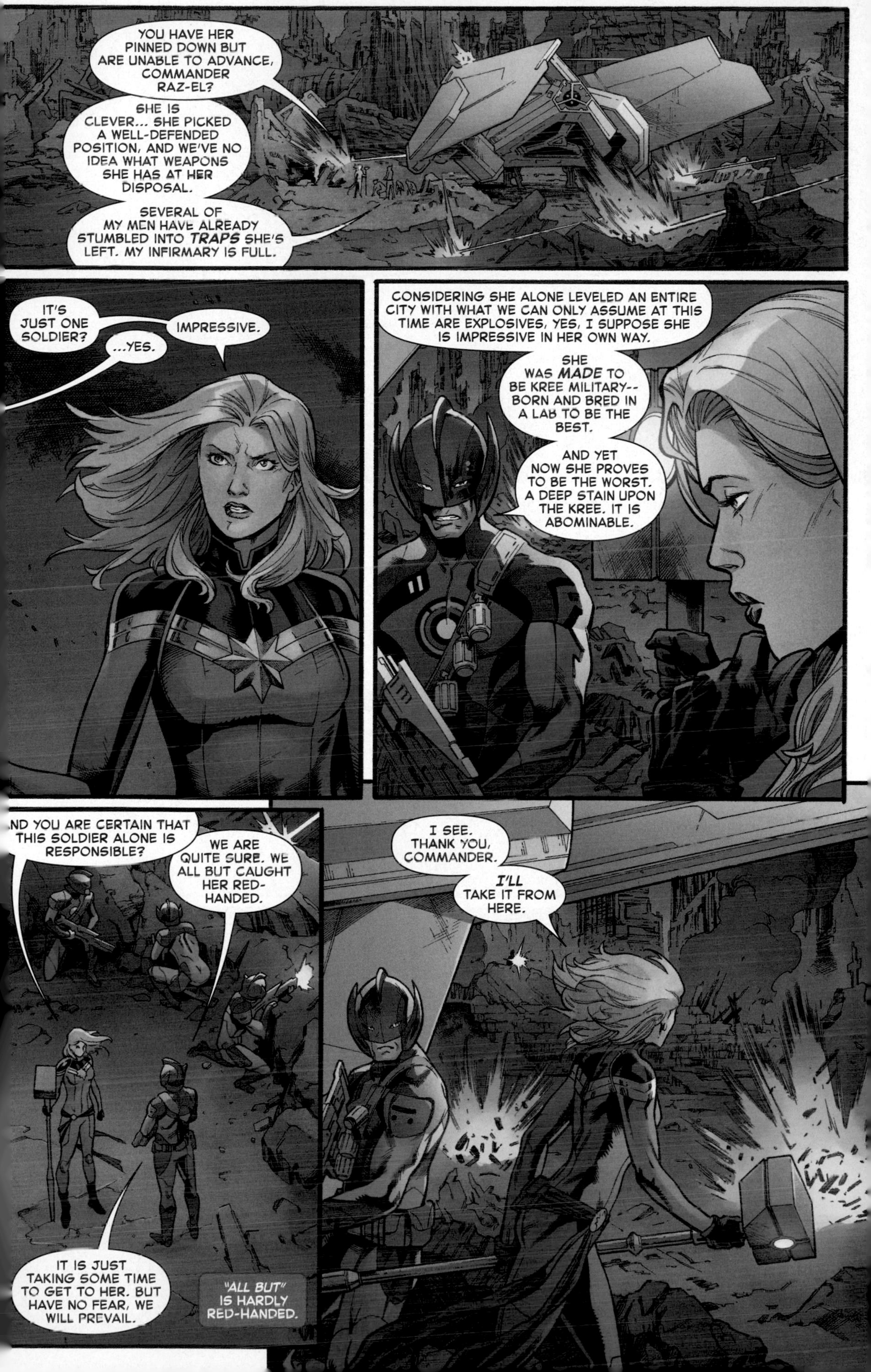

YOU HAVE HER PINNED DOWN BUT ARE UNABLE TO ADVANCE, COMMANDER RAZ-EL?
SHE IS CLEVER... SHE PICKED A WELL-DEFENDED POSITION, AND WE'VE NO IDEA WHAT WEAPONS SHE HAS AT HER DISPOSAL.
SEVERAL OF MY MEN HAVE ALREADY STUMBLED INTO TRAPS SHE'S LEFT. MY INFIRMARY IS FULL.
IT'S JUST ONE SOLDIER?
...YES.
IMPRESSIVE.
CONSIDERING SHE ALONE LEVELED AN ENTIRE CITY WITH WHAT WE CAN ONLY ASSUME AT THIS TIME ARE EXPLOSIVES, YES, I SUPPOSE SHE IS IMPRESSIVE IN HER OWN WAY.
SHE WAS MADE TO BE KREE MILITARY--BORN AND BRED IN A LAB TO BE THE BEST.
AND YET NOW SHE PROVES TO BE THE WORST. A DEEP STAIN UPON THE KREE. IT IS ABOMINABLE.
ND YOU ARE CERTAIN THAT THIS SOLDIER ALONE IS RESPONSIBLE?
WE ARE QUITE SURE. WE ALL BUT CAUGHT HER RED-HANDED.
IT IS JUST TAKING SOME TIME TO GET TO HER. BUT HAVE NO FEAR, WE WILL PREVAIL.
"ALL BUT" IS HARDLY RED-HANDED.
I SEE. THANK YOU, COMMANDER.
I'LL TAKE IT FROM HERE.

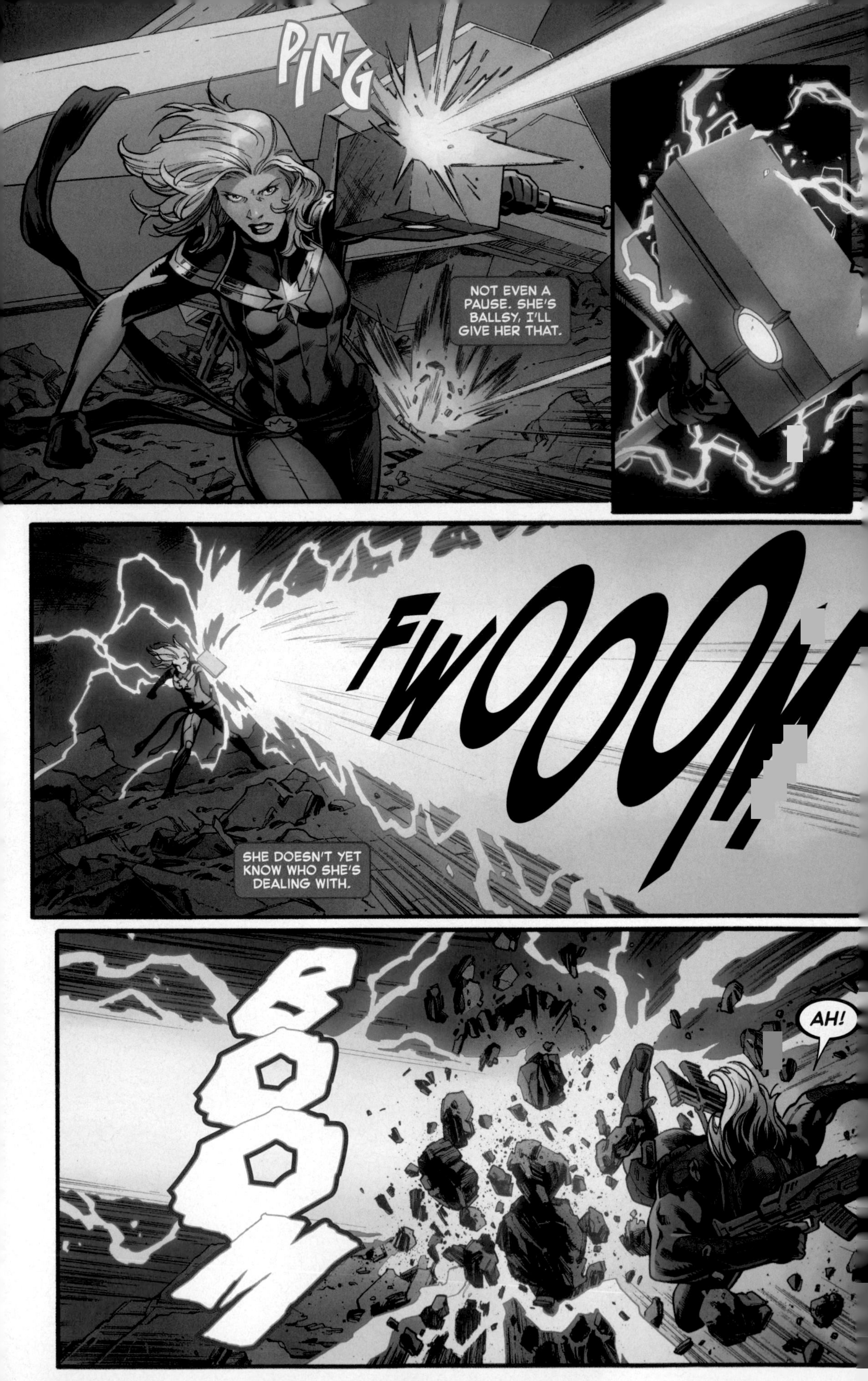
PING
NOT EVEN A PAUSE. SHE'S BALLSY, I'LL GIVE HER THAT.
FWOOOM
SHE DOESN'T YET KNOW WHO SHE'S DEALING WITH.
BOOM
AH!

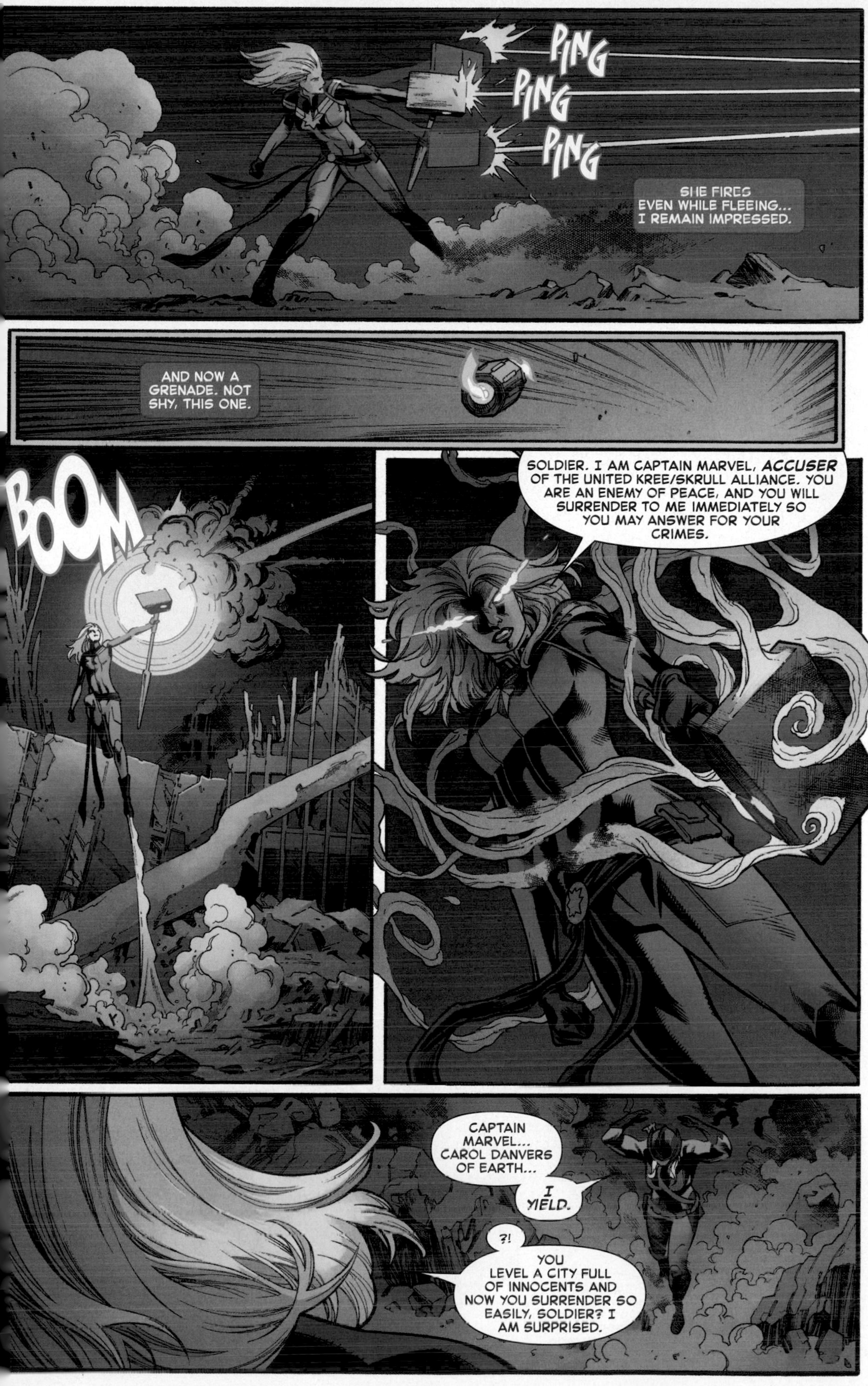
PING
PING
PING
SHE FIRES EVEN WHILE FLEEING... I REMAIN IMPRESSED.
AND NOW A GRENADE. NOT SHY, THIS ONE.
BOOM
SOLDIER. I AM CAPTAIN MARVEL, ACCUSER OF THE UNITED KREE/SKRULL ALLIANCE. YOU ARE AN ENEMY OF PEACE, AND YOU WILL SURRENDER TO ME IMMEDIATELY SO YOU MAY ANSWER FOR YOUR CRIMES.
CAPTAIN MARVEL... CAROL DANVERS OF EARTH...
I YIELD.
?!
YOU LEVEL A CITY FULL OF INNOCENTS AND NOW YOU SURRENDER SO EASILY, SOLDIER? I AM SURPRISED.

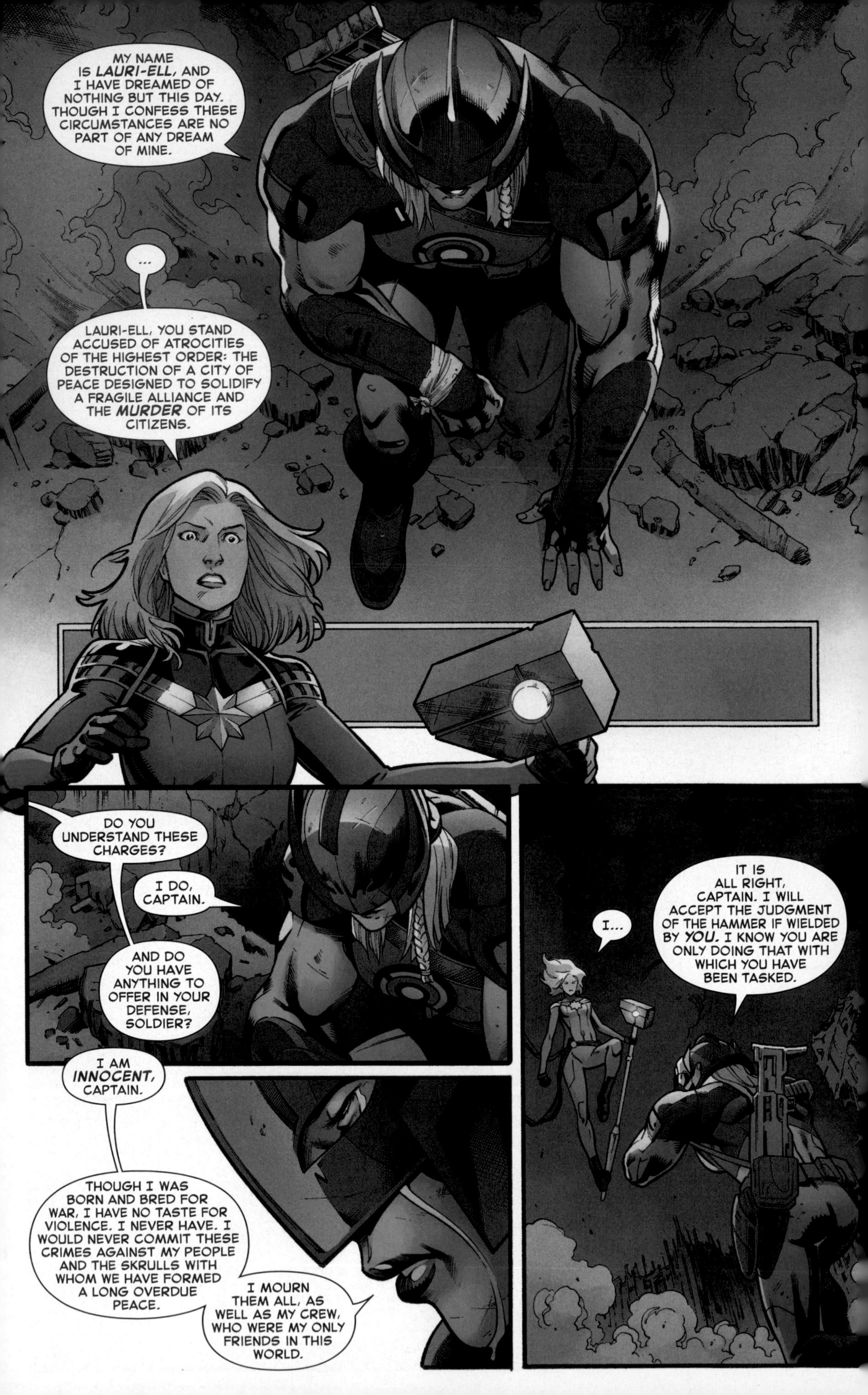
MY NAME IS *LAURI-ELL*, AND I HAVE DREAMED OF NOTHING BUT THIS DAY. THOUGH I CONFESS THESE CIRCUMSTANCES ARE NO PART OF ANY DREAM OF MINE.
...
LAURI-ELL, YOU STAND ACCUSED OF ATROCITIES OF THE HIGHEST ORDER: THE DESTRUCTION OF A CITY OF PEACE DESIGNED TO SOLIDIFY A FRAGILE ALLIANCE AND THE *MURDER* OF ITS CITIZENS.
DO YOU UNDERSTAND THESE CHARGES?
I DO, CAPTAIN.
AND DO YOU HAVE ANYTHING TO OFFER IN YOUR DEFENSE, SOLDIER?
I AM *INNOCENT*, CAPTAIN.
THOUGH I WAS BORN AND BRED FOR WAR, I HAVE NO TASTE FOR VIOLENCE. I NEVER HAVE. I WOULD NEVER COMMIT THESE CRIMES AGAINST MY PEOPLE AND THE SKRULLS WITH WHOM WE HAVE FORMED A LONG OVERDUE PEACE.
I MOURN THEM ALL, AS WELL AS MY CREW, WHO WERE MY ONLY FRIENDS IN THIS WORLD.
I...
IT IS ALL RIGHT, CAPTAIN. I WILL ACCEPT THE JUDGMENT OF THE HAMMER IF WIELDED BY *YOU*. I KNOW YOU ARE ONLY DOING THAT WITH WHICH YOU HAVE BEEN TASKED.

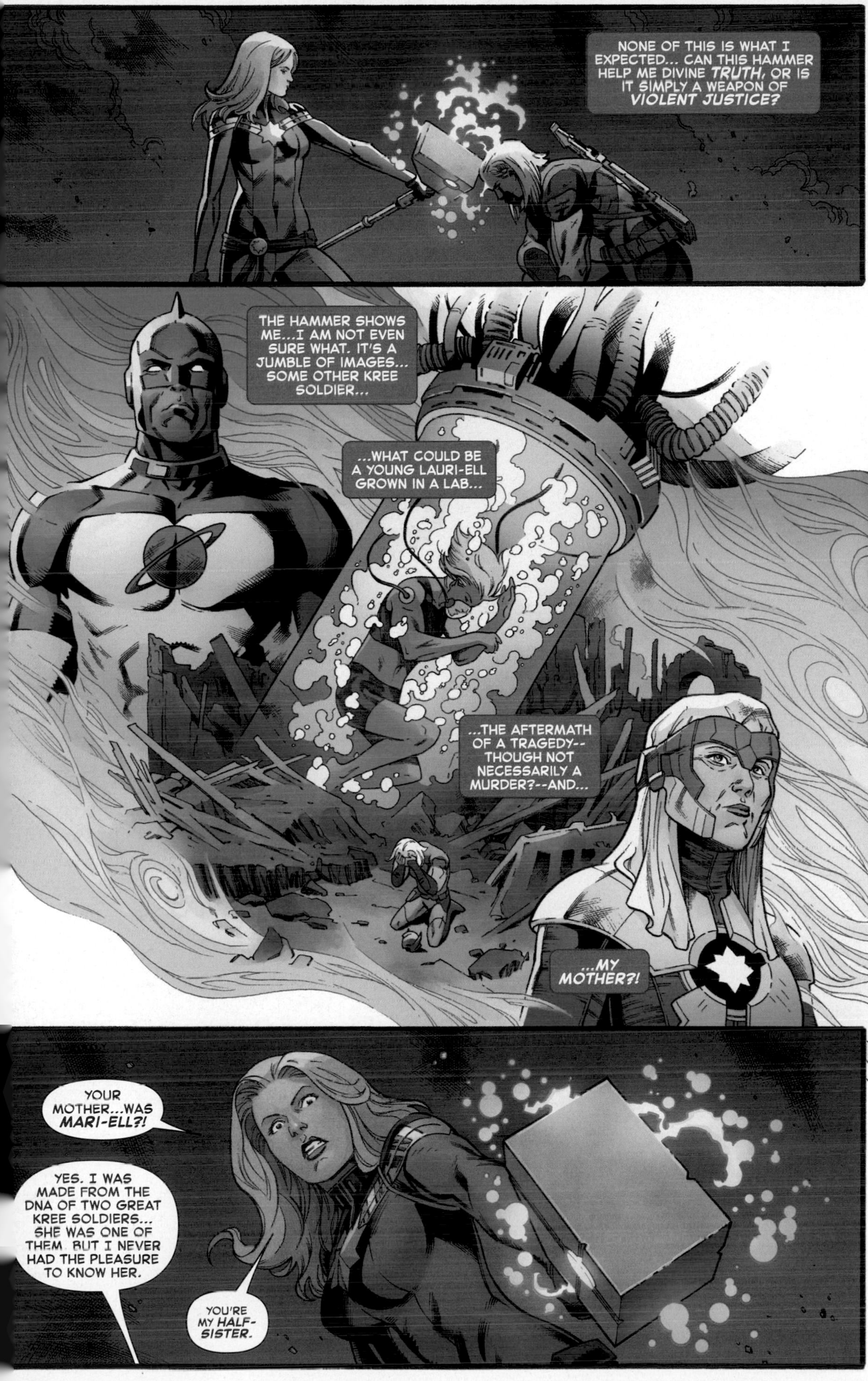
NONE OF THIS IS WHAT I EXPECTED... CAN THIS HAMMER HELP ME DIVINE TRUTH, OR IS IT SIMPLY A WEAPON OF VIOLENT JUSTICE?
THE HAMMER SHOWS ME...I AM NOT EVEN SURE WHAT. IT'S A JUMBLE OF IMAGES... SOME OTHER KREE SOLDIER...
...WHAT COULD BE A YOUNG LAURI-ELL GROWN IN A LAB...
...THE AFTERMATH OF A TRAGEDY-- THOUGH NOT NECESSARILY A MURDER?--AND...
...MY MOTHER?!
YOUR MOTHER...WAS MARI-ELL?!
YES. I WAS MADE FROM THE DNA OF TWO GREAT KREE SOLDIERS... SHE WAS ONE OF THEM. BUT I NEVER HAD THE PLEASURE TO KNOW HER.
YOU'RE MY HALF-SISTER.

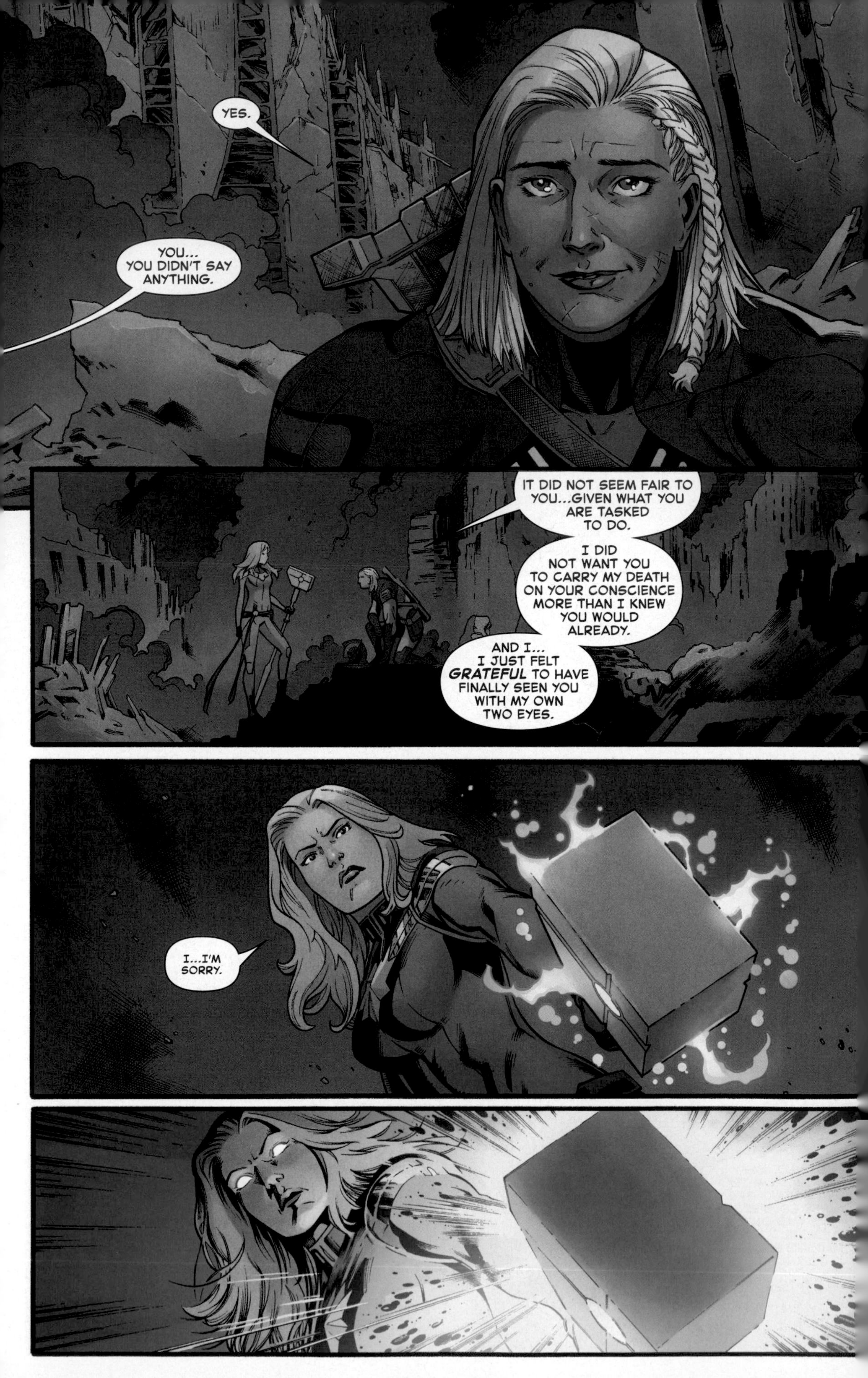
YES.
YOU... YOU DIDN'T SAY ANYTHING.
IT DID NOT SEEM FAIR TO YOU...GIVEN WHAT YOU ARE TASKED TO DO.
I DID NOT WANT YOU TO CARRY MY DEATH ON YOUR CONSCIENCE MORE THAN I KNEW YOU WOULD ALREADY.
AND I... I JUST FELT GRATEFUL TO HAVE FINALLY SEEN YOU WITH MY OWN TWO EYES.
I...I'M SORRY.

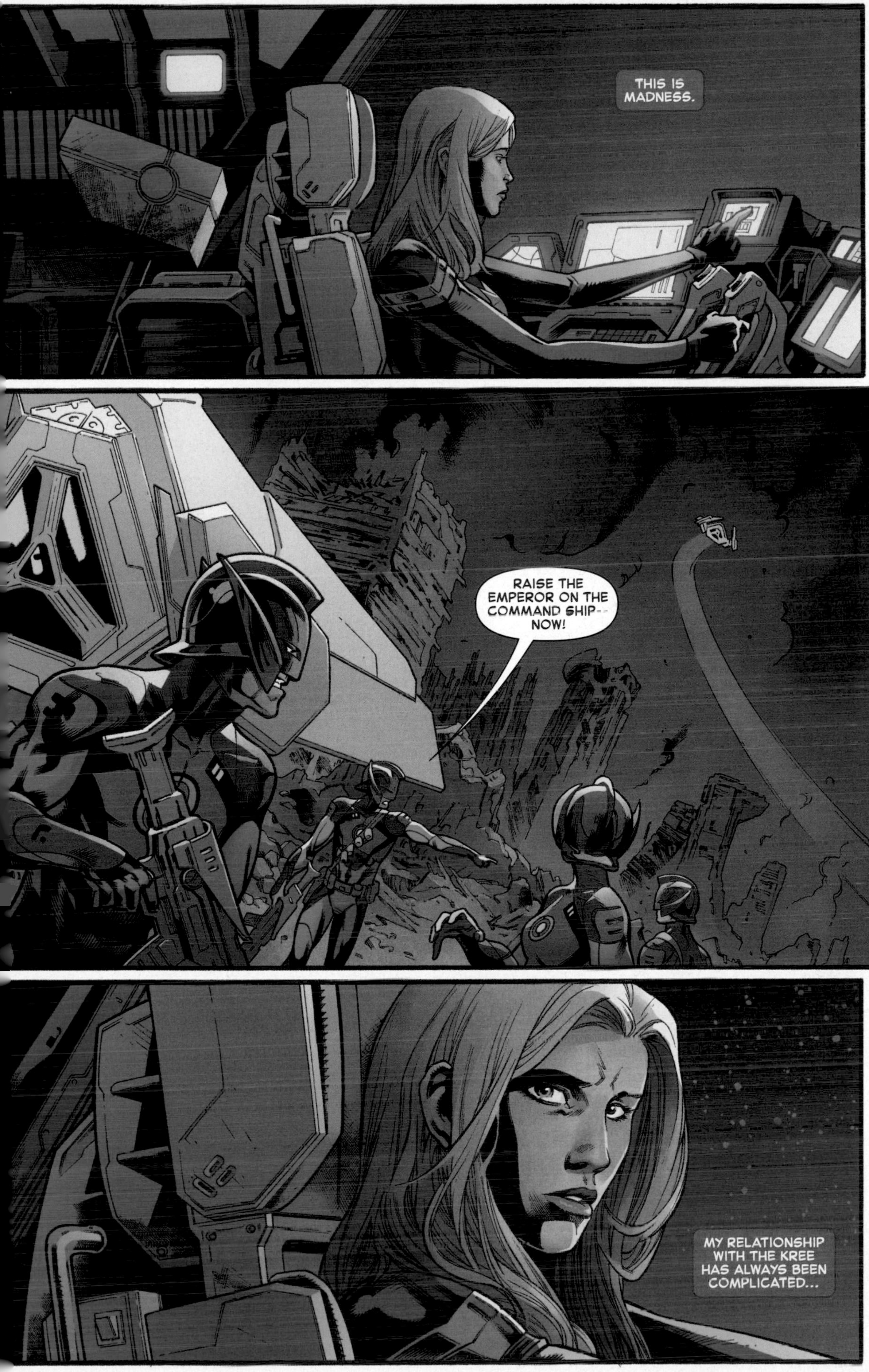
THIS IS MADNESS.
RAISE THE EMPEROR ON THE COMMAND SHIP-- NOW!
MY RELATIONSHIP WITH THE KREE HAS ALWAYS BEEN COMPLICATED...

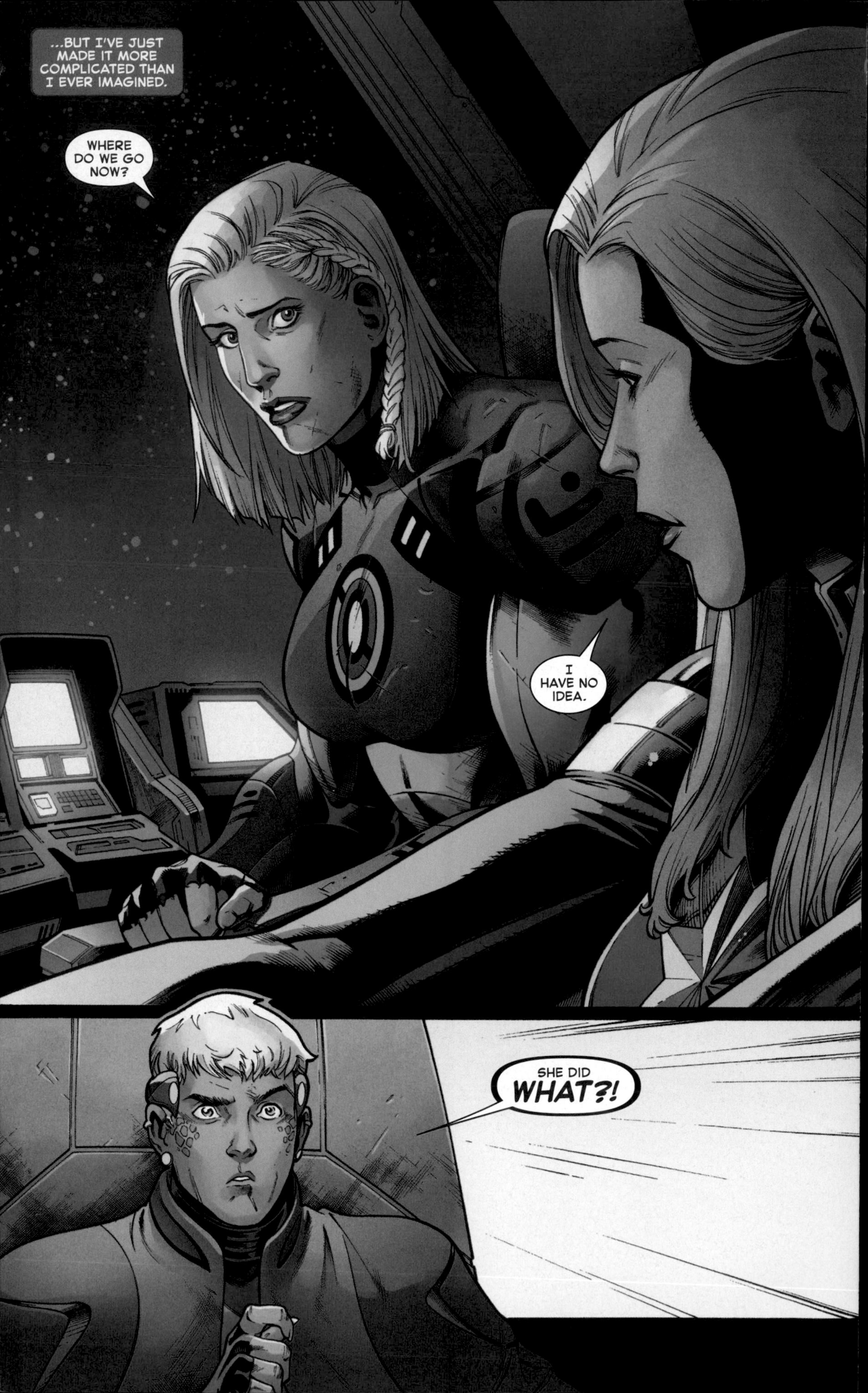
...BUT I'VE JUST MADE IT MORE COMPLICATED THAN I EVER IMAGINED.
WHERE DO WE GO NOW?
I HAVE NO IDEA.
SHE DID WHAT?!

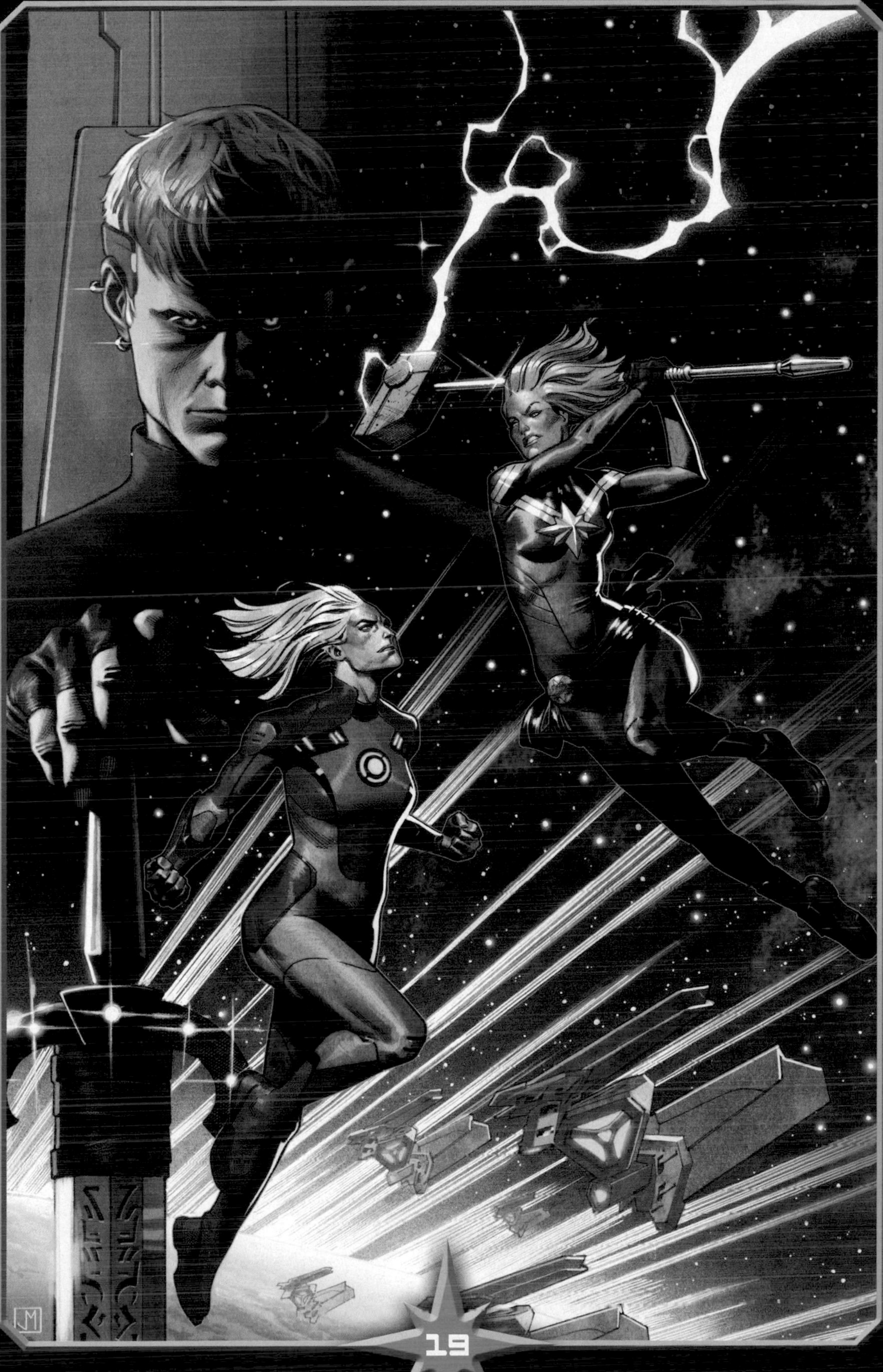

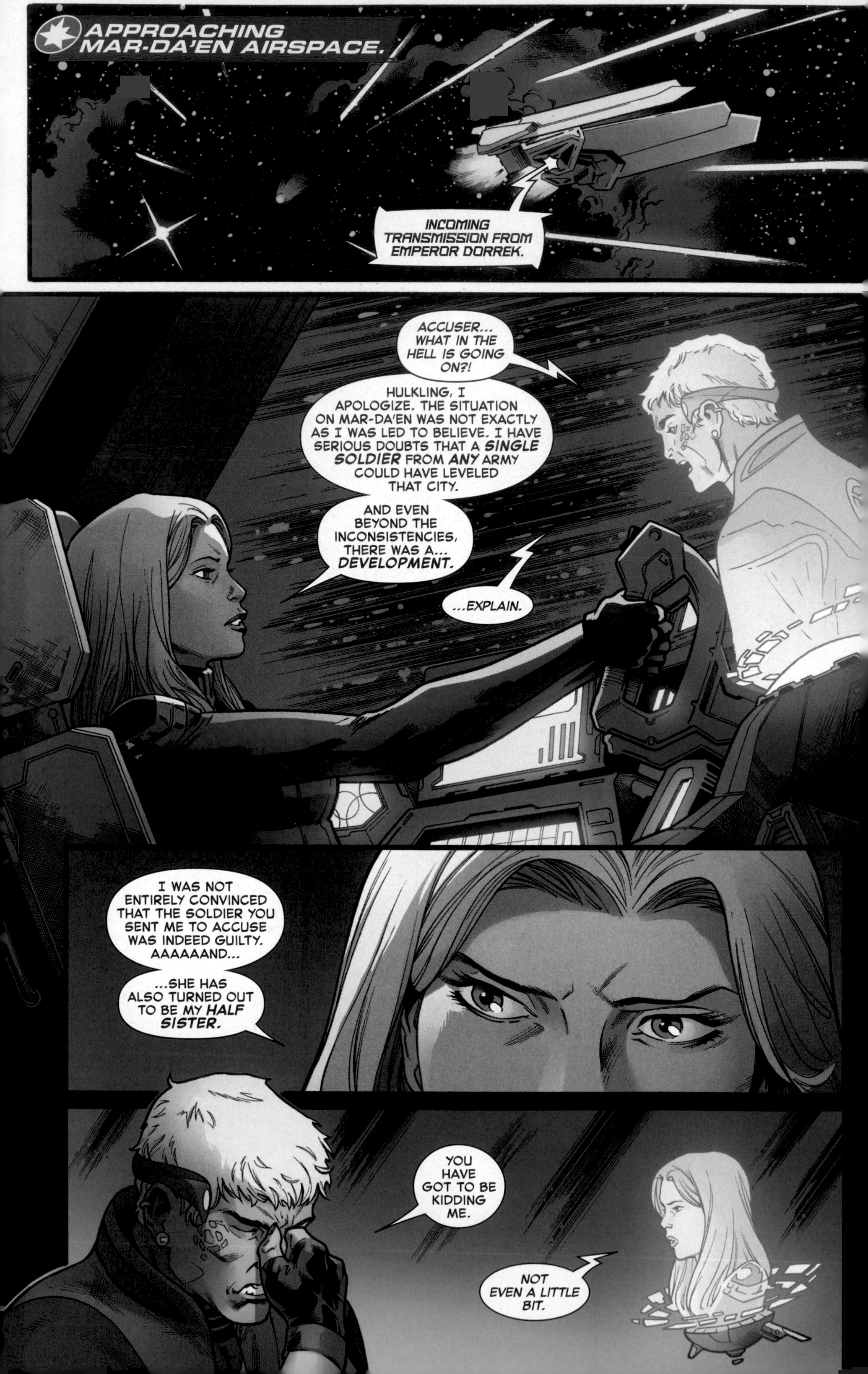
APPROACHING MAR-DA'EN AIRSPACE.
INCOMING TRANSMISSION FROM EMPEROR DORREK.
ACCUSER... WHAT IN THE HELL IS GOING ON?!
HULKLING, I APOLOGIZE. THE SITUATION ON MAR-DA'EN WAS NOT EXACTLY AS I WAS LED TO BELIEVE. I HAVE SERIOUS DOUBTS THAT A SINGLE SOLDIER FROM ANY ARMY COULD HAVE LEVELED THAT CITY.
AND EVEN BEYOND THE INCONSISTENCIES, THERE WAS A... DEVELOPMENT.
...EXPLAIN.
I WAS NOT ENTIRELY CONVINCED THAT THE SOLDIER YOU SENT ME TO ACCUSE WAS INDEED GUILTY. AAAAAAND...
...SHE HAS ALSO TURNED OUT TO BE MY HALF SISTER.
YOU HAVE GOT TO BE KIDDING ME.
NOT EVEN A LITTLE BIT.

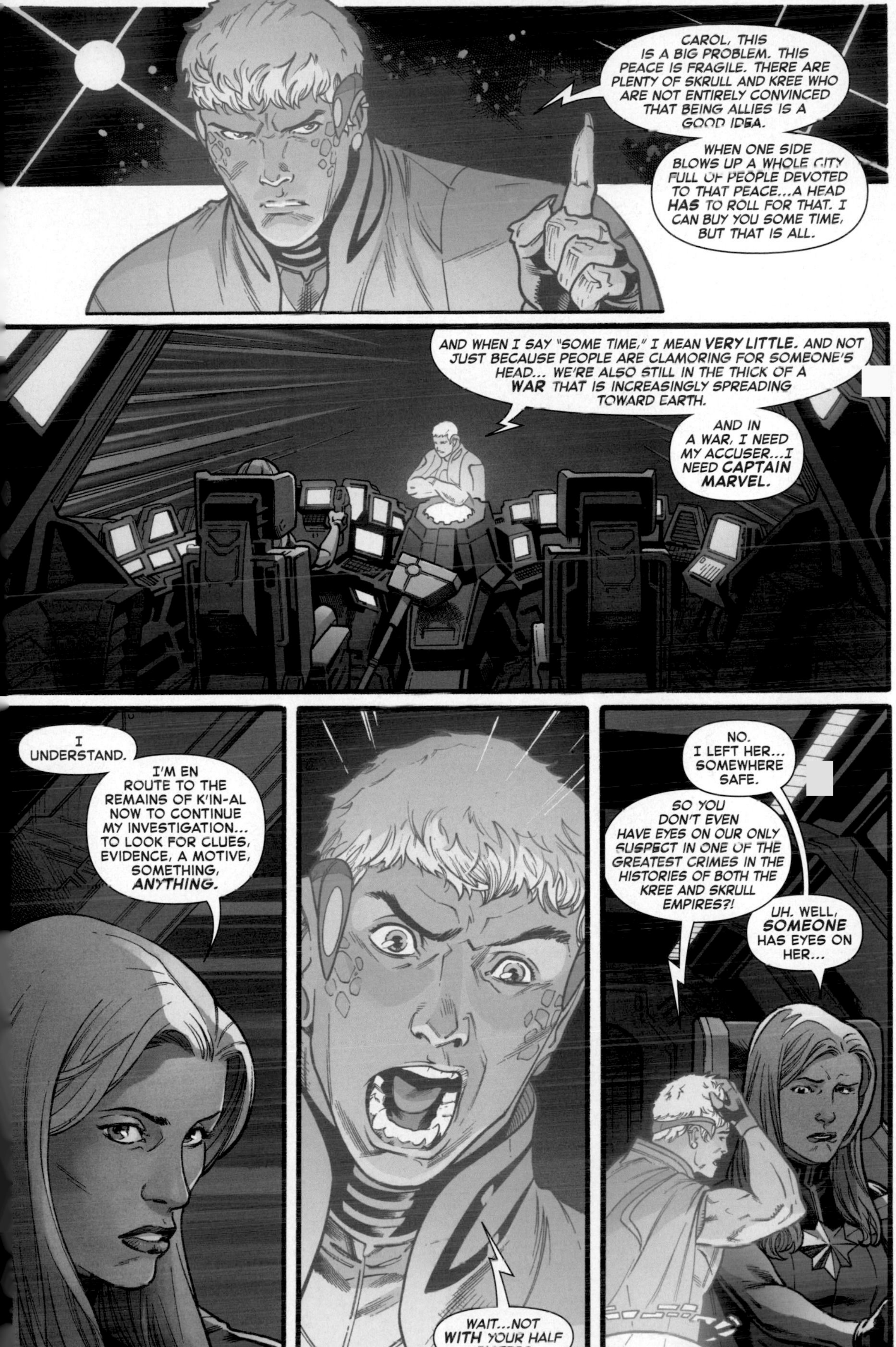
CAROL, THIS IS A BIG PROBLEM. THIS PEACE IS FRAGILE. THERE ARE PLENTY OF SKRULL AND KREE WHO ARE NOT ENTIRELY CONVINCED THAT BEING ALLIES IS A GOOD IDEA.
WHEN ONE SIDE BLOWS UP A WHOLE CITY FULL OF PEOPLE DEVOTED TO THAT PEACE...A HEAD HAS TO ROLL FOR THAT. I CAN BUY YOU SOME TIME, BUT THAT IS ALL.
AND WHEN I SAY "SOME TIME," I MEAN VERY LITTLE. AND NOT JUST BECAUSE PEOPLE ARE CLAMORING FOR SOMEONE'S HEAD... WE'RE ALSO STILL IN THE THICK OF A WAR THAT IS INCREASINGLY SPREADING TOWARD EARTH.
AND IN A WAR, I NEED MY ACCUSER...I NEED CAPTAIN MARVEL.
I UNDERSTAND.
I'M EN ROUTE TO THE REMAINS OF K'IN-AL NOW TO CONTINUE MY INVESTIGATION... TO LOOK FOR CLUES, EVIDENCE, A MOTIVE, SOMETHING, ANYTHING.
WAIT...NOT WITH YOUR HALF SISTER?
NO. I LEFT HER... SOMEWHERE SAFE.
SO YOU DON'T EVEN HAVE EYES ON OUR ONLY SUSPECT IN ONE OF THE GREATEST CRIMES IN THE HISTORIES OF BOTH THE KREE AND SKRULL EMPIRES?!
UH. WELL, SOMEONE HAS EYES ON HER...

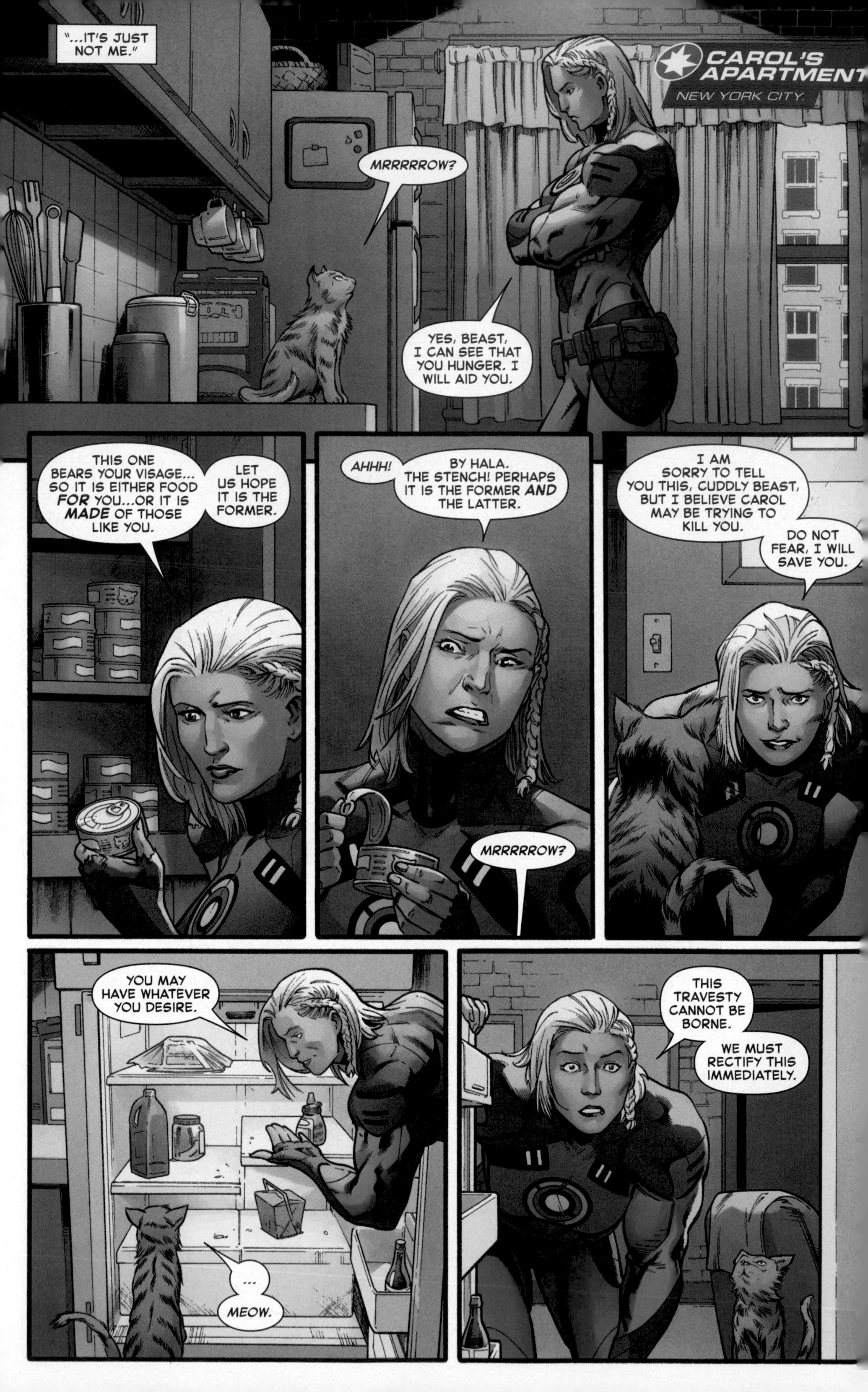
"...IT'S JUST NOT ME."
CAROL'S APARTMENT
NEW YORK CITY.
MRRRRROW?
YES, BEAST, I CAN SEE THAT YOU HUNGER. I WILL AID YOU.
THIS ONE BEARS YOUR VISAGE... SO IT IS EITHER FOOD FOR YOU...OR IT IS MADE OF THOSE LIKE YOU.
LET US HOPE IT IS THE FORMER.
AHHH!
BY HALA. THE STENCH! PERHAPS IT IS THE FORMER AND THE LATTER.
MRRRRROW?
I AM SORRY TO TELL YOU THIS, CUDDLY BEAST, BUT I BELIEVE CAROL MAY BE TRYING TO KILL YOU.
DO NOT FEAR, I WILL SAVE YOU.
YOU MAY HAVE WHATEVER YOU DESIRE.
...
MEOW.
THIS TRAVESTY CANNOT BE BORNE.
WE MUST RECTIFY THIS IMMEDIATELY.

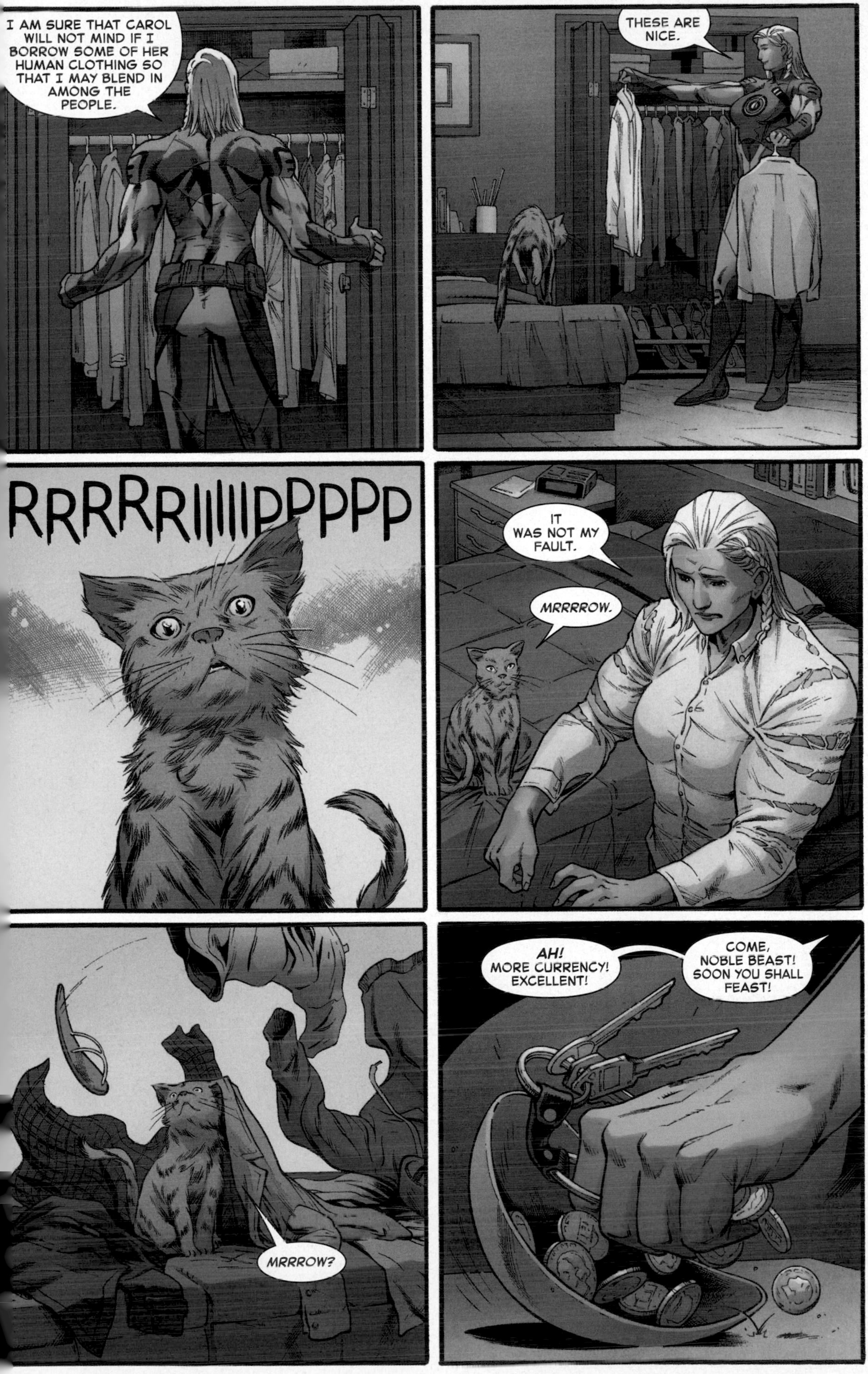
I AM SURE THAT CAROL WILL NOT MIND IF I BORROW SOME OF HER HUMAN CLOTHING SO THAT I MAY BLEND IN AMONG THE PEOPLE.
THESE ARE NICE.
RRRRRIIIIIIPPPPP
IT WAS NOT MY FAULT.
MRRRROW.
MRRROW?
AH! MORE CURRENCY! EXCELLENT!
COME, NOBLE BEAST! SOON YOU SHALL FEAST!

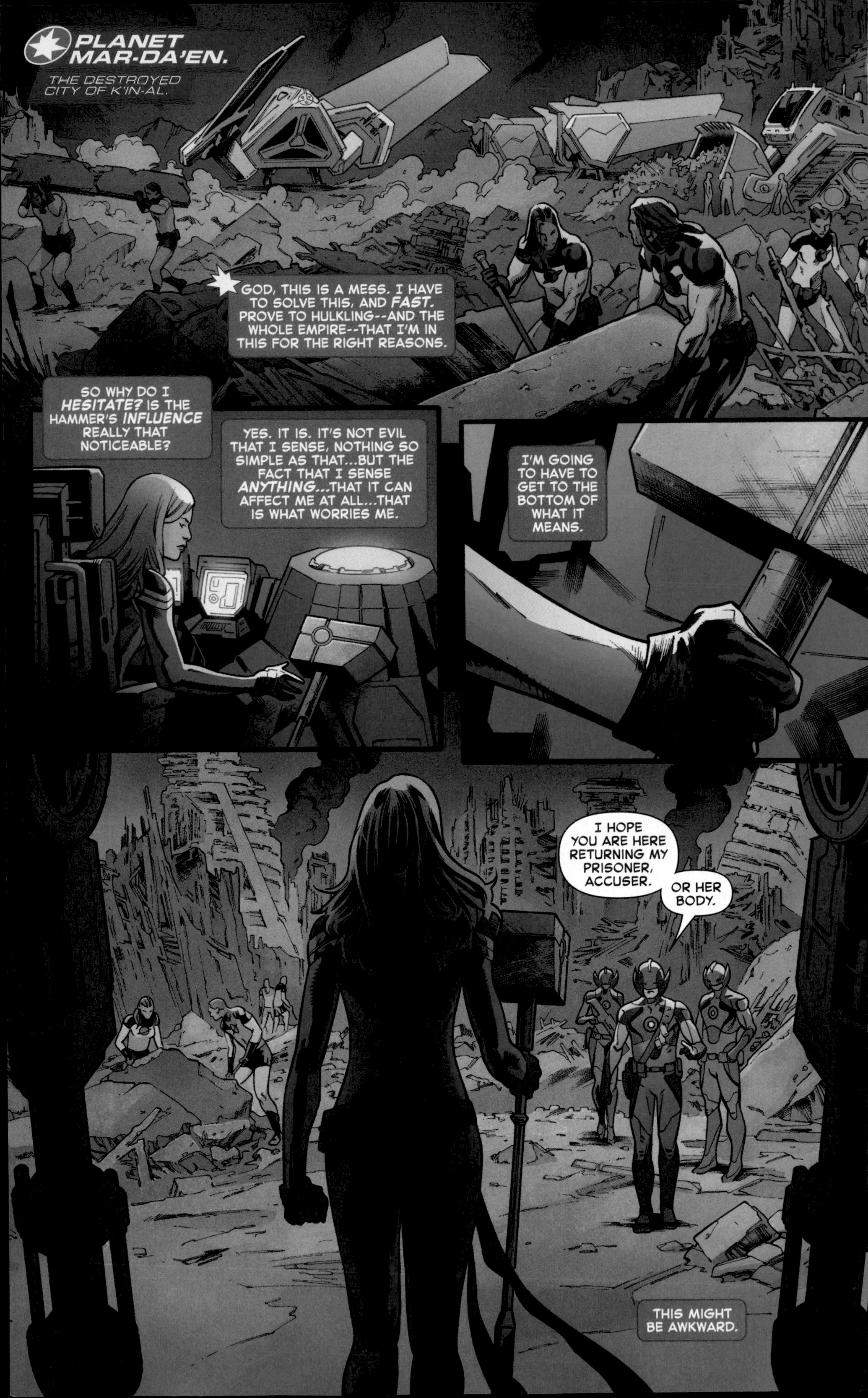
PLANET MAR-DA'EN.
THE DESTROYED CITY OF K'IN-AL.
GOD, THIS IS A MESS. I HAVE TO SOLVE THIS, AND FAST. PROVE TO HULKLING--AND THE WHOLE EMPIRE--THAT I'M IN THIS FOR THE RIGHT REASONS.
SO WHY DO I HESITATE? IS THE HAMMER'S INFLUENCE REALLY THAT NOTICEABLE?
YES. IT IS. IT'S NOT EVIL THAT I SENSE, NOTHING SO SIMPLE AS THAT...BUT THE FACT THAT I SENSE ANYTHING...THAT IT CAN AFFECT ME AT ALL...THAT IS WHAT WORRIES ME.
I'M GOING TO HAVE TO GET TO THE BOTTOM OF WHAT IT MEANS.
I HOPE YOU ARE HERE RETURNING MY PRISONER, ACCUSER.
OR HER BODY.
THIS MIGHT BE AWKWARD.

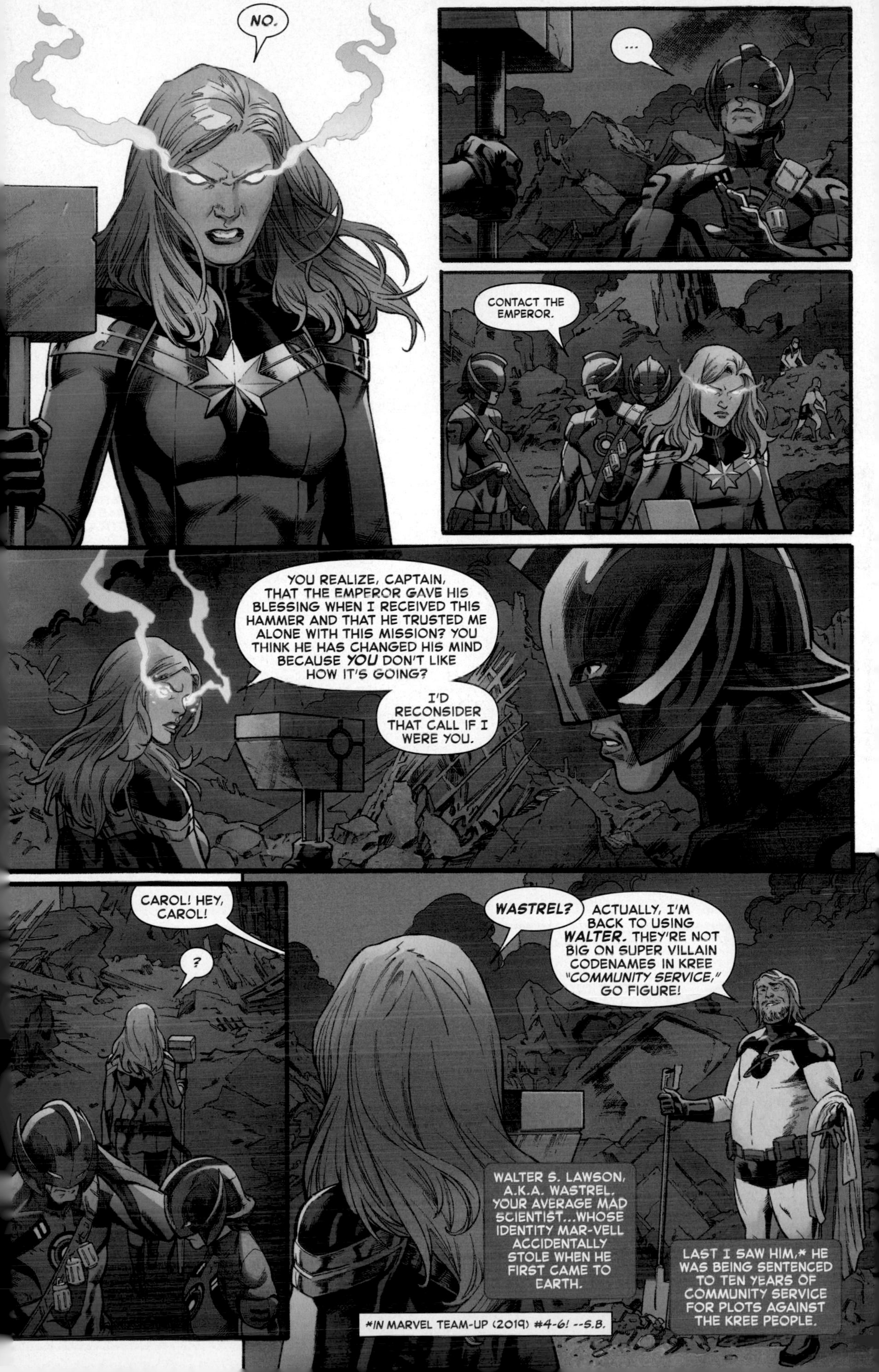
NO.
...
CONTACT THE EMPEROR.
YOU REALIZE, CAPTAIN, THAT THE EMPEROR GAVE HIS BLESSING WHEN I RECEIVED THIS HAMMER AND THAT HE TRUSTED ME ALONE WITH THIS MISSION? YOU THINK HE HAS CHANGED HIS MIND BECAUSE YOU DON'T LIKE HOW IT'S GOING?
I'D RECONSIDER THAT CALL IF I WERE YOU.
CAROL! HEY, CAROL!
?
WASTREL?
ACTUALLY, I'M BACK TO USING WALTER. THEY'RE NOT BIG ON SUPER VILLAIN CODENAMES IN KREE "COMMUNITY SERVICE," GO FIGURE!
WALTER S. LAWSON, A.K.A. WASTREL. YOUR AVERAGE MAD SCIENTIST...WHOSE IDENTITY MAR-VELL ACCIDENTALLY STOLE WHEN HE FIRST CAME TO EARTH.
LAST I SAW HIM,* HE WAS BEING SENTENCED TO TEN YEARS OF COMMUNITY SERVICE FOR PLOTS AGAINST THE KREE PEOPLE.
*IN MARVEL TEAM-UP (2019) #4-6! --S.B.

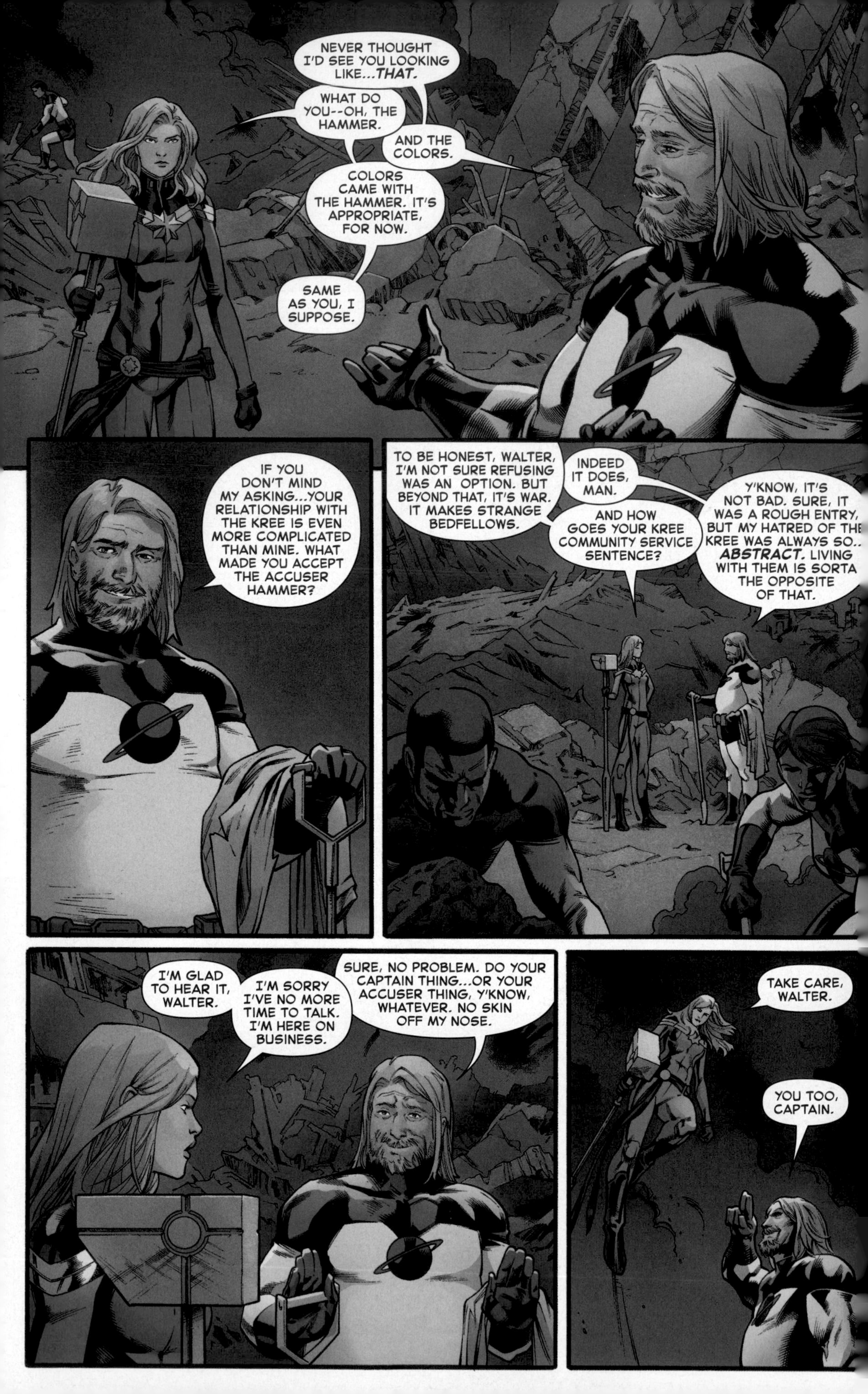
NEVER THOUGHT I'D SEE YOU LOOKING LIKE...THAT.
WHAT DO YOU--OH, THE HAMMER.
AND THE COLORS.
COLORS CAME WITH THE HAMMER. IT'S APPROPRIATE, FOR NOW.
SAME AS YOU, I SUPPOSE.
IF YOU DON'T MIND MY ASKING...YOUR RELATIONSHIP WITH THE KREE IS EVEN MORE COMPLICATED THAN MINE. WHAT MADE YOU ACCEPT THE ACCUSER HAMMER?
TO BE HONEST, WALTER, I'M NOT SURE REFUSING WAS AN OPTION. BUT BEYOND THAT, IT'S WAR. IT MAKES STRANGE BEDFELLOWS.
INDEED IT DOES, MAN.
AND HOW GOES YOUR KREE COMMUNITY SERVICE SENTENCE?
Y'KNOW, IT'S NOT BAD. SURE, IT WAS A ROUGH ENTRY, BUT MY HATRED OF THE KREE WAS ALWAYS SO... ABSTRACT. LIVING WITH THEM IS SORTA THE OPPOSITE OF THAT.
I'M GLAD TO HEAR IT, WALTER.
I'M SORRY I'VE NO MORE TIME TO TALK. I'M HERE ON BUSINESS.
SURE, NO PROBLEM. DO YOUR CAPTAIN THING...OR YOUR ACCUSER THING, Y'KNOW, WHATEVER. NO SKIN OFF MY NOSE.
TAKE CARE, WALTER.
YOU TOO, CAPTAIN.

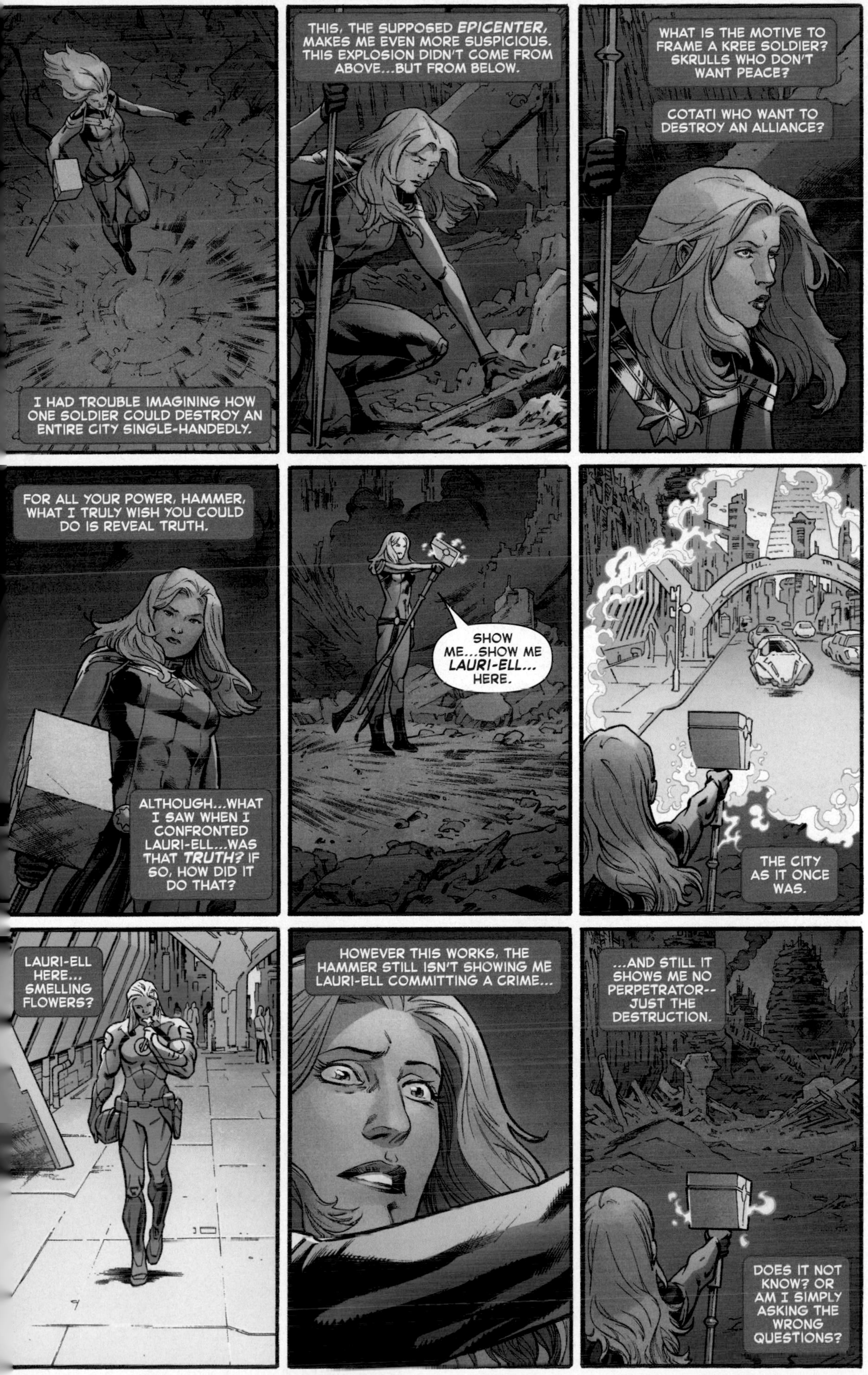
I HAD TROUBLE IMAGINING HOW ONE SOLDIER COULD DESTROY AN ENTIRE CITY SINGLE-HANDEDLY.
THIS, THE SUPPOSED *EPICENTER,* MAKES ME EVEN MORE SUSPICIOUS. THIS EXPLOSION DIDN'T COME FROM ABOVE...BUT FROM BELOW.
WHAT IS THE MOTIVE TO FRAME A KREE SOLDIER? SKRULLS WHO DON'T WANT PEACE?
COTATI WHO WANT TO DESTROY AN ALLIANCE?
FOR ALL YOUR POWER, HAMMER, WHAT I TRULY WISH YOU COULD DO IS REVEAL TRUTH.
ALTHOUGH...WHAT I SAW WHEN I CONFRONTED LAURI-ELL...WAS THAT *TRUTH?* IF SO, HOW DID IT DO THAT?
SHOW ME...SHOW ME *LAURI-ELL...* HERE.
THE CITY AS IT ONCE WAS.
LAURI-ELL HERE... SMELLING FLOWERS?
HOWEVER THIS WORKS, THE HAMMER STILL ISN'T SHOWING ME LAURI-ELL COMMITTING A CRIME...
...AND STILL IT SHOWS ME NO PERPETRATOR--JUST THE DESTRUCTION.
DOES IT NOT KNOW? OR AM I SIMPLY ASKING THE WRONG QUESTIONS?

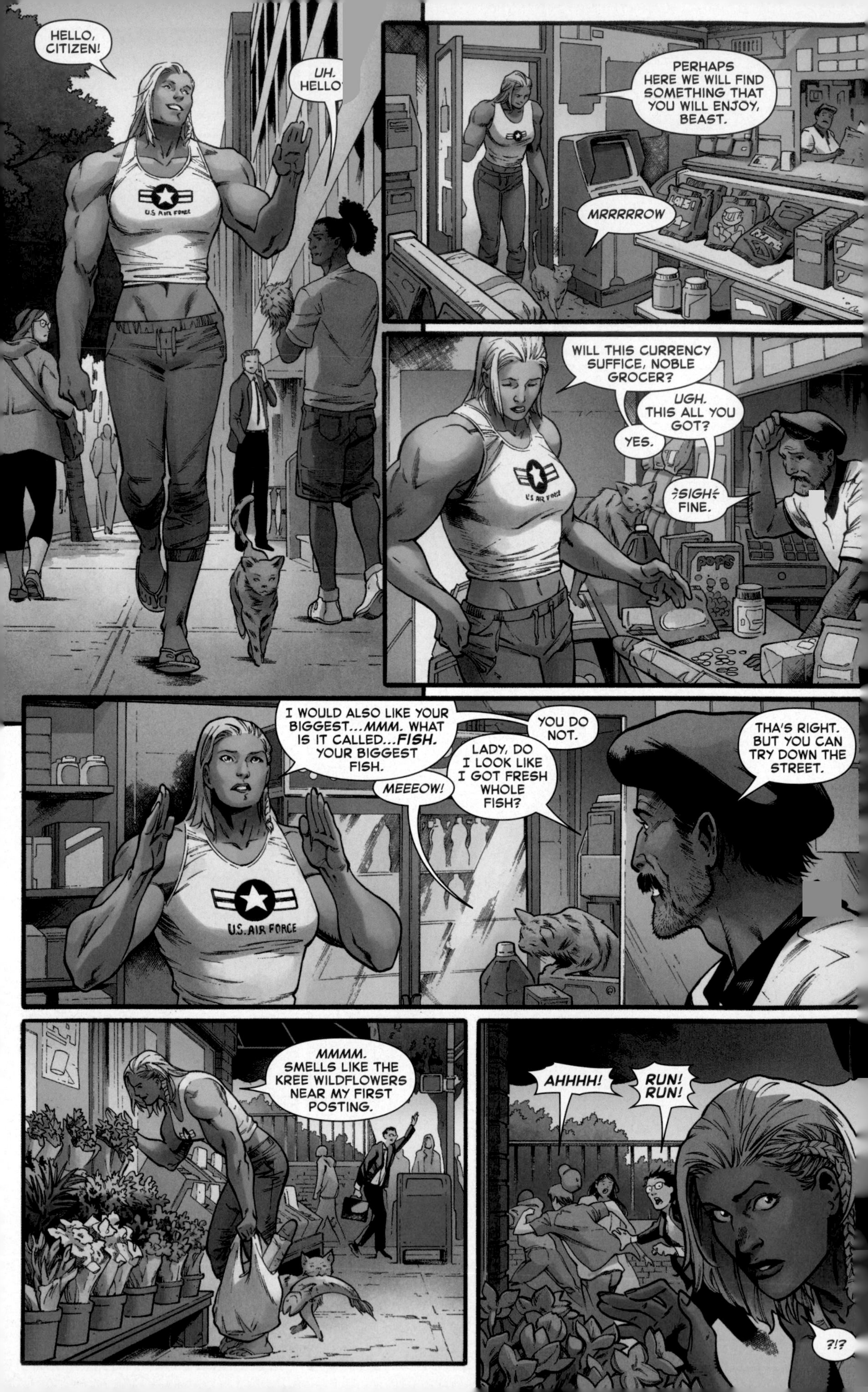
HELLO, CITIZEN!
UH. HELLO
PERHAPS HERE WE WILL FIND SOMETHING THAT YOU WILL ENJOY, BEAST.
MRRRRROW
WILL THIS CURRENCY SUFFICE, NOBLE GROCER?
UGH. THIS ALL YOU GOT?
YES.
SIGH FINE.
I WOULD ALSO LIKE YOUR BIGGEST...MMM. WHAT IS IT CALLED...FISH. YOUR BIGGEST FISH.
MEEEOW!
YOU DO NOT.
LADY, DO I LOOK LIKE I GOT FRESH WHOLE FISH?
THA'S RIGHT. BUT YOU CAN TRY DOWN THE STREET.
MMMM. SMELLS LIKE THE KREE WILDFLOWERS NEAR MY FIRST POSTING.
AHHHH!
RUN! RUN!
?!?

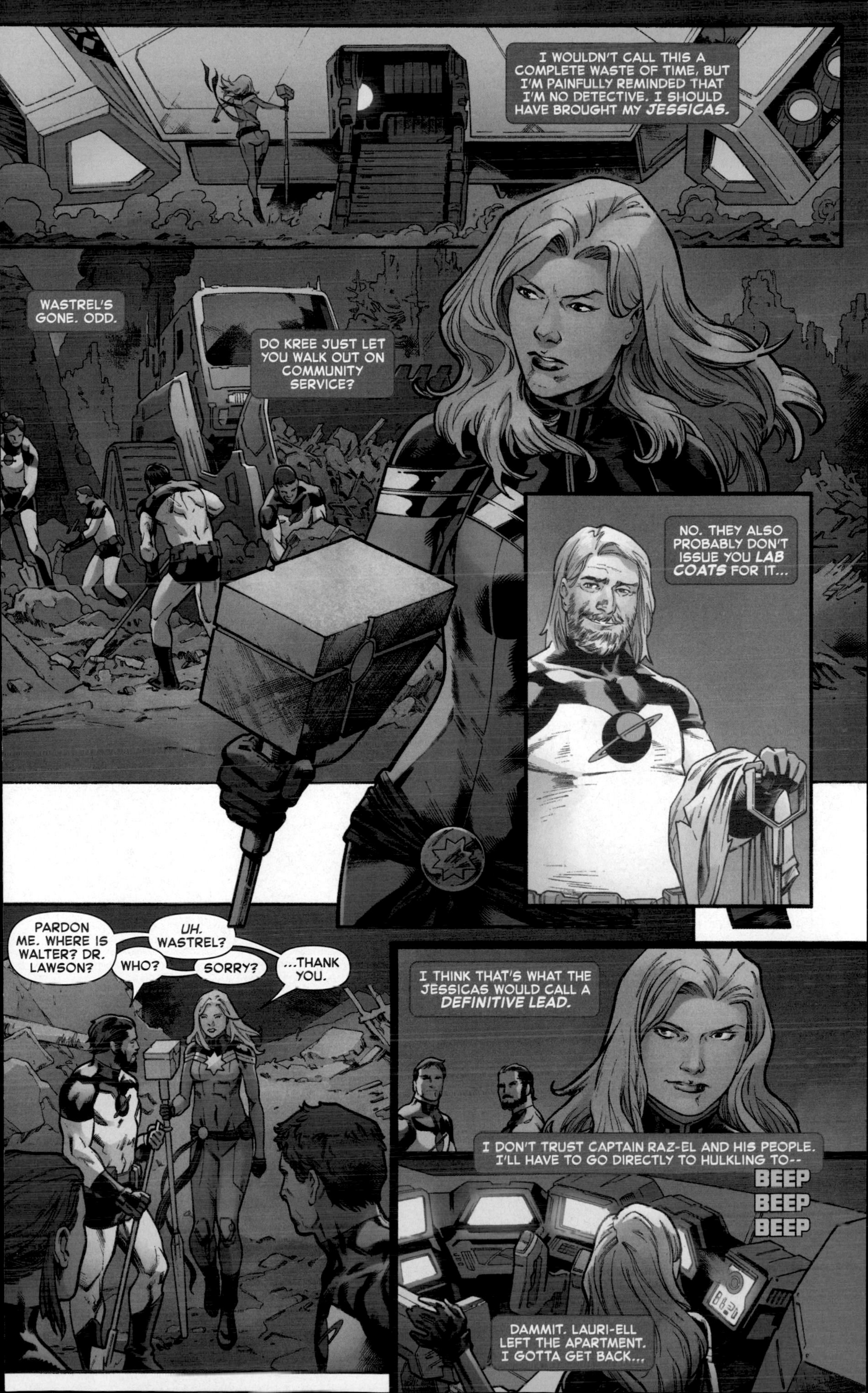
I WOULDN'T CALL THIS A COMPLETE WASTE OF TIME, BUT I'M PAINFULLY REMINDED THAT I'M NO DETECTIVE. I SHOULD HAVE BROUGHT MY JESSICAS.
WASTREL'S GONE. ODD.
DO KREE JUST LET YOU WALK OUT ON COMMUNITY SERVICE?
NO. THEY ALSO PROBABLY DON'T ISSUE YOU LAB COATS FOR IT...
PARDON ME. WHERE IS WALTER? DR. LAWSON?
WHO?
UH. WASTREL?
SORRY?
...THANK YOU.
I THINK THAT'S WHAT THE JESSICAS WOULD CALL A DEFINITIVE LEAD.
I DON'T TRUST CAPTAIN RAZ-EL AND HIS PEOPLE. I'LL HAVE TO GO DIRECTLY TO HULKLING TO--
BEEP
BEEP
BEEP
DAMMIT. LAURI-ELL LEFT THE APARTMENT. I GOTTA GET BACK...

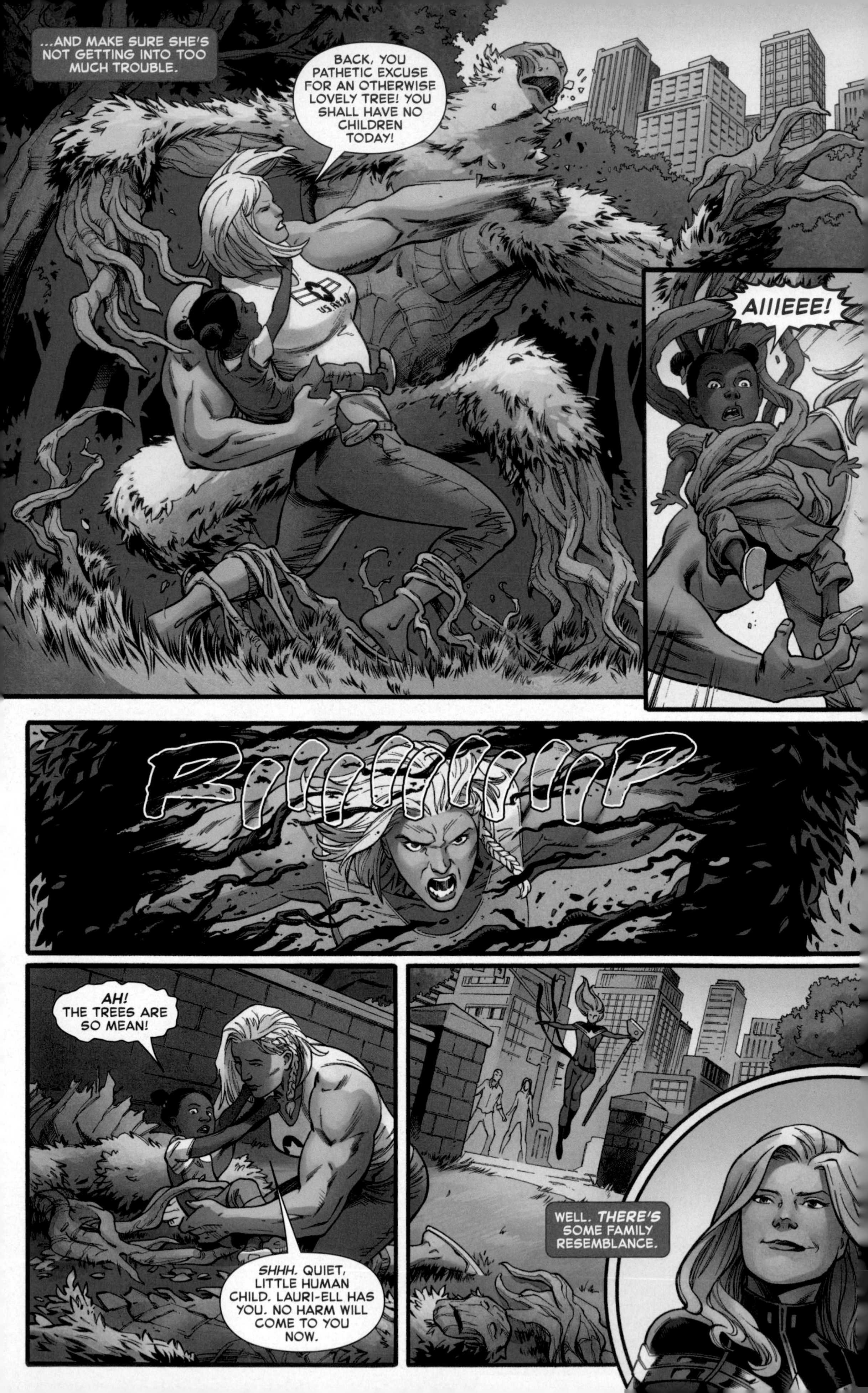
...AND MAKE SURE SHE'S NOT GETTING INTO TOO MUCH TROUBLE.
BACK, YOU PATHETIC EXCUSE FOR AN OTHERWISE LOVELY TREE! YOU SHALL HAVE NO CHILDREN TODAY!
AIIIEEE!
RIIIIIIIIP
AH! THE TREES ARE SO MEAN!
SHHH. QUIET, LITTLE HUMAN CHILD. LAURI-ELL HAS YOU. NO HARM WILL COME TO YOU NOW.
WELL. THERE'S SOME FAMILY RESEMBLANCE.

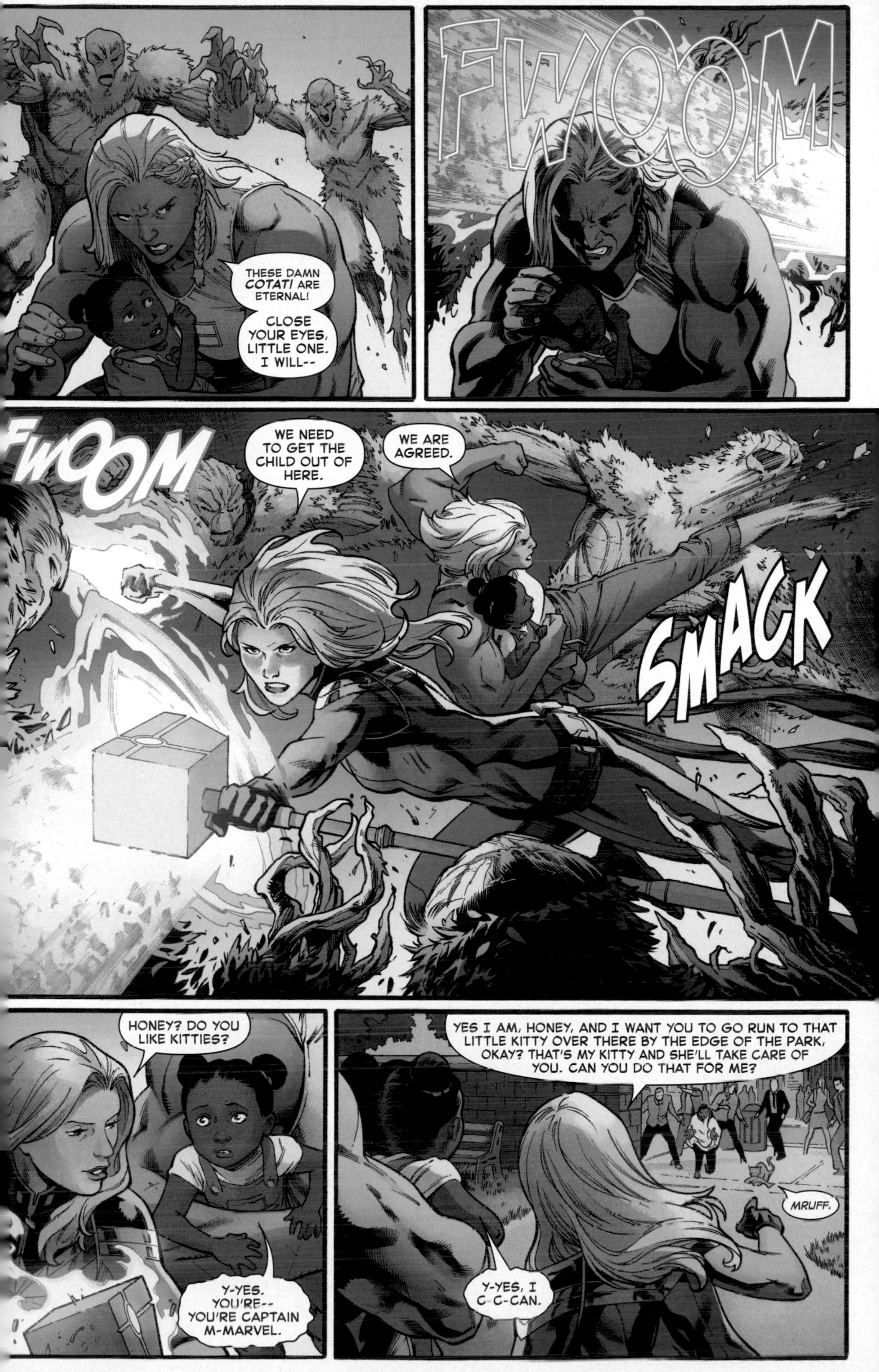
THESE DAMN *COTATI* ARE ETERNAL!
CLOSE YOUR EYES, LITTLE ONE. I WILL--
FWOOOM
FWOOOM
WE NEED TO GET THE CHILD OUT OF HERE.
WE ARE AGREED.
SMACK
HONEY? DO YOU LIKE KITTIES?
Y-YES. YOU'RE-- YOU'RE CAPTAIN M-MARVEL.
YES I AM, HONEY, AND I WANT YOU TO GO RUN TO THAT LITTLE KITTY OVER THERE BY THE EDGE OF THE PARK, OKAY? THAT'S MY KITTY AND SHE'LL TAKE CARE OF YOU. CAN YOU DO THAT FOR ME?
MRUFF.
Y-YES, I C-C-CAN.

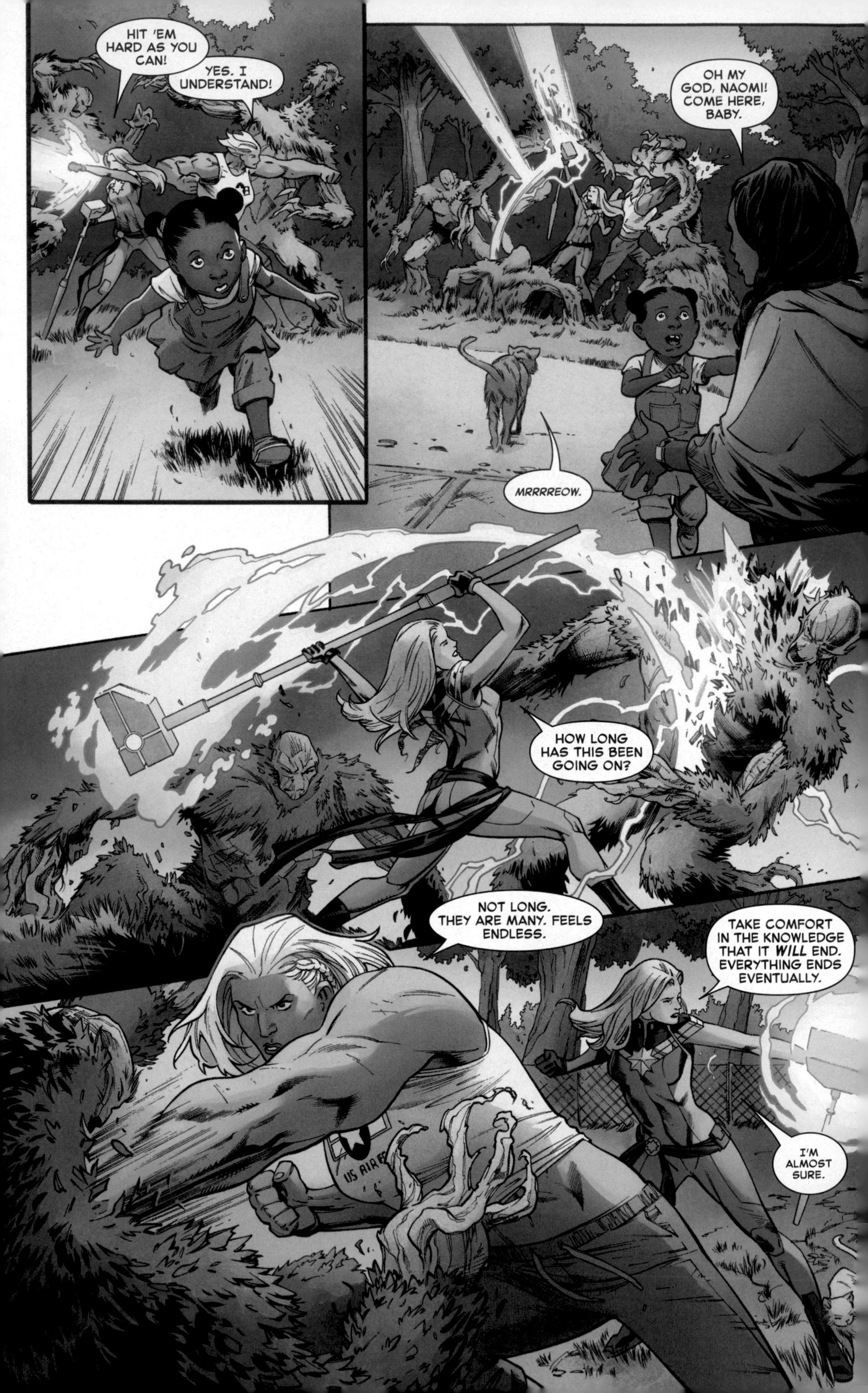
HIT 'EM HARD AS YOU CAN!
YES. I UNDERSTAND!
OH MY GOD, NAOMI! COME HERE, BABY.
MRRRREOW.
HOW LONG HAS THIS BEEN GOING ON?
NOT LONG. THEY ARE MANY. FEELS ENDLESS.
TAKE COMFORT IN THE KNOWLEDGE THAT IT WILL END. EVERYTHING ENDS EVENTUALLY.
I'M ALMOST SURE.

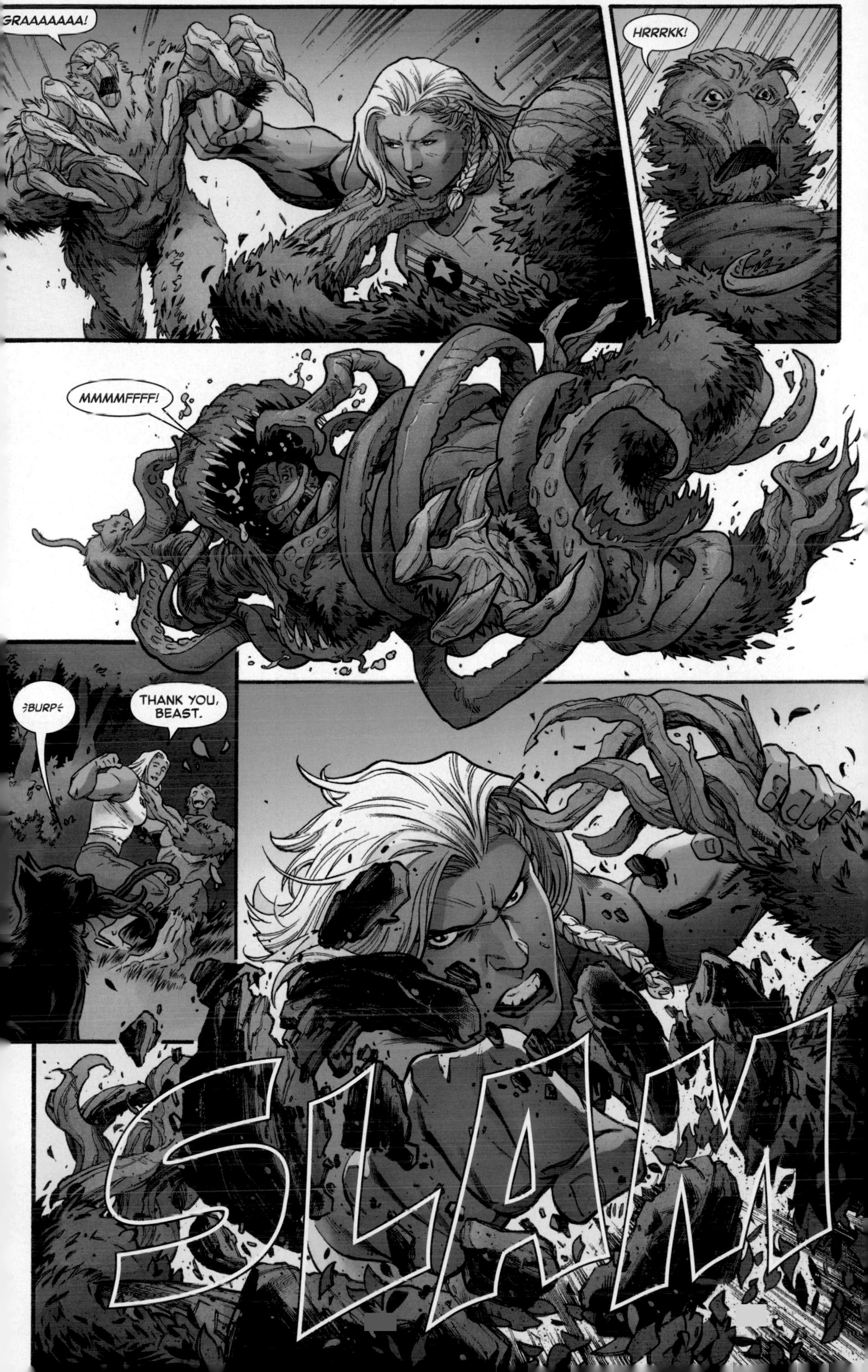
GRAAAAAAA!
HRRRKK!
MMMMFFFF!
BURP
THANK YOU, BEAST.
SLAM

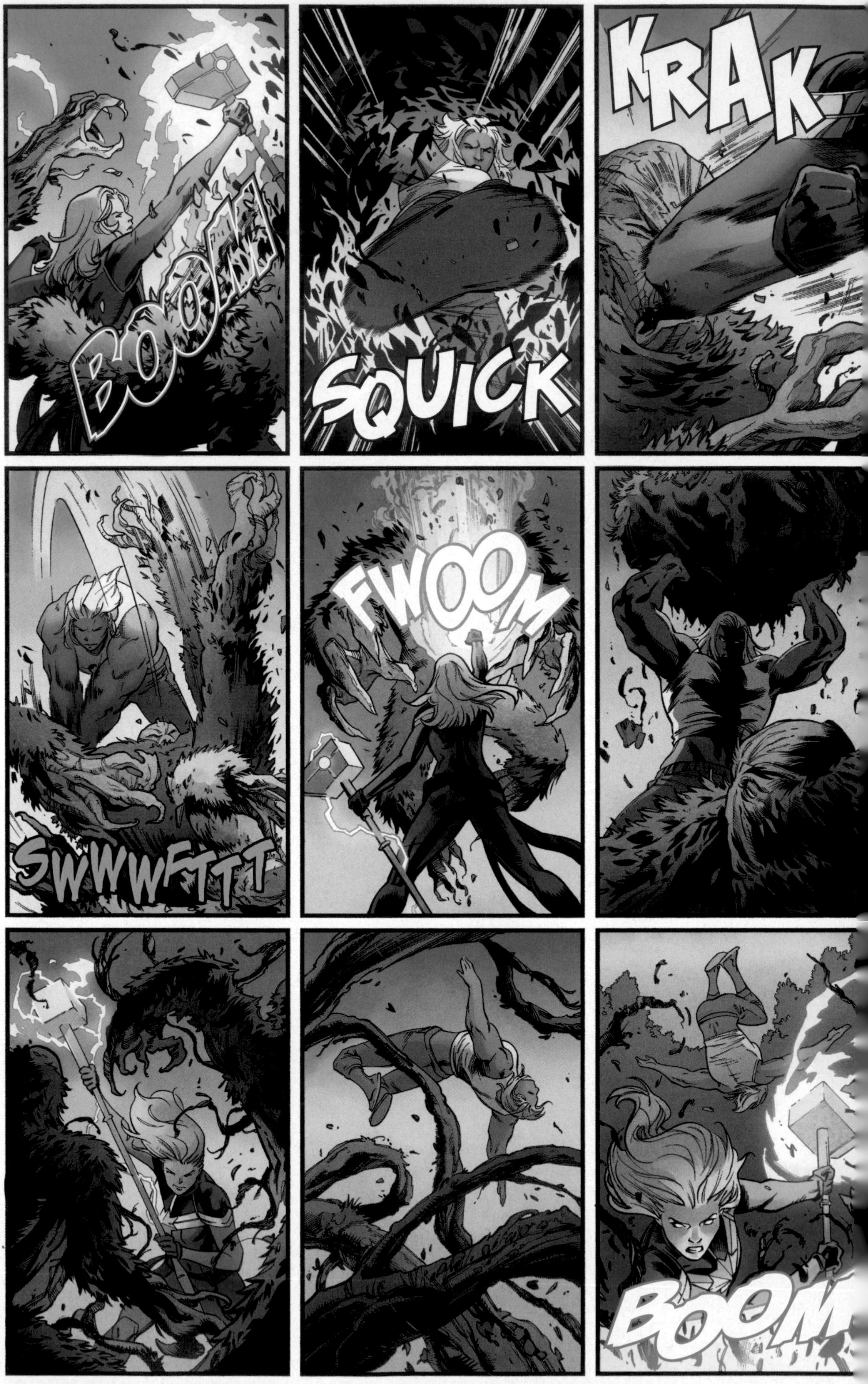
BOOM
SQUICK
KRAK
SWWWFTTT
FWOOM
BOOM

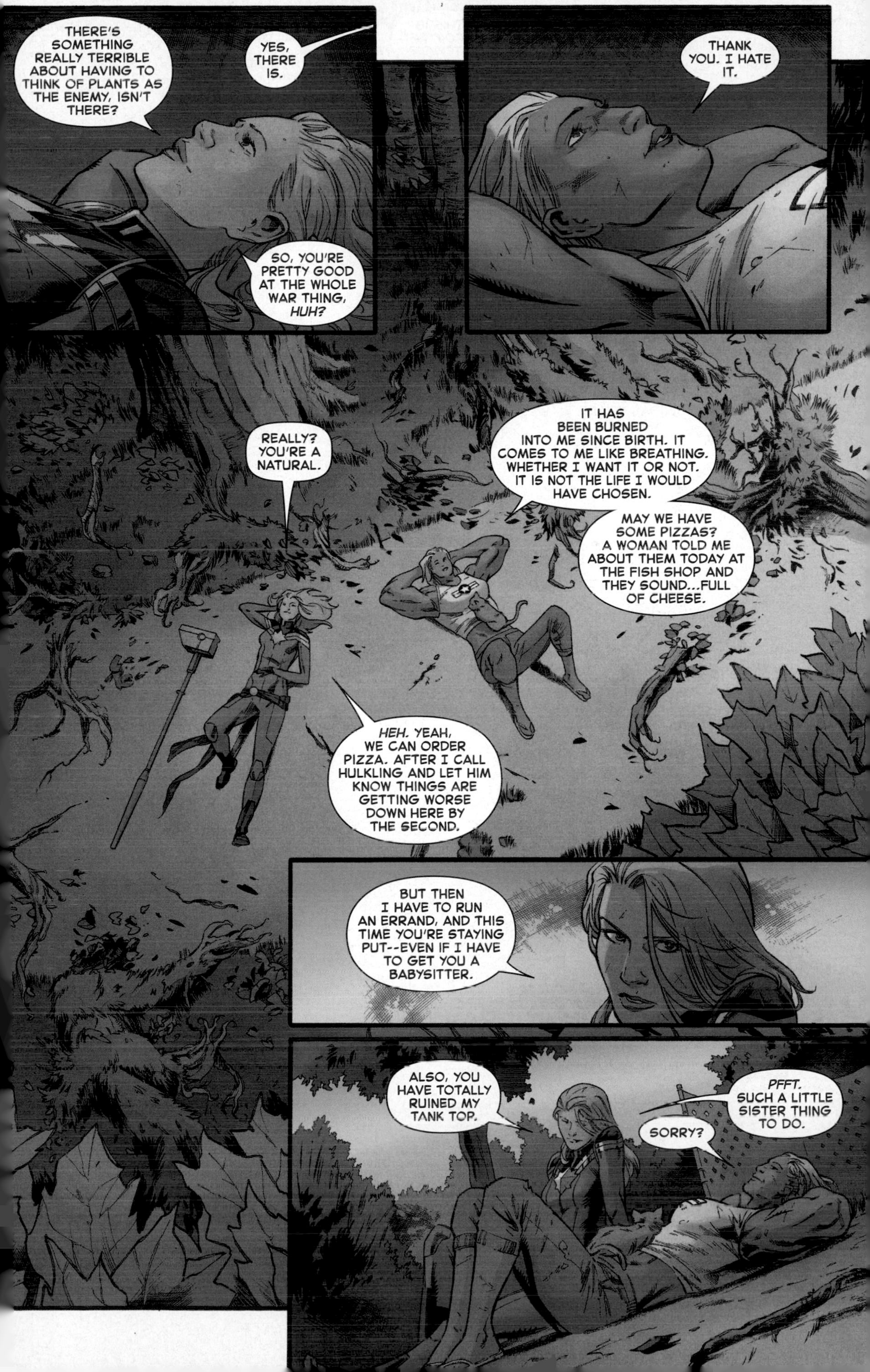
THERE'S SOMETHING REALLY TERRIBLE ABOUT HAVING TO THINK OF PLANTS AS THE ENEMY, ISN'T THERE?
YES, THERE IS.
SO, YOU'RE PRETTY GOOD AT THE WHOLE WAR THING, *HUH?*
THANK YOU. I HATE IT.
REALLY? YOU'RE A NATURAL.
IT HAS BEEN BURNED INTO ME SINCE BIRTH. IT COMES TO ME LIKE BREATHING. WHETHER I WANT IT OR NOT. IT IS NOT THE LIFE I WOULD HAVE CHOSEN.
MAY WE HAVE SOME PIZZAS? A WOMAN TOLD ME ABOUT THEM TODAY AT THE FISH SHOP AND THEY SOUND...FULL OF CHEESE.
HEH. YEAH, WE CAN ORDER PIZZA. AFTER I CALL HULKLING AND LET HIM KNOW THINGS ARE GETTING WORSE DOWN HERE BY THE SECOND.
BUT THEN I HAVE TO RUN AN ERRAND, AND THIS TIME YOU'RE STAYING PUT--EVEN IF I HAVE TO GET YOU A BABYSITTER.
ALSO, YOU HAVE TOTALLY RUINED MY TANK TOP.
SORRY?
PFFT. SUCH A LITTLE SISTER THING TO DO.

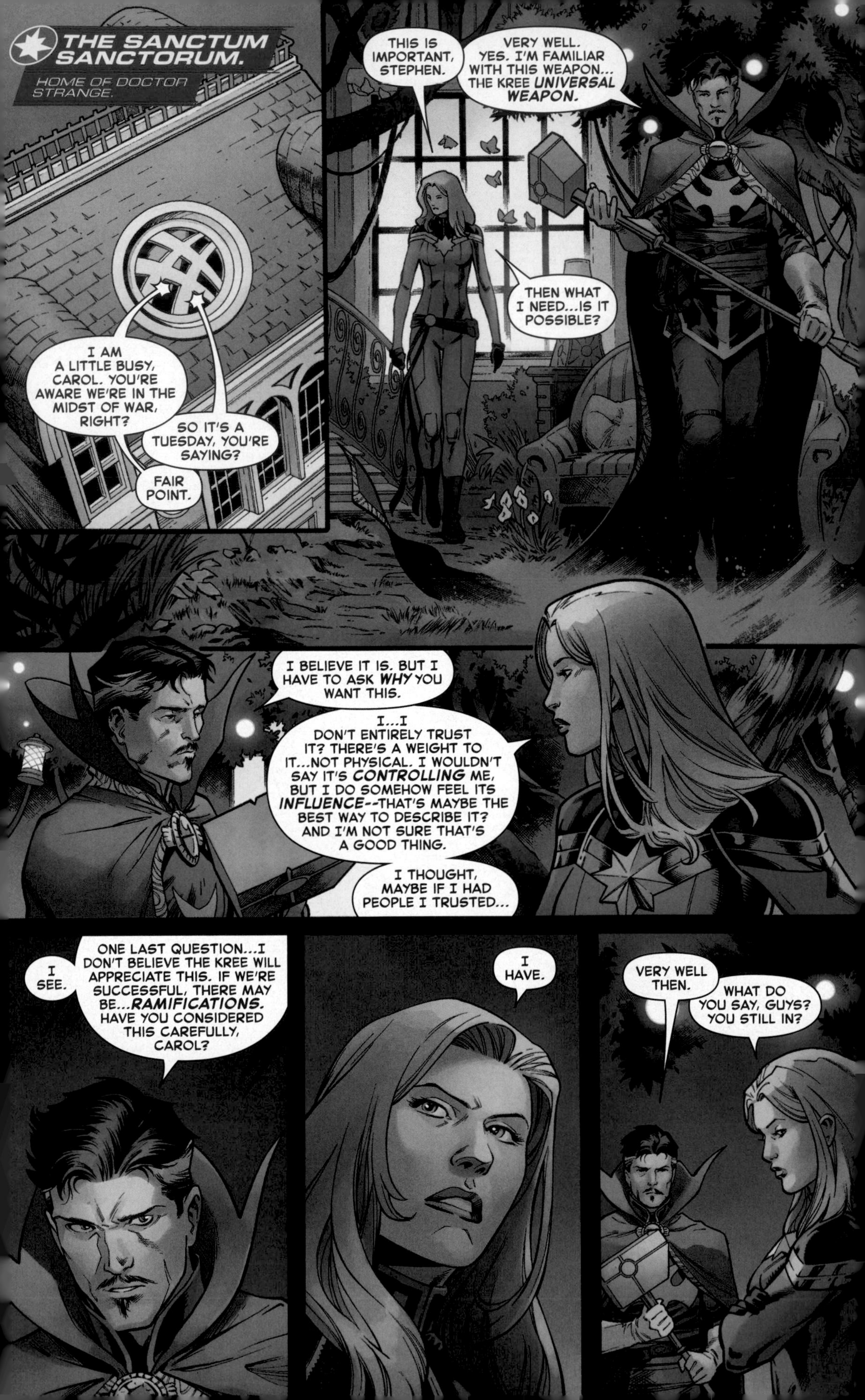
THE SANCTUM SANCTORUM.
HOME OF DOCTOR STRANGE.
I AM A LITTLE BUSY, CAROL. YOU'RE AWARE WE'RE IN THE MIDST OF WAR, RIGHT?
SO IT'S A TUESDAY, YOU'RE SAYING?
FAIR POINT.
THIS IS IMPORTANT, STEPHEN.
VERY WELL. YES. I'M FAMILIAR WITH THIS WEAPON... THE KREE UNIVERSAL WEAPON.
THEN WHAT I NEED...IS IT POSSIBLE?
I BELIEVE IT IS. BUT I HAVE TO ASK WHY YOU WANT THIS.
I...I DON'T ENTIRELY TRUST IT? THERE'S A WEIGHT TO IT...NOT PHYSICAL. I WOULDN'T SAY IT'S CONTROLLING ME, BUT I DO SOMEHOW FEEL ITS INFLUENCE--THAT'S MAYBE THE BEST WAY TO DESCRIBE IT? AND I'M NOT SURE THAT'S A GOOD THING.
I THOUGHT, MAYBE IF I HAD PEOPLE I TRUSTED...
I SEE.
ONE LAST QUESTION...I DON'T BELIEVE THE KREE WILL APPRECIATE THIS. IF WE'RE SUCCESSFUL, THERE MAY BE...RAMIFICATIONS. HAVE YOU CONSIDERED THIS CAREFULLY, CAROL?
I HAVE.
VERY WELL THEN.
WHAT DO YOU SAY, GUYS? YOU STILL IN?

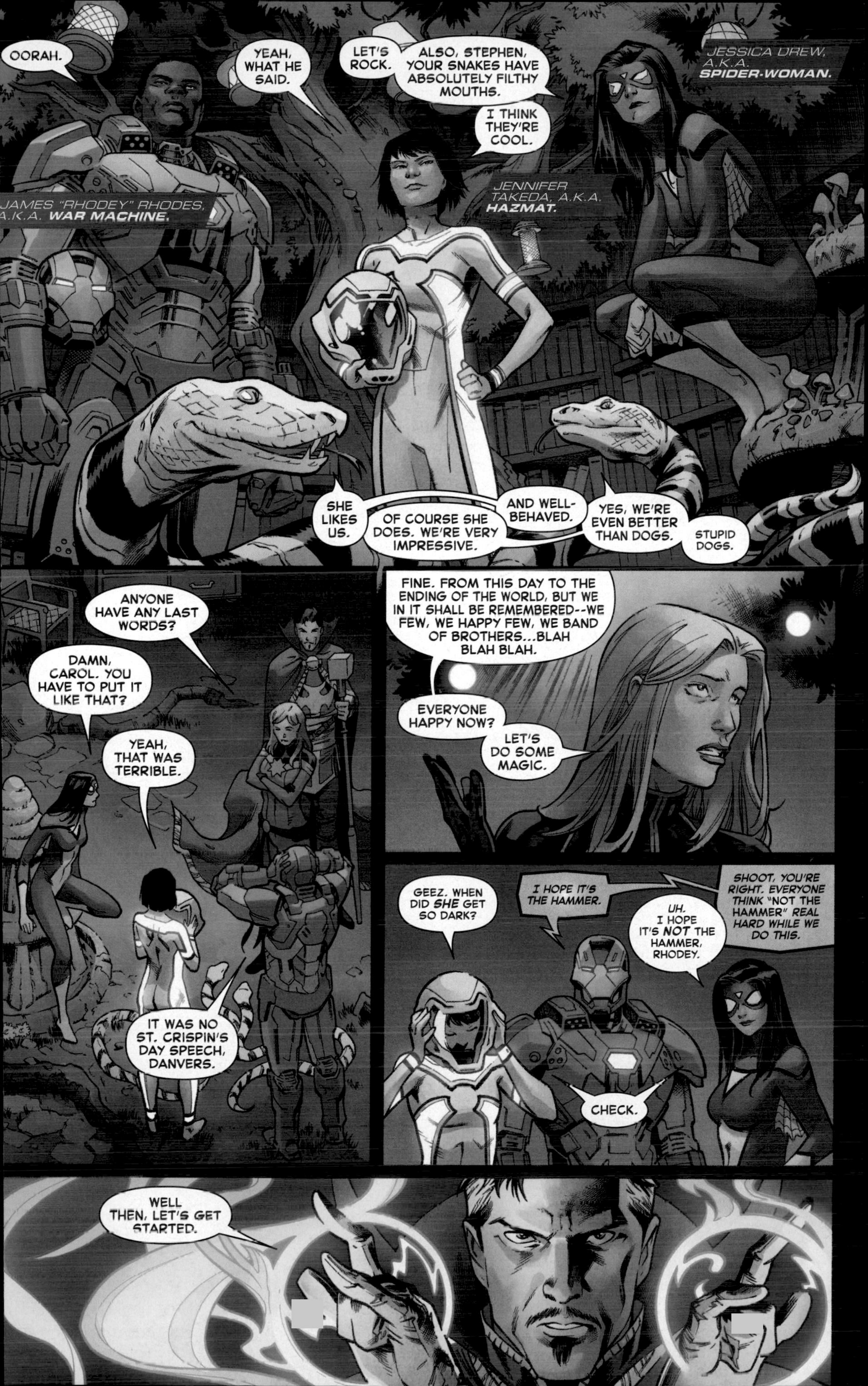
OORAH.
YEAH, WHAT HE SAID.
LET'S ROCK.
ALSO, STEPHEN, YOUR SNAKES HAVE ABSOLUTELY FILTHY MOUTHS.
I THINK THEY'RE COOL.
JESSICA DREW, A.K.A. SPIDER-WOMAN.
JAMES "RHODEY" RHODES, A.K.A. WAR MACHINE.
JENNIFER TAKEDA, A.K.A. HAZMAT.
SHE LIKES US.
OF COURSE SHE DOES. WE'RE VERY IMPRESSIVE.
AND WELL-BEHAVED.
YES, WE'RE EVEN BETTER THAN DOGS.
STUPID DOGS.
ANYONE HAVE ANY LAST WORDS?
DAMN, CAROL. YOU HAVE TO PUT IT LIKE THAT?
YEAH, THAT WAS TERRIBLE.
IT WAS NO ST. CRISPIN'S DAY SPEECH, DANVERS.
FINE. FROM THIS DAY TO THE ENDING OF THE WORLD, BUT WE IN IT SHALL BE REMEMBERED--WE FEW, WE HAPPY FEW, WE BAND OF BROTHERS...BLAH BLAH BLAH.
EVERYONE HAPPY NOW?
LET'S DO SOME MAGIC.
GEEZ. WHEN DID SHE GET SO DARK?
I HOPE IT'S THE HAMMER.
UH. I HOPE IT'S NOT THE HAMMER, RHODEY.
SHOOT, YOU'RE RIGHT. EVERYONE THINK "NOT THE HAMMER" REAL HARD WHILE WE DO THIS.
CHECK.
WELL THEN, LET'S GET STARTED.

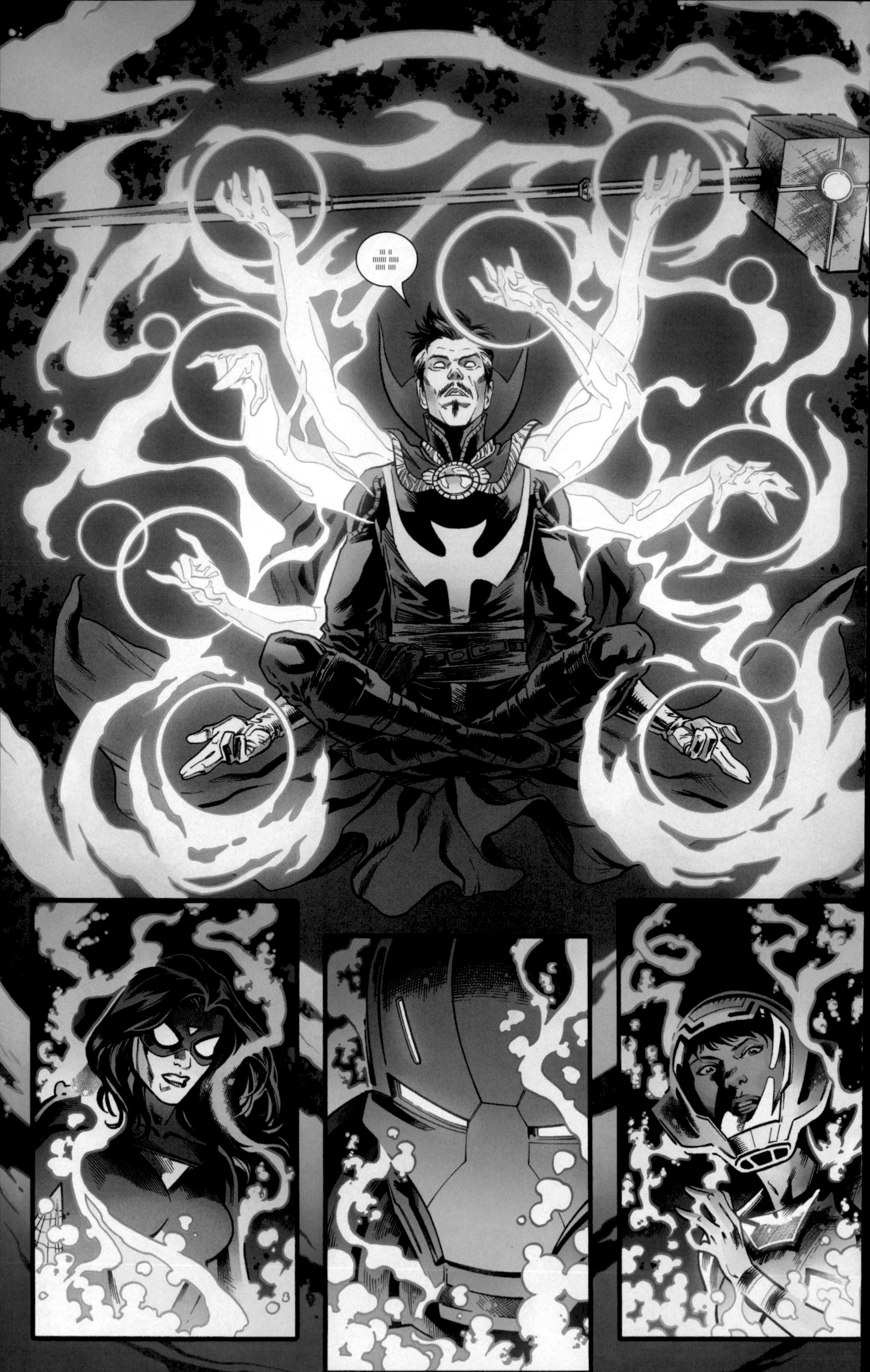

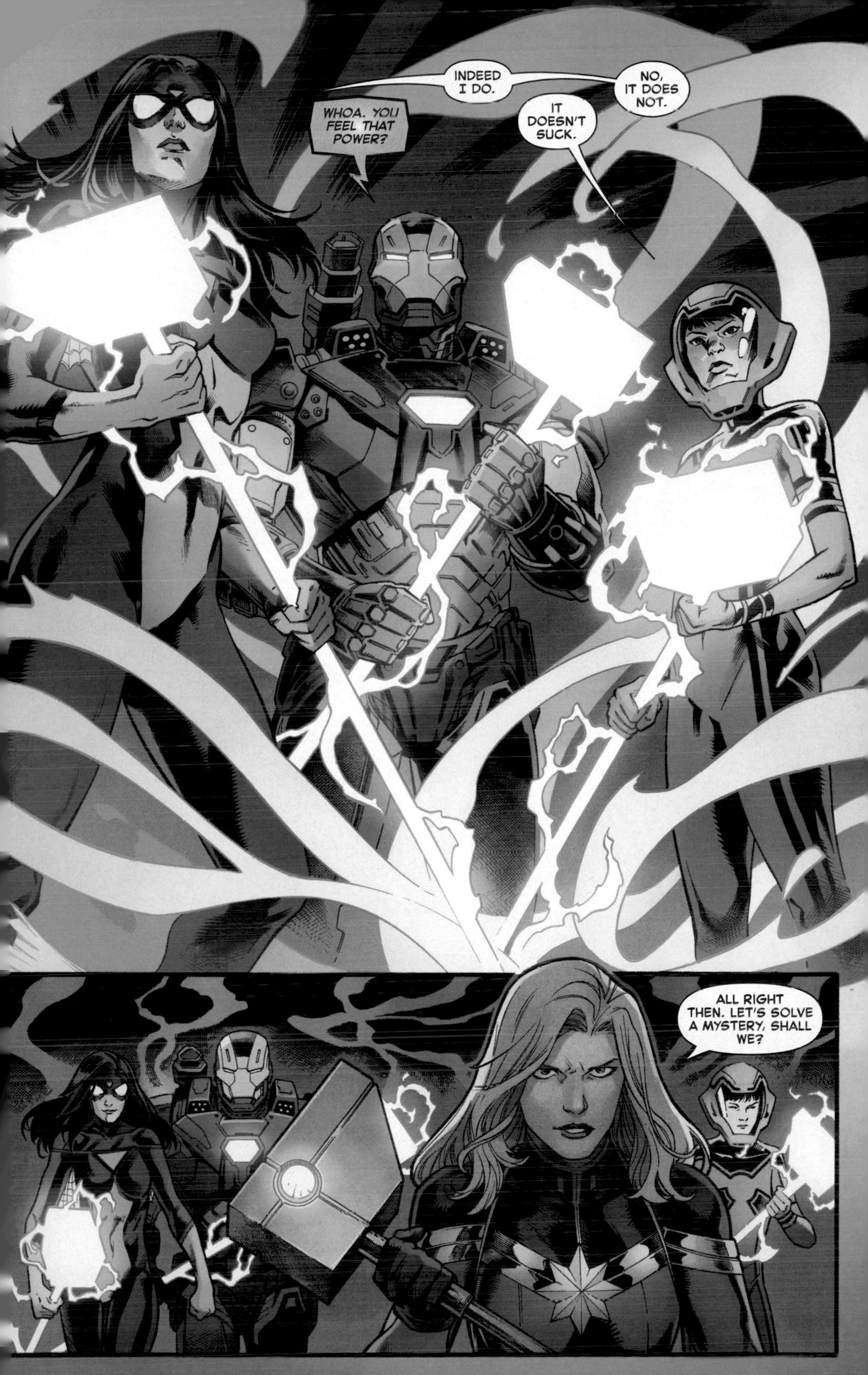
WHOA. YOU FEEL THAT POWER?
INDEED I DO.
IT DOESN'T SUCK.
NO, IT DOES NOT.
ALL RIGHT THEN. LET'S SOLVE A MYSTERY, SHALL WE?

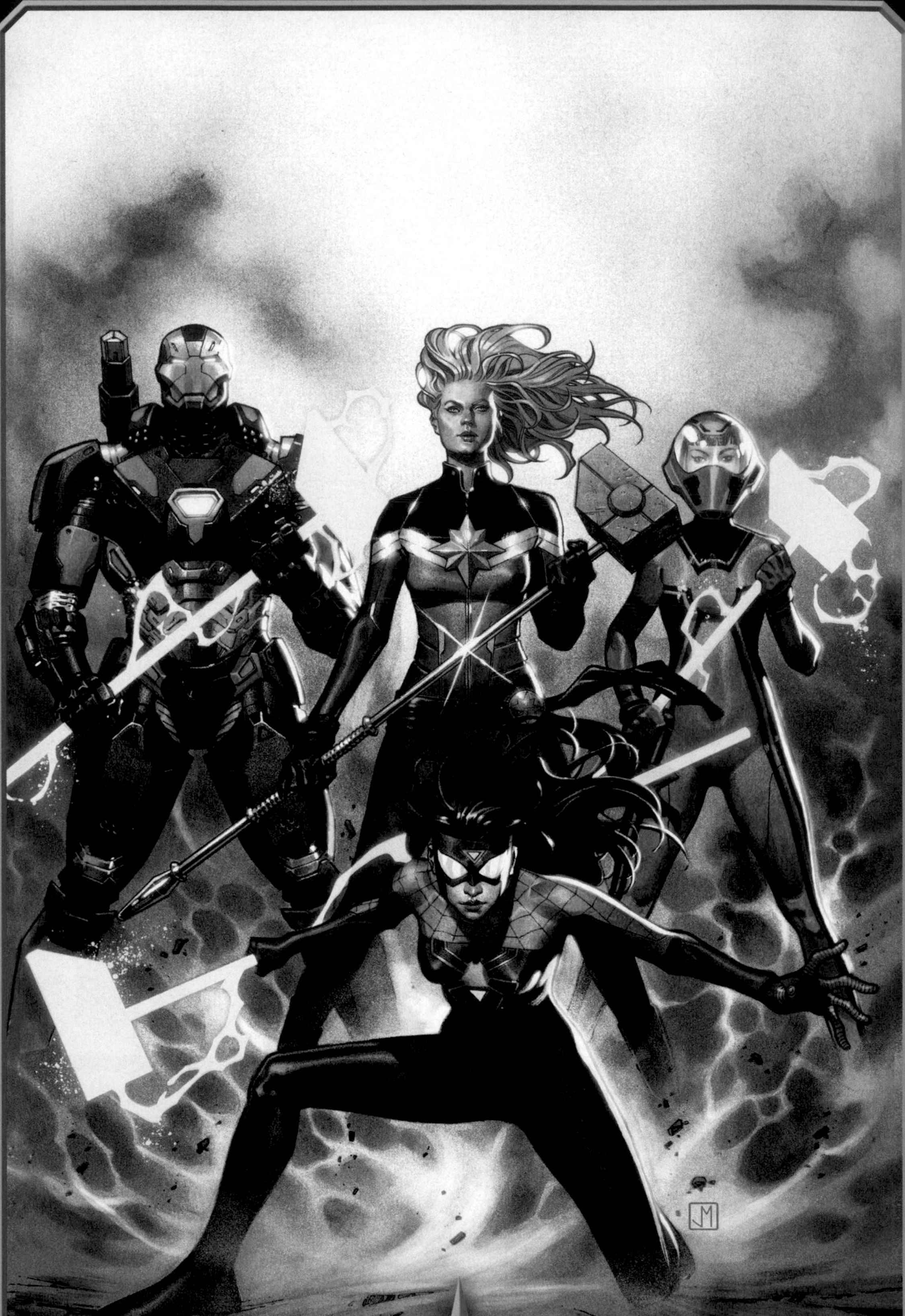

20

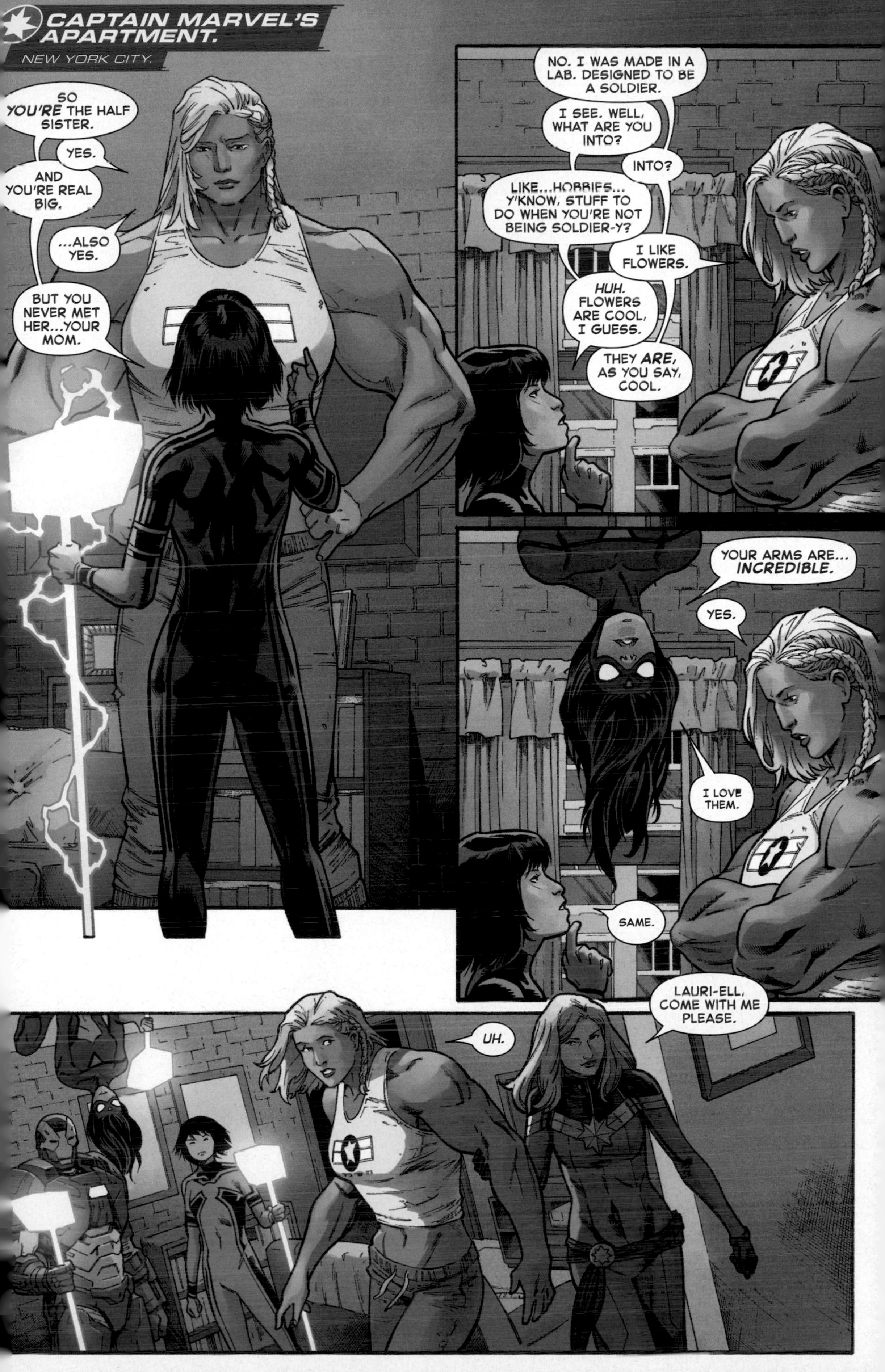
CAPTAIN MARVEL'S APARTMENT.
NEW YORK CITY.
SO YOU'RE THE HALF SISTER.
YES.
AND YOU'RE REAL BIG.
...ALSO YES.
BUT YOU NEVER MET HER...YOUR MOM.
NO. I WAS MADE IN A LAB. DESIGNED TO BE A SOLDIER.
I SEE. WELL, WHAT ARE YOU INTO?
INTO?
LIKE...HOBBIES... Y'KNOW, STUFF TO DO WHEN YOU'RE NOT BEING SOLDIER-Y?
I LIKE FLOWERS.
HUH. FLOWERS ARE COOL, I GUESS.
THEY ARE, AS YOU SAY, COOL.
YOUR ARMS ARE... INCREDIBLE.
YES.
I LOVE THEM.
SAME.
LAURI-ELL, COME WITH ME PLEASE.
UH.

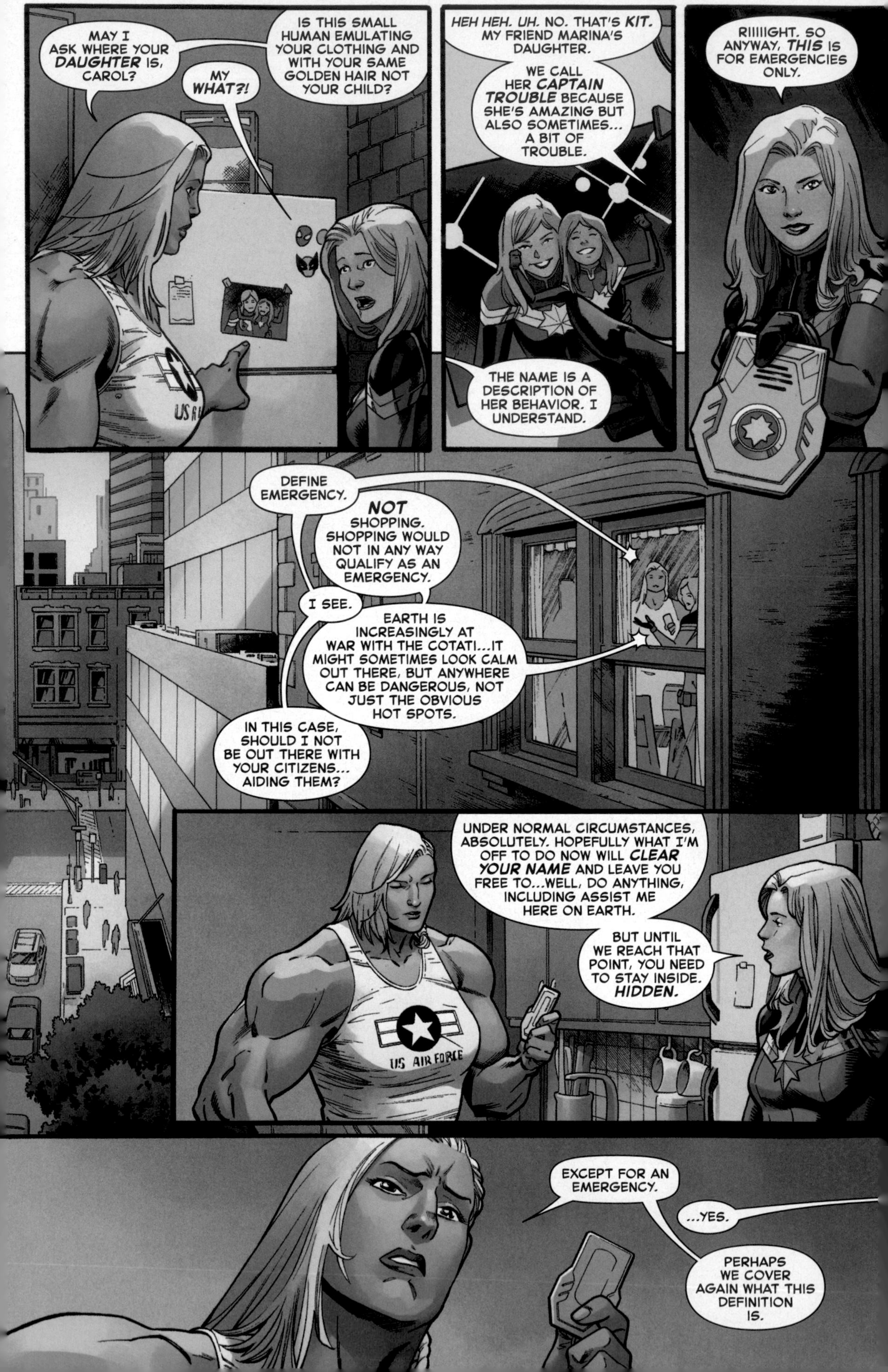
MAY I ASK WHERE YOUR DAUGHTER IS, CAROL?
MY WHAT?!
IS THIS SMALL HUMAN EMULATING YOUR CLOTHING AND WITH YOUR SAME GOLDEN HAIR NOT YOUR CHILD?
HEH HEH. UH. NO. THAT'S KIT. MY FRIEND MARINA'S DAUGHTER.
WE CALL HER CAPTAIN TROUBLE BECAUSE SHE'S AMAZING BUT ALSO SOMETIMES... A BIT OF TROUBLE.
THE NAME IS A DESCRIPTION OF HER BEHAVIOR. I UNDERSTAND.
RIIIIIGHT. SO ANYWAY, THIS IS FOR EMERGENCIES ONLY.
DEFINE EMERGENCY.
NOT SHOPPING. SHOPPING WOULD NOT IN ANY WAY QUALIFY AS AN EMERGENCY.
I SEE.
EARTH IS INCREASINGLY AT WAR WITH THE COTATI...IT MIGHT SOMETIMES LOOK CALM OUT THERE, BUT ANYWHERE CAN BE DANGEROUS, NOT JUST THE OBVIOUS HOT SPOTS.
IN THIS CASE, SHOULD I NOT BE OUT THERE WITH YOUR CITIZENS... AIDING THEM?
UNDER NORMAL CIRCUMSTANCES, ABSOLUTELY. HOPEFULLY WHAT I'M OFF TO DO NOW WILL CLEAR YOUR NAME AND LEAVE YOU FREE TO...WELL, DO ANYTHING, INCLUDING ASSIST ME HERE ON EARTH.
BUT UNTIL WE REACH THAT POINT, YOU NEED TO STAY INSIDE. HIDDEN.
US AIR FORCE
EXCEPT FOR AN EMERGENCY.
...YES.
PERHAPS WE COVER AGAIN WHAT THIS DEFINITION IS.

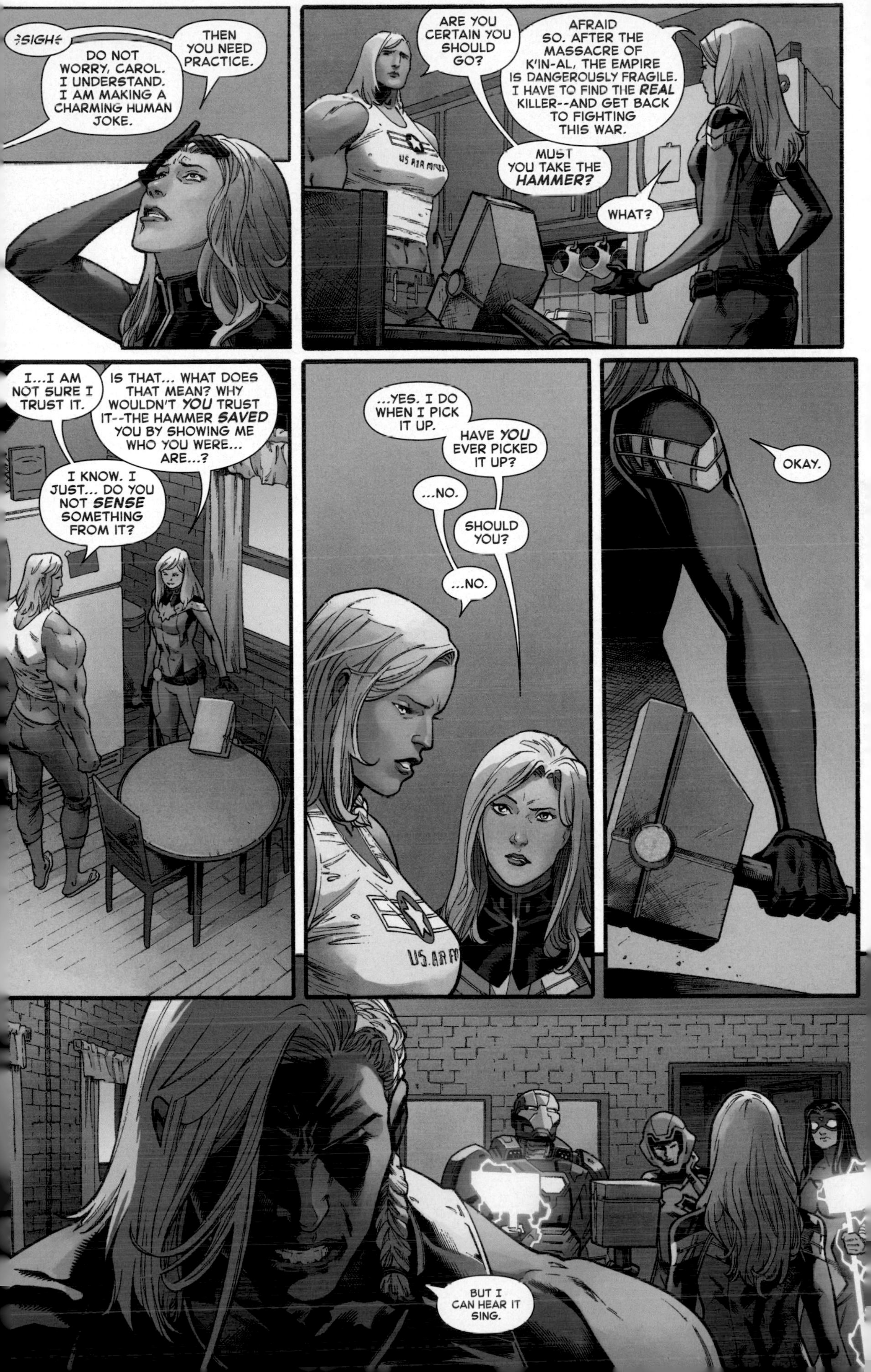

SIGH
DO NOT WORRY, CAROL. I UNDERSTAND. I AM MAKING A CHARMING HUMAN JOKE.
THEN YOU NEED PRACTICE.
ARE YOU CERTAIN YOU SHOULD GO?
AFRAID SO. AFTER THE MASSACRE OF K'IN-AL, THE EMPIRE IS DANGEROUSLY FRAGILE. I HAVE TO FIND THE REAL KILLER--AND GET BACK TO FIGHTING THIS WAR.
MUST YOU TAKE THE HAMMER?
WHAT?
I...I AM NOT SURE I TRUST IT.
IS THAT... WHAT DOES THAT MEAN? WHY WOULDN'T YOU TRUST IT--THE HAMMER SAVED YOU BY SHOWING ME WHO YOU WERE... ARE...?
I KNOW. I JUST... DO YOU NOT SENSE SOMETHING FROM IT?
...YES. I DO WHEN I PICK IT UP.
HAVE YOU EVER PICKED IT UP?
...NO.
SHOULD YOU?
...NO.
OKAY.
BUT I CAN HEAR IT SING.

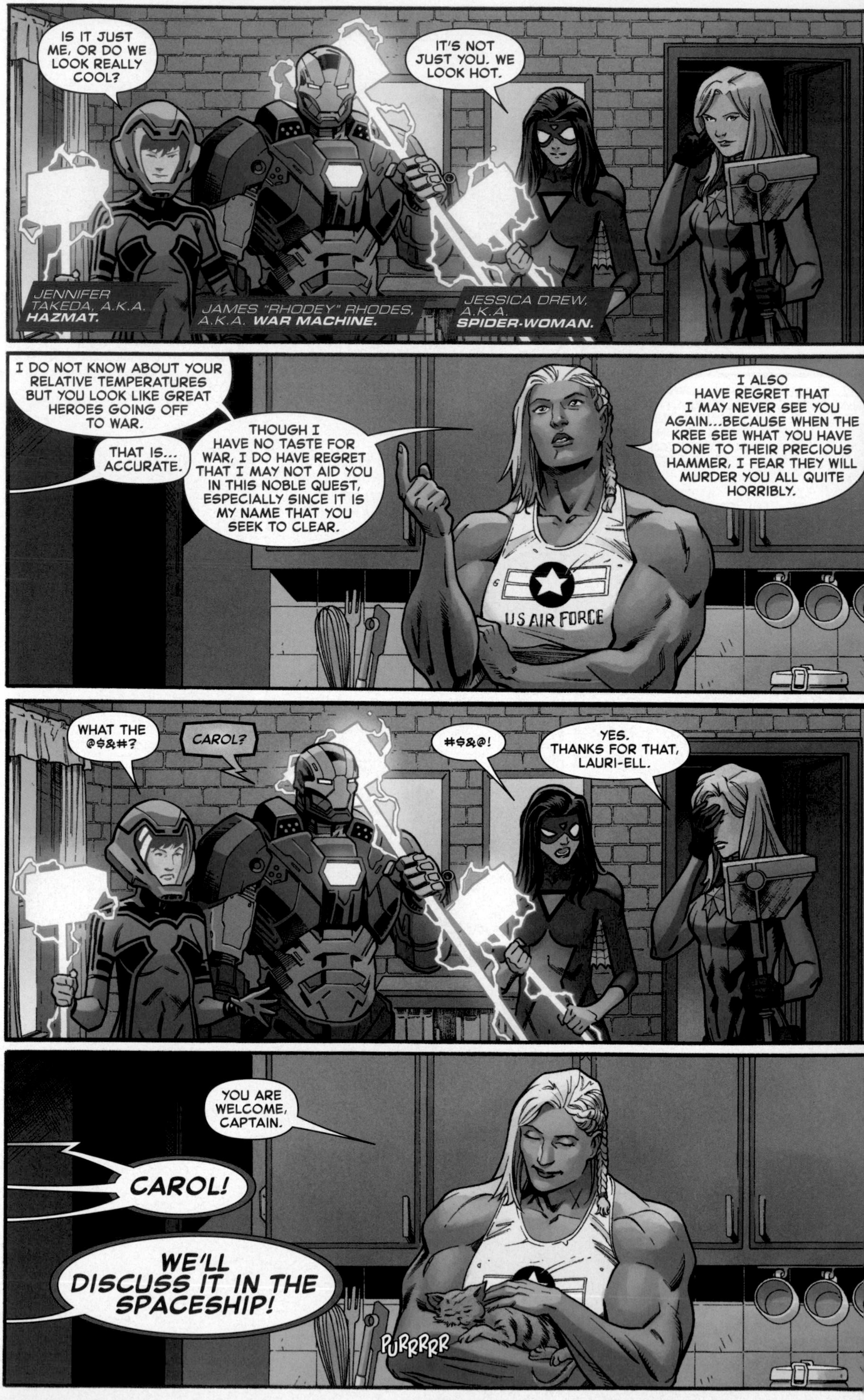
IS IT JUST ME, OR DO WE LOOK REALLY COOL?
IT'S NOT JUST YOU. WE LOOK HOT.
JENNIFER TAKEDA, A.K.A. HAZMAT.
JAMES "RHODEY" RHODES, A.K.A. WAR MACHINE.
JESSICA DREW, A.K.A. SPIDER-WOMAN.
I DO NOT KNOW ABOUT YOUR RELATIVE TEMPERATURES BUT YOU LOOK LIKE GREAT HEROES GOING OFF TO WAR.
THAT IS... ACCURATE.
THOUGH I HAVE NO TASTE FOR WAR, I DO HAVE REGRET THAT I MAY NOT AID YOU IN THIS NOBLE QUEST, ESPECIALLY SINCE IT IS MY NAME THAT YOU SEEK TO CLEAR.
I ALSO HAVE REGRET THAT I MAY NEVER SEE YOU AGAIN...BECAUSE WHEN THE KREE SEE WHAT YOU HAVE DONE TO THEIR PRECIOUS HAMMER, I FEAR THEY WILL MURDER YOU ALL QUITE HORRIBLY.
US AIR FORCE
WHAT THE @$&#?
CAROL?
#$&@!
YES. THANKS FOR THAT, LAURI-ELL.
YOU ARE WELCOME, CAPTAIN.
CAROL!
WE'LL DISCUSS IT IN THE SPACESHIP!
PURRRRR

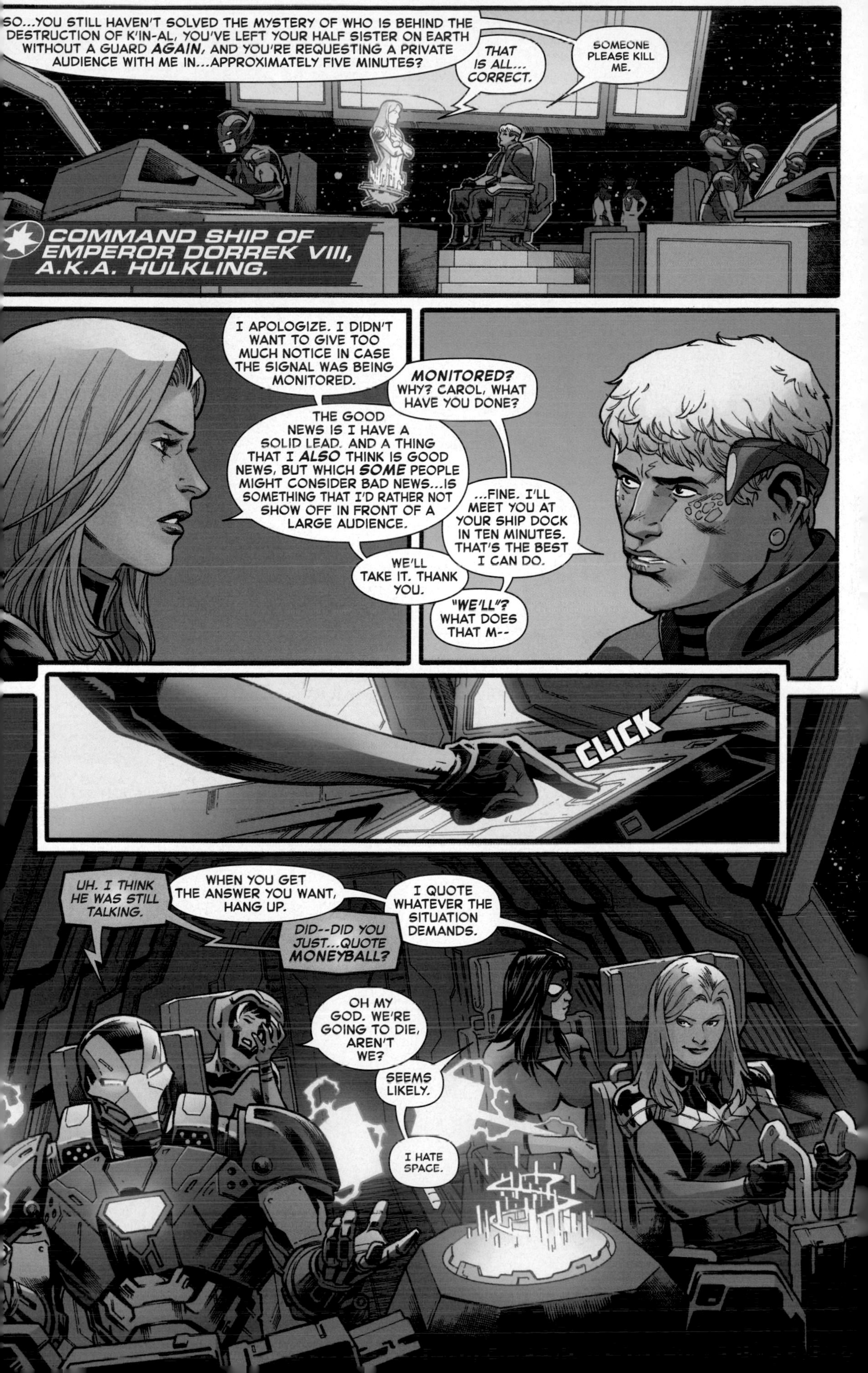
SO...YOU STILL HAVEN'T SOLVED THE MYSTERY OF WHO IS BEHIND THE DESTRUCTION OF K'IN-AL, YOU'VE LEFT YOUR HALF SISTER ON EARTH WITHOUT A GUARD AGAIN, AND YOU'RE REQUESTING A PRIVATE AUDIENCE WITH ME IN...APPROXIMATELY FIVE MINUTES?
THAT IS ALL... CORRECT.
SOMEONE PLEASE KILL ME.
COMMAND SHIP OF EMPEROR DORREK VIII, A.K.A. HULKLING.
I APOLOGIZE. I DIDN'T WANT TO GIVE TOO MUCH NOTICE IN CASE THE SIGNAL WAS BEING MONITORED.
MONITORED? WHY? CAROL, WHAT HAVE YOU DONE?
THE GOOD NEWS IS I HAVE A SOLID LEAD. AND A THING THAT I ALSO THINK IS GOOD NEWS, BUT WHICH SOME PEOPLE MIGHT CONSIDER BAD NEWS...IS SOMETHING THAT I'D RATHER NOT SHOW OFF IN FRONT OF A LARGE AUDIENCE.
...FINE. I'LL MEET YOU AT YOUR SHIP DOCK IN TEN MINUTES. THAT'S THE BEST I CAN DO.
WE'LL TAKE IT. THANK YOU.
"WE'LL"? WHAT DOES THAT M--
CLICK
UH. I THINK HE WAS STILL TALKING.
WHEN YOU GET THE ANSWER YOU WANT, HANG UP.
DID--DID YOU JUST...QUOTE MONEYBALL?
I QUOTE WHATEVER THE SITUATION DEMANDS.
OH MY GOD. WE'RE GOING TO DIE, AREN'T WE?
SEEMS LIKELY.
I HATE SPACE.

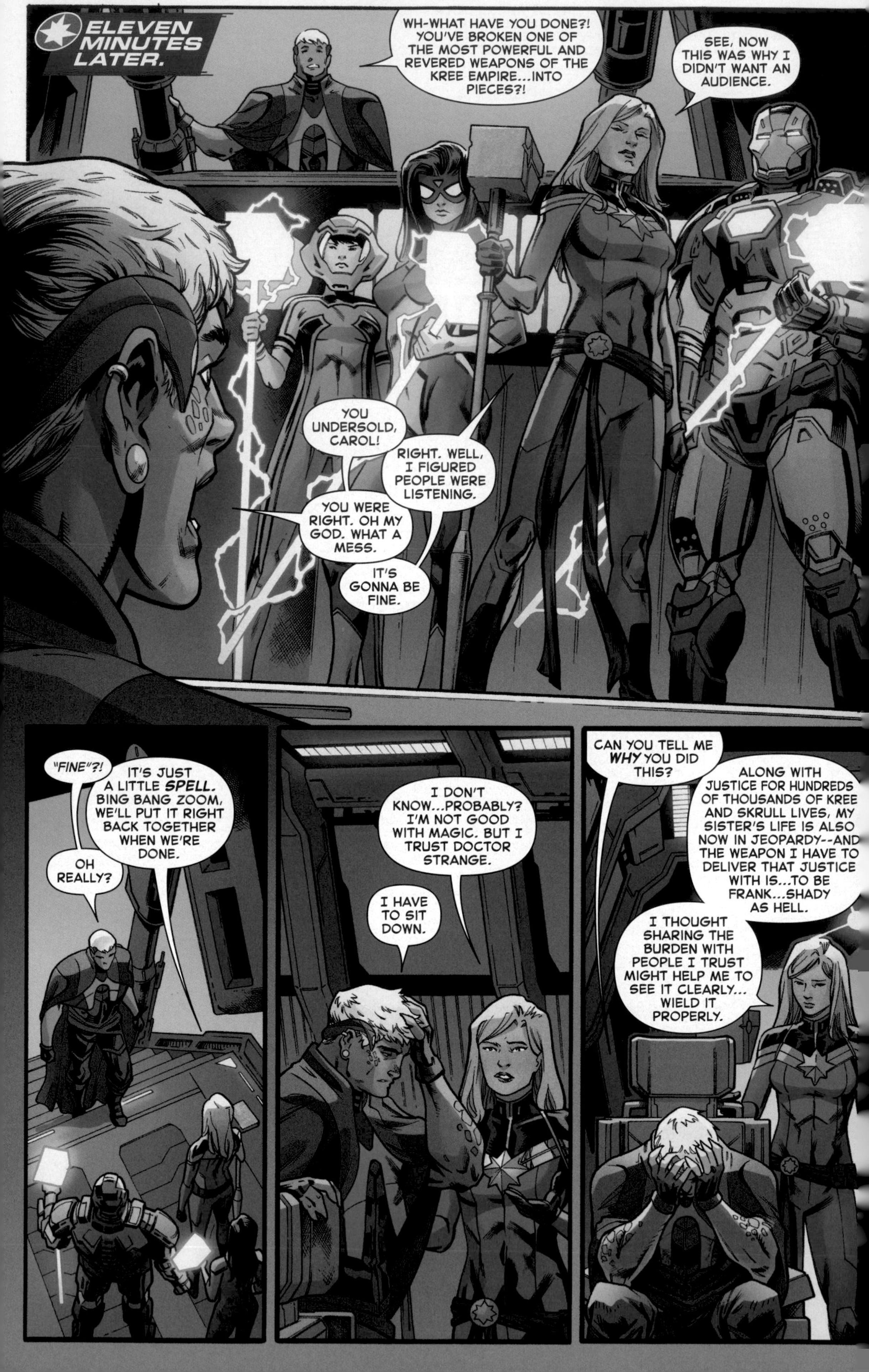
ELEVEN MINUTES LATER.
WH-WHAT HAVE YOU DONE?! YOU'VE BROKEN ONE OF THE MOST POWERFUL AND REVERED WEAPONS OF THE KREE EMPIRE...INTO PIECES?!
SEE, NOW THIS WAS WHY I DIDN'T WANT AN AUDIENCE.
YOU UNDERSOLD, CAROL!
RIGHT. WELL, I FIGURED PEOPLE WERE LISTENING.
YOU WERE RIGHT. OH MY GOD. WHAT A MESS.
IT'S GONNA BE FINE.
"FINE"?!
IT'S JUST A LITTLE SPELL. BING BANG ZOOM, WE'LL PUT IT RIGHT BACK TOGETHER WHEN WE'RE DONE.
OH REALLY?
I DON'T KNOW...PROBABLY? I'M NOT GOOD WITH MAGIC. BUT I TRUST DOCTOR STRANGE.
I HAVE TO SIT DOWN.
CAN YOU TELL ME WHY YOU DID THIS?
ALONG WITH JUSTICE FOR HUNDREDS OF THOUSANDS OF KREE AND SKRULL LIVES, MY SISTER'S LIFE IS ALSO NOW IN JEOPARDY--AND THE WEAPON I HAVE TO DELIVER THAT JUSTICE WITH IS...TO BE FRANK...SHADY AS HELL.
I THOUGHT SHARING THE BURDEN WITH PEOPLE I TRUST MIGHT HELP ME TO SEE IT CLEARLY... WIELD IT PROPERLY.

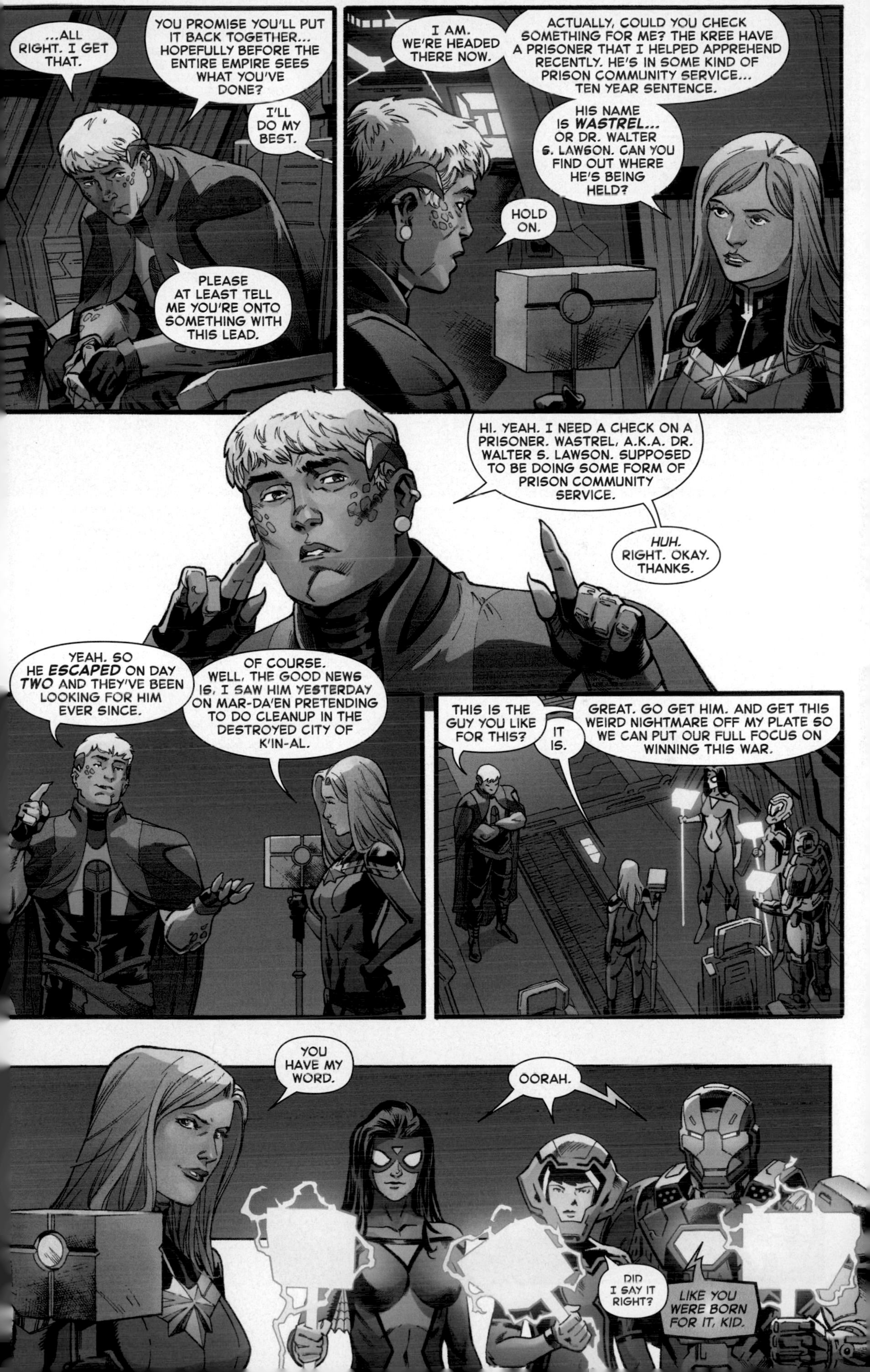
...ALL RIGHT. I GET THAT.
YOU PROMISE YOU'LL PUT IT BACK TOGETHER... HOPEFULLY BEFORE THE ENTIRE EMPIRE SEES WHAT YOU'VE DONE?
I'LL DO MY BEST.
PLEASE AT LEAST TELL ME YOU'RE ONTO SOMETHING WITH THIS LEAD.
I AM. WE'RE HEADED THERE NOW.
ACTUALLY, COULD YOU CHECK SOMETHING FOR ME? THE KREE HAVE A PRISONER THAT I HELPED APPREHEND RECENTLY. HE'S IN SOME KIND OF PRISON COMMUNITY SERVICE... TEN YEAR SENTENCE.
HIS NAME IS ***WASTREL...*** OR DR. WALTER S. LAWSON. CAN YOU FIND OUT WHERE HE'S BEING HELD?
HOLD ON.
HI. YEAH. I NEED A CHECK ON A PRISONER. WASTREL, A.K.A. DR. WALTER S. LAWSON. SUPPOSED TO BE DOING SOME FORM OF PRISON COMMUNITY SERVICE.
HUH. RIGHT. OKAY. THANKS.
YEAH. SO HE ***ESCAPED*** ON DAY ***TWO*** AND THEY'VE BEEN LOOKING FOR HIM EVER SINCE.
OF COURSE. WELL, THE GOOD NEWS IS, I SAW HIM YESTERDAY ON MAR-DA'EN PRETENDING TO DO CLEANUP IN THE DESTROYED CITY OF K'IN-AL.
THIS IS THE GUY YOU LIKE FOR THIS?
IT IS.
GREAT. GO GET HIM. AND GET THIS WEIRD NIGHTMARE OFF MY PLATE SO WE CAN PUT OUR FULL FOCUS ON WINNING THIS WAR.
YOU HAVE MY WORD.
OORAH.
DID I SAY IT RIGHT?
LIKE YOU WERE BORN FOR IT, KID.

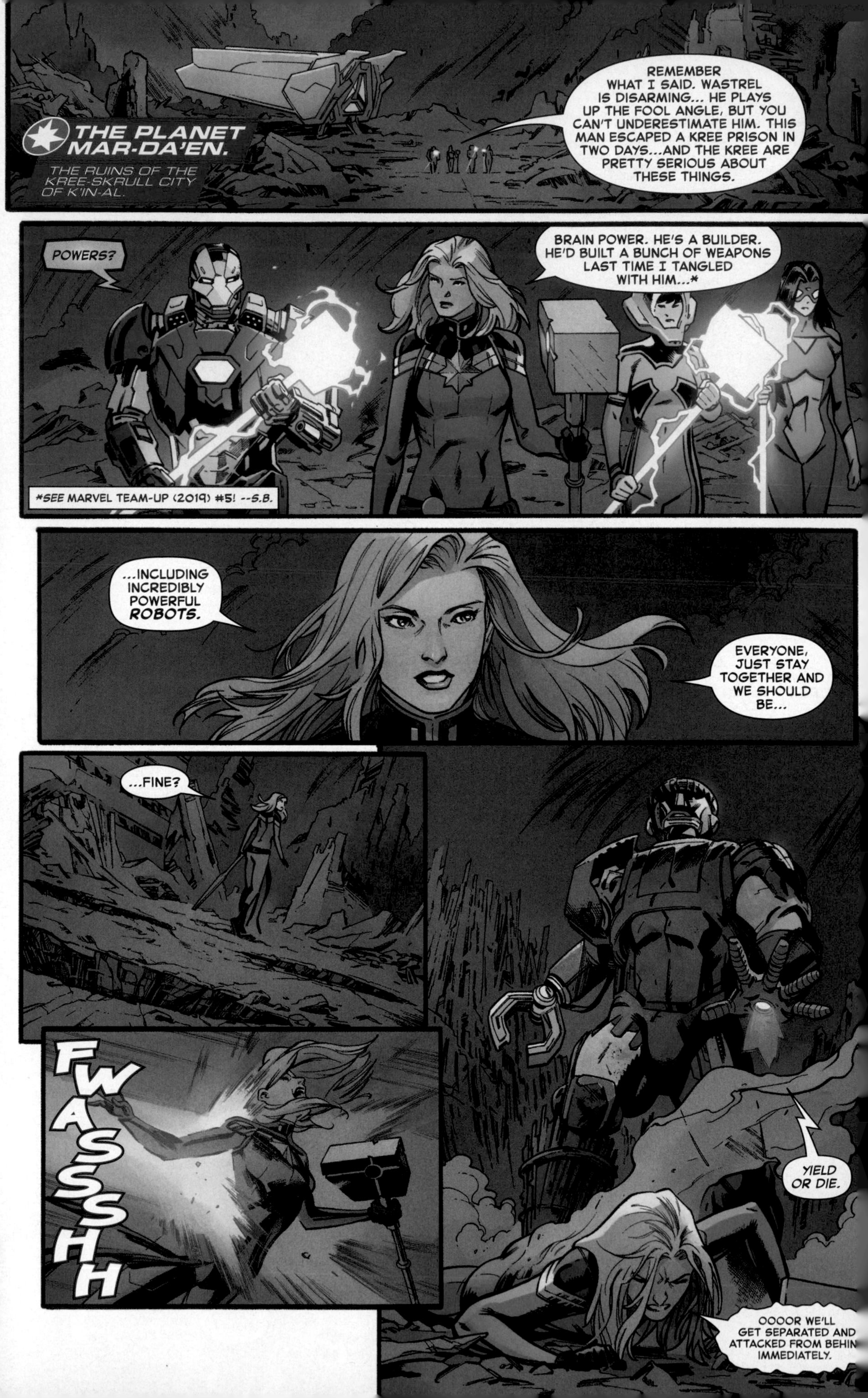
THE PLANET MAR-DA'EN.
THE RUINS OF THE KREE-SKRULL CITY OF K'IN-AL.
REMEMBER WHAT I SAID. WASTREL IS DISARMING... HE PLAYS UP THE FOOL ANGLE, BUT YOU CAN'T UNDERESTIMATE HIM. THIS MAN ESCAPED A KREE PRISON IN TWO DAYS...AND THE KREE ARE PRETTY SERIOUS ABOUT THESE THINGS.
POWERS?
BRAIN POWER. HE'S A BUILDER. HE'D BUILT A BUNCH OF WEAPONS LAST TIME I TANGLED WITH HIM...*
*SEE MARVEL TEAM-UP (2019) #5! --S.B.
...INCLUDING INCREDIBLY POWERFUL ROBOTS.
EVERYONE, JUST STAY TOGETHER AND WE SHOULD BE...
...FINE?
FWASSHH
YIELD OR DIE.
OOOOR WE'LL GET SEPARATED AND ATTACKED FROM BEHIN IMMEDIATELY.

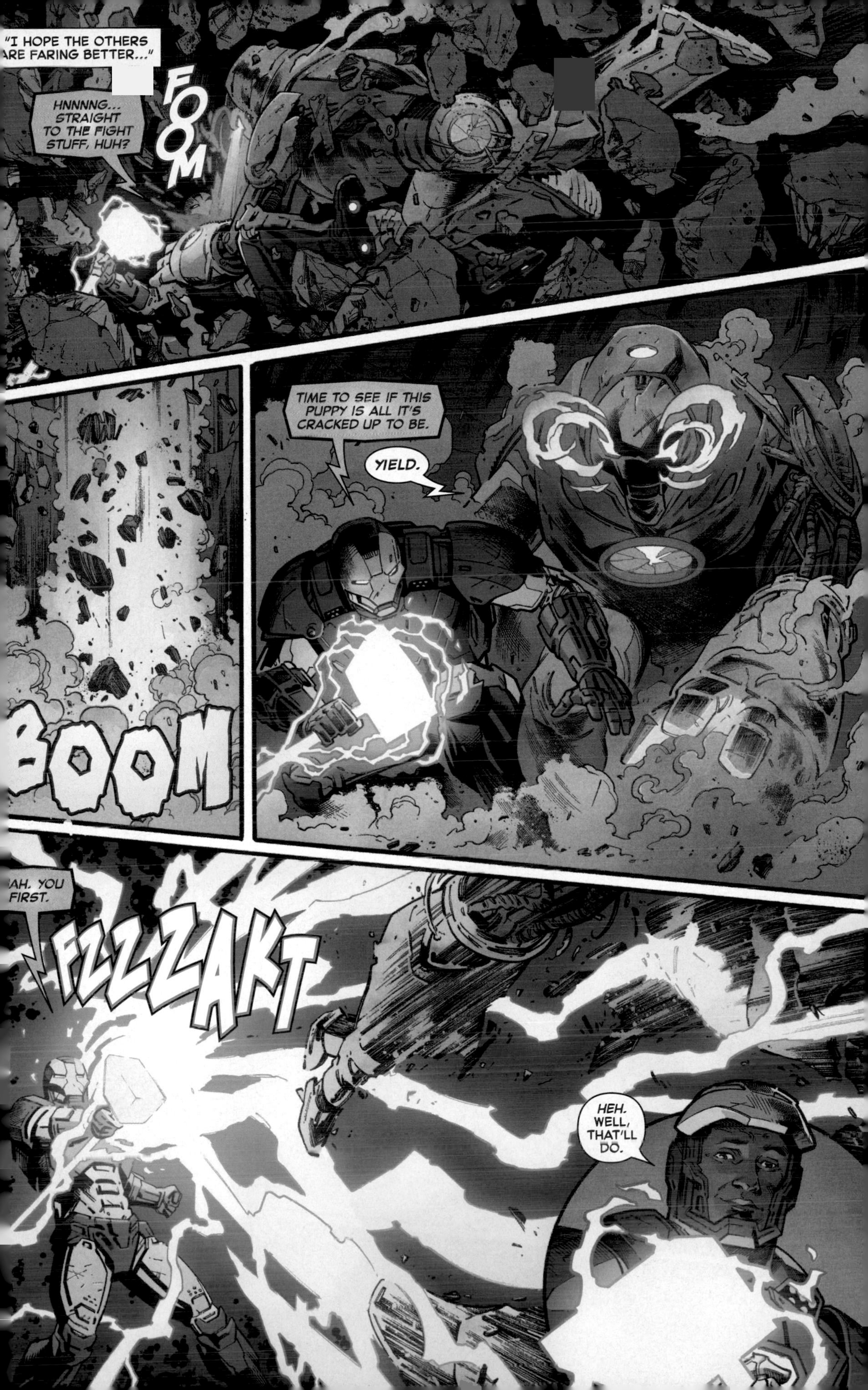
"I HOPE THE OTHERS
ARE FARING BETTER..."
HNNNNG... STRAIGHT TO THE FIGHT STUFF, HUH?
FOOM
BOOM
TIME TO SEE IF THIS PUPPY IS ALL IT'S CRACKED UP TO BE.
YIELD.
AH. YOU FIRST.
FZZZAKT
HEH. WELL, THAT'LL DO.

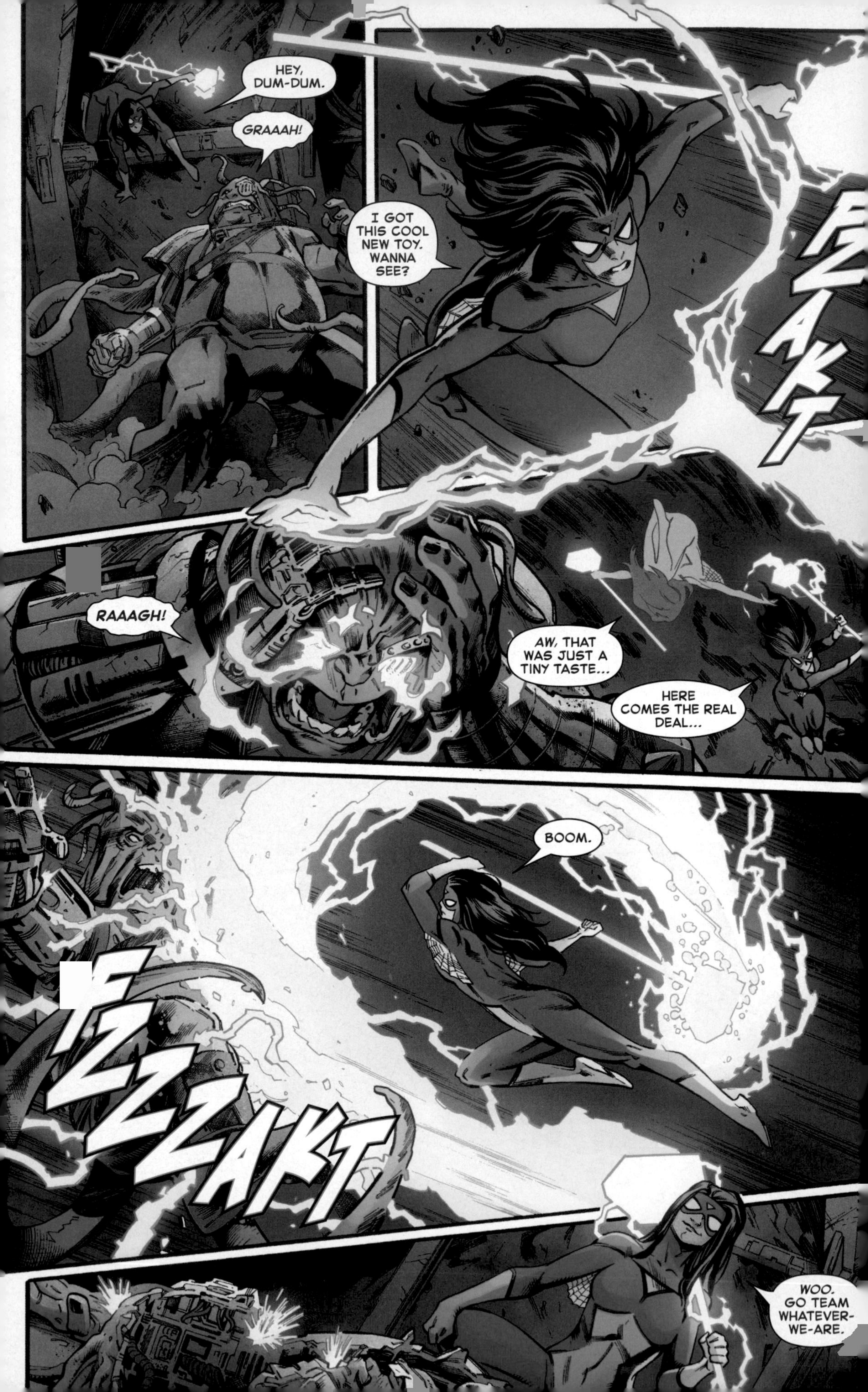
HEY, DUM-DUM.
GRAAAH!
I GOT THIS COOL NEW TOY. WANNA SEE?
FZZAKT
RAAAGH!
AW, THAT WAS JUST A TINY TASTE...
HERE COMES THE REAL DEAL...
BOOM.
FZZZAKT
WOO. GO TEAM WHATEVER-WE-ARE.

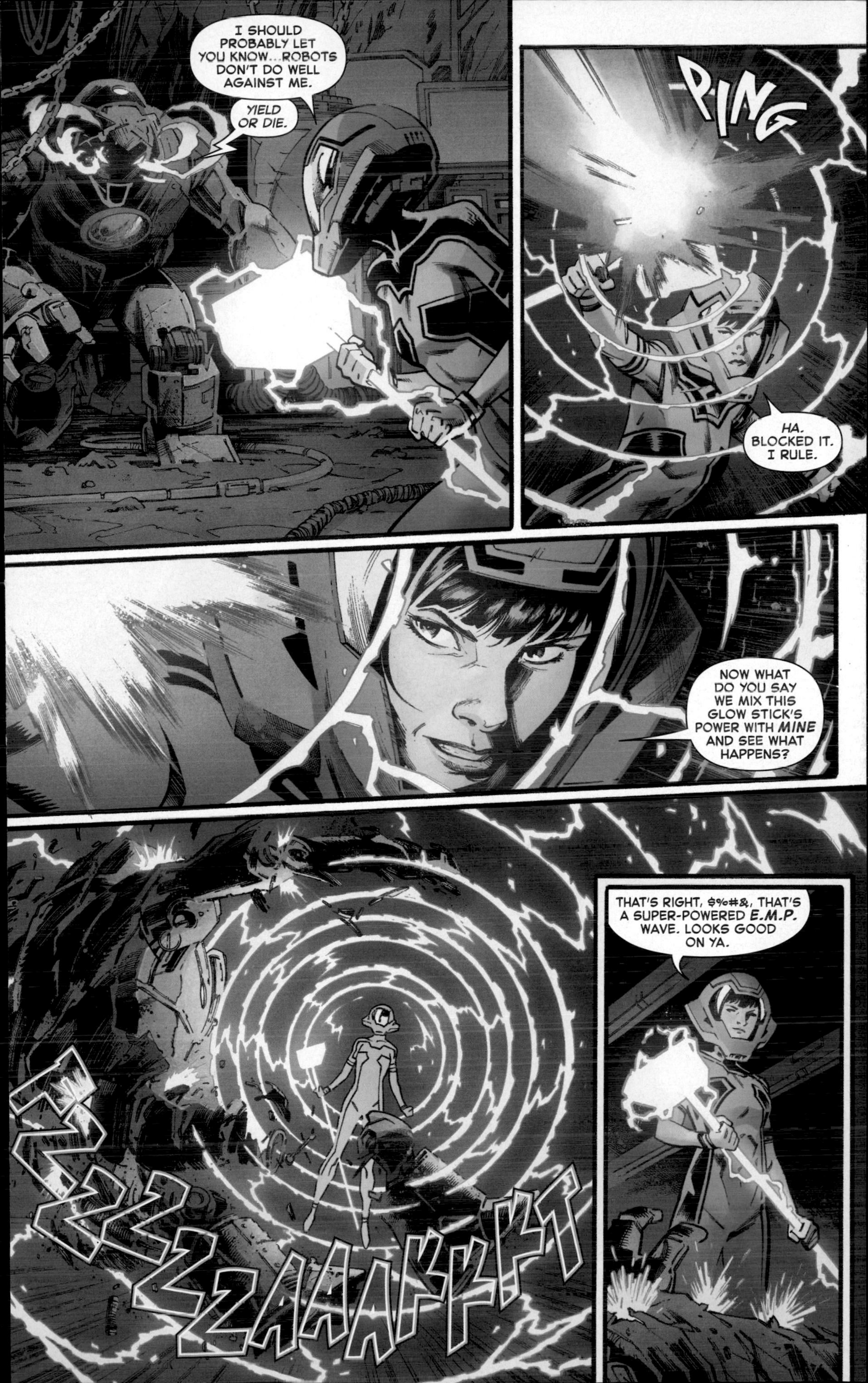
I SHOULD PROBABLY LET YOU KNOW...ROBOTS DON'T DO WELL AGAINST ME.
YIELD OR DIE.
PING
HA. BLOCKED IT. I RULE.
NOW WHAT DO YOU SAY WE MIX THIS GLOW STICK'S POWER WITH MINE AND SEE WHAT HAPPENS?
ZZZZAAAKKKT
THAT'S RIGHT, $%#&, THAT'S A SUPER-POWERED E.M.P. WAVE. LOOKS GOOD ON YA.

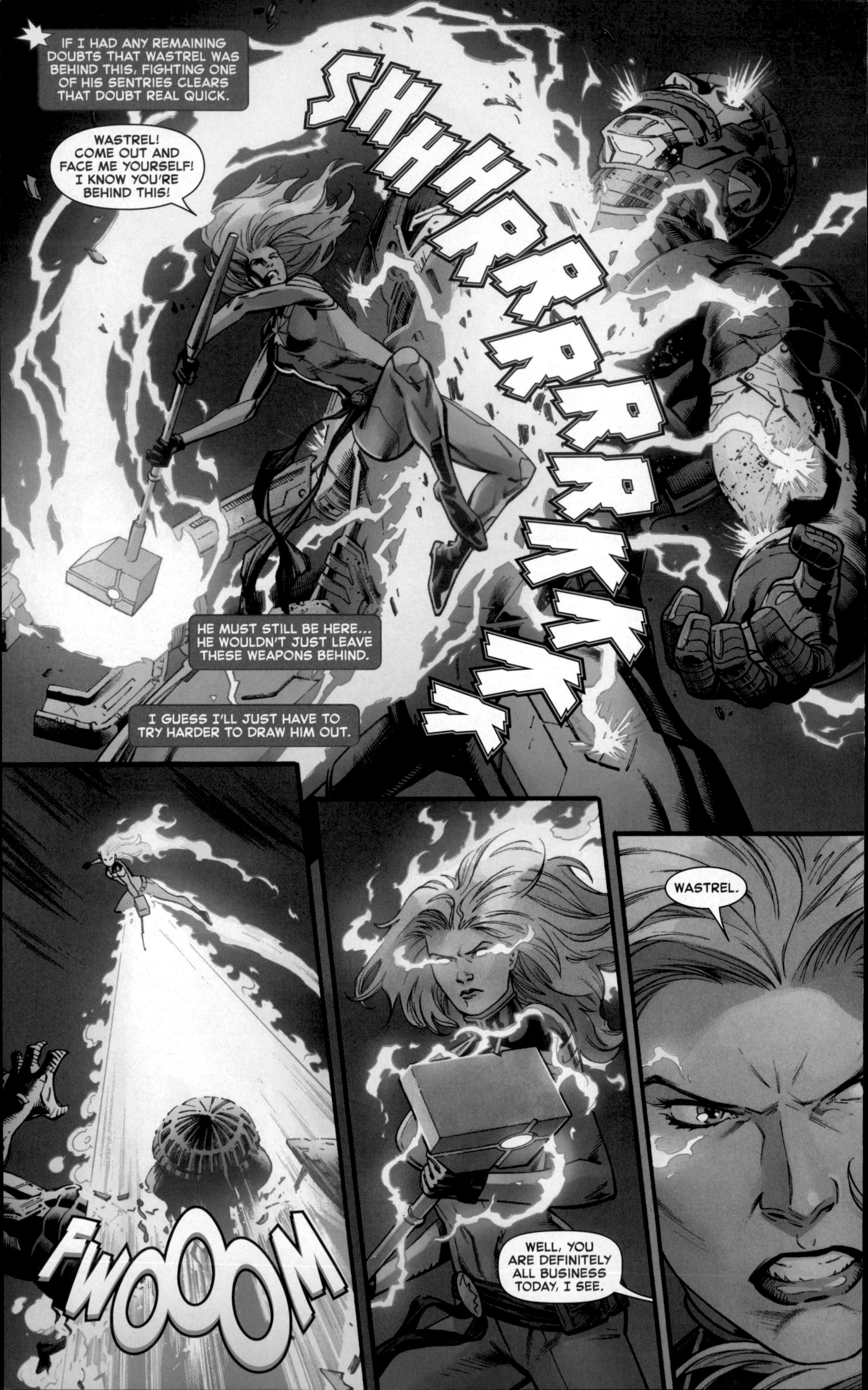
IF I HAD ANY REMAINING DOUBTS THAT WASTREL WAS BEHIND THIS, FIGHTING ONE OF HIS SENTRIES CLEARS THAT DOUBT REAL QUICK.
WASTREL! COME OUT AND FACE ME YOURSELF! I KNOW YOU'RE BEHIND THIS!
SHHHRRRRRKKKK
HE MUST STILL BE HERE... HE WOULDN'T JUST LEAVE THESE WEAPONS BEHIND.
I GUESS I'LL JUST HAVE TO TRY HARDER TO DRAW HIM OUT.
FWOOOM
WASTREL.
WELL, YOU ARE DEFINITELY ALL BUSINESS TODAY, I SEE.

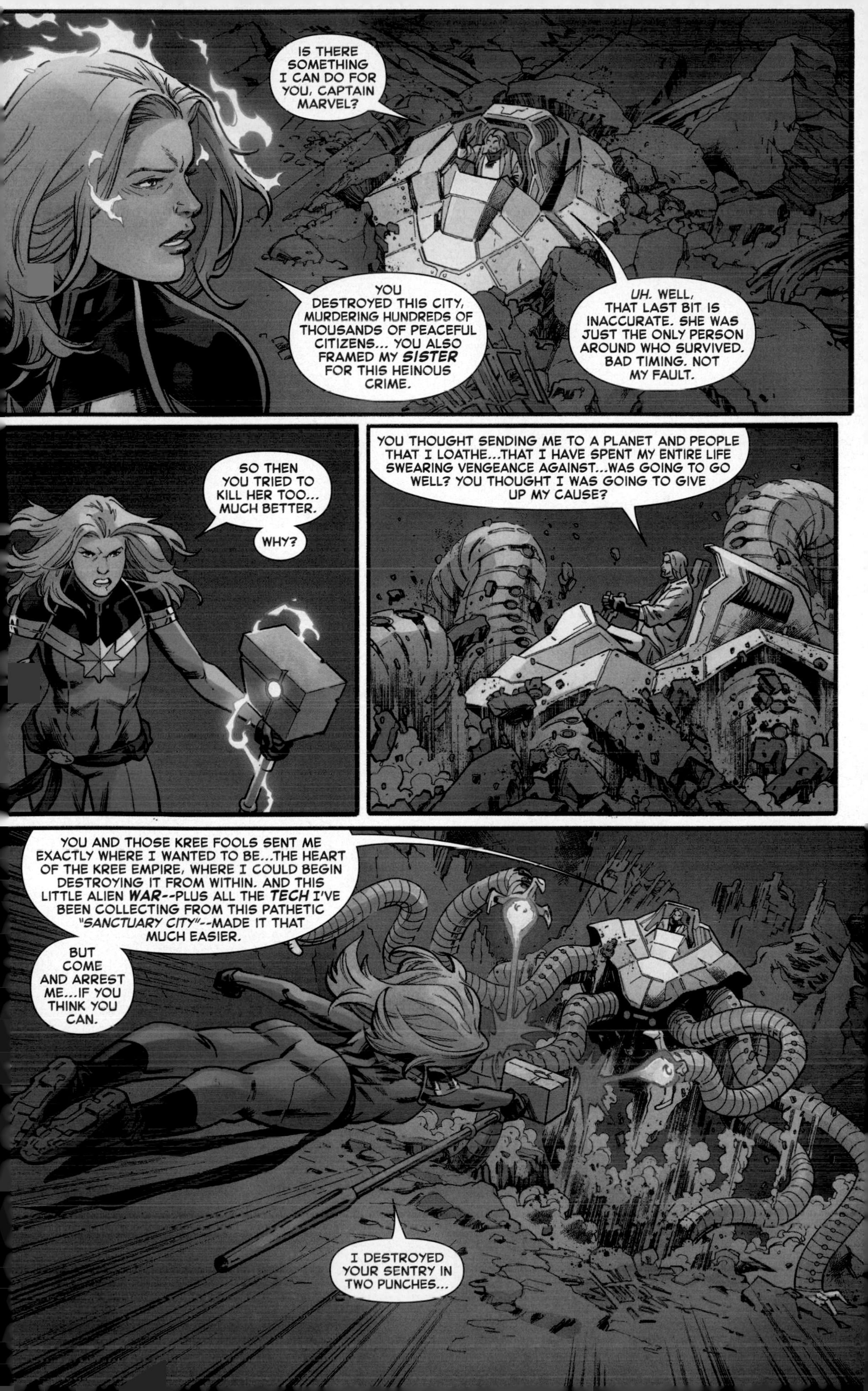
IS THERE SOMETHING I CAN DO FOR YOU, CAPTAIN MARVEL?
YOU DESTROYED THIS CITY, MURDERING HUNDREDS OF THOUSANDS OF PEACEFUL CITIZENS... YOU ALSO FRAMED MY *SISTER* FOR THIS HEINOUS CRIME.
UH. WELL, THAT LAST BIT IS INACCURATE. SHE WAS JUST THE ONLY PERSON AROUND WHO SURVIVED. BAD TIMING. NOT MY FAULT.
SO THEN YOU TRIED TO KILL HER TOO... MUCH BETTER.
WHY?
YOU THOUGHT SENDING ME TO A PLANET AND PEOPLE THAT I LOATHE...THAT I HAVE SPENT MY ENTIRE LIFE SWEARING VENGEANCE AGAINST...WAS GOING TO GO WELL? YOU THOUGHT I WAS GOING TO GIVE UP MY CAUSE?
YOU AND THOSE KREE FOOLS SENT ME EXACTLY WHERE I WANTED TO BE...THE HEART OF THE KREE EMPIRE, WHERE I COULD BEGIN DESTROYING IT FROM WITHIN. AND THIS LITTLE ALIEN *WAR*--PLUS ALL THE *TECH* I'VE BEEN COLLECTING FROM THIS PATHETIC *"SANCTUARY CITY"*--MADE IT THAT MUCH EASIER.
BUT COME AND ARREST ME...IF YOU THINK YOU CAN.
I DESTROYED YOUR SENTRY IN TWO PUNCHES...

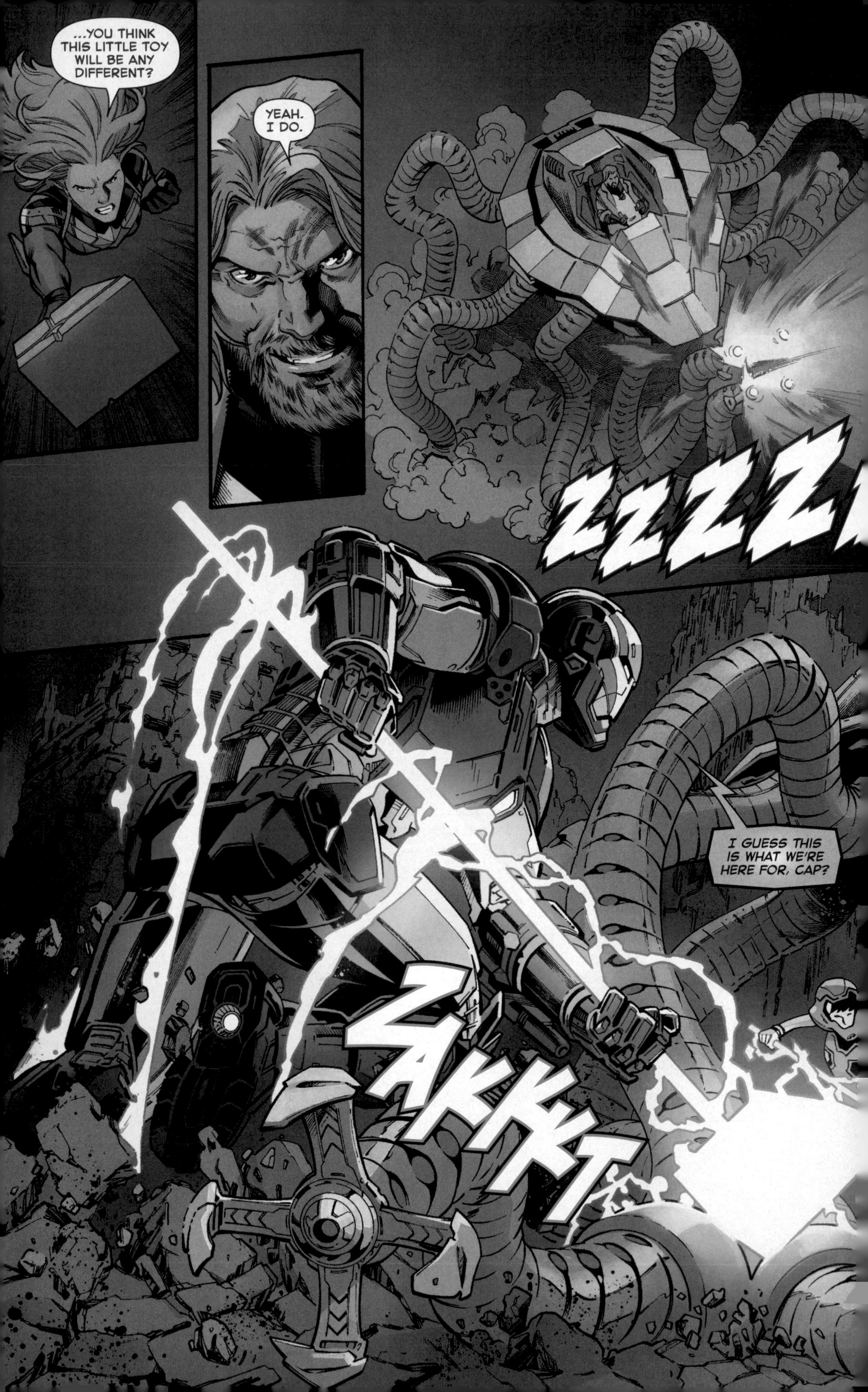
...YOU THINK THIS LITTLE TOY WILL BE ANY DIFFERENT?
YEAH. I DO.
ZZZZ
I GUESS THIS IS WHAT WE'RE HERE FOR, CAP?
ZAKKKT

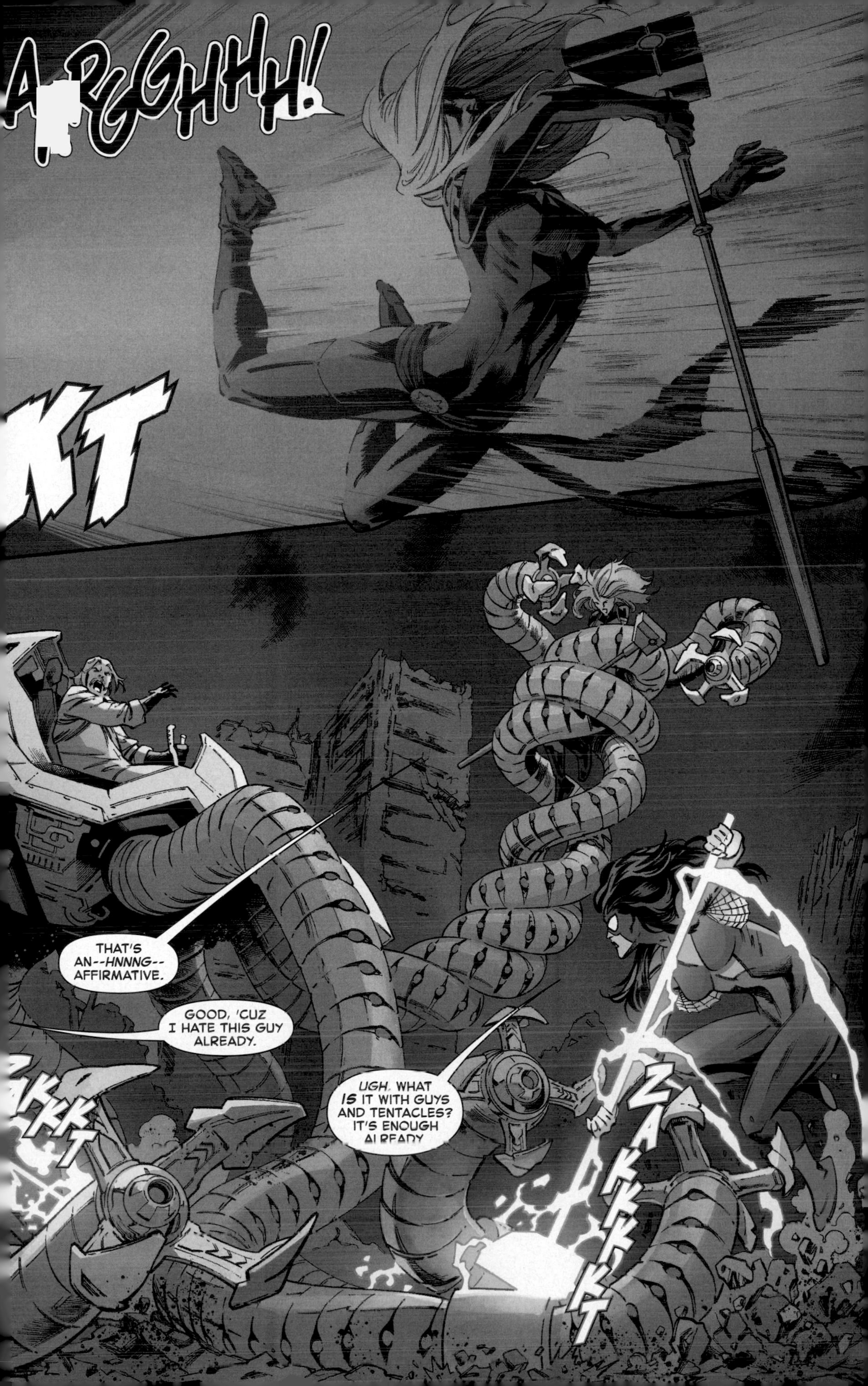
ARGGHHH!
KT
THAT'S AN--HNNNG-- AFFIRMATIVE.
GOOD, 'CUZ I HATE THIS GUY ALREADY.
UGH. WHAT IS IT WITH GUYS AND TENTACLES? IT'S ENOUGH ALREADY
KKKT
ZAKKKKKKKT

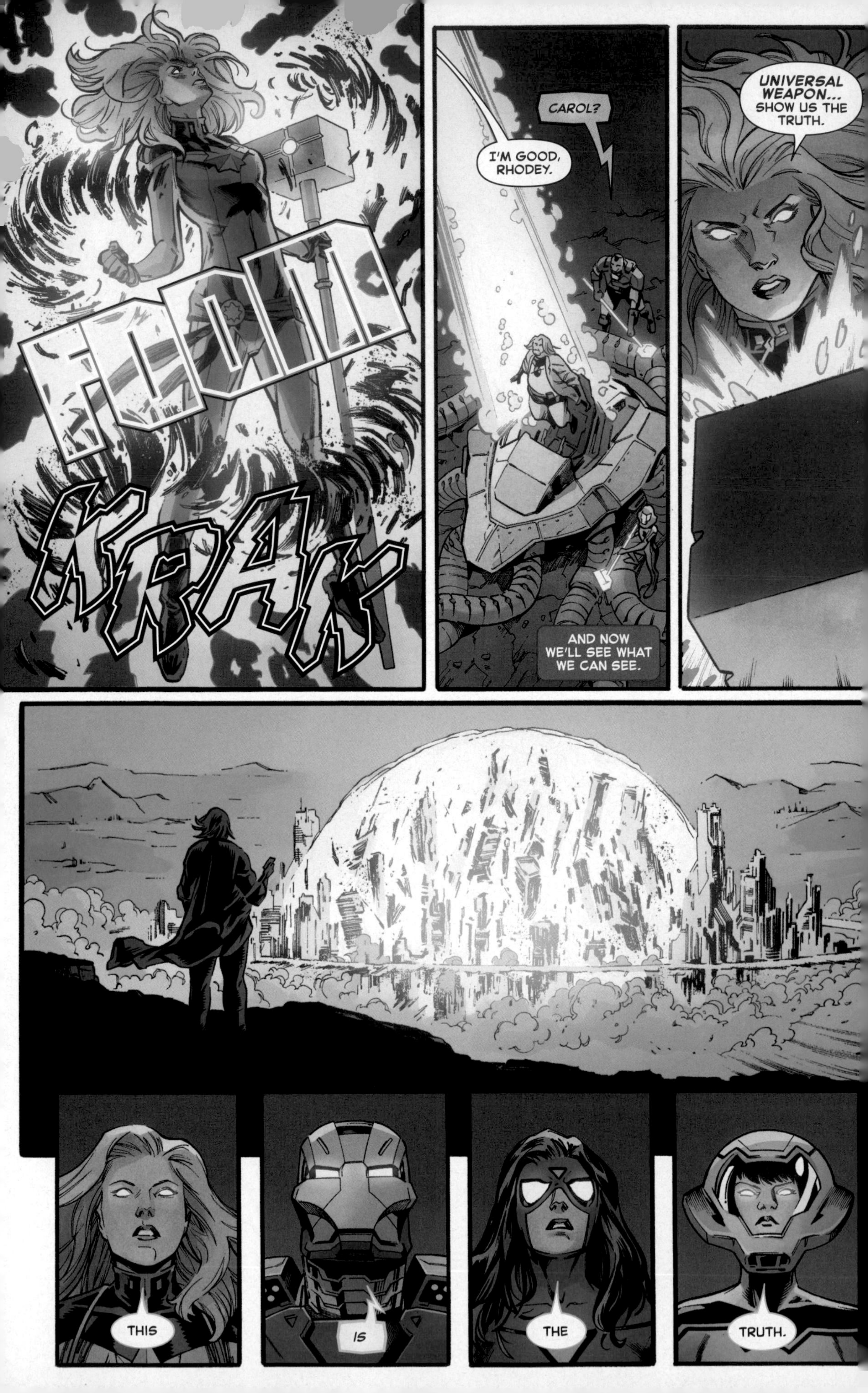
FOOM
KRAK
CAROL?
I'M GOOD, RHODEY.
AND NOW WE'LL SEE WHAT WE CAN SEE.
UNIVERSAL WEAPON... SHOW US THE TRUTH.
THIS
IS
THE
TRUTH.

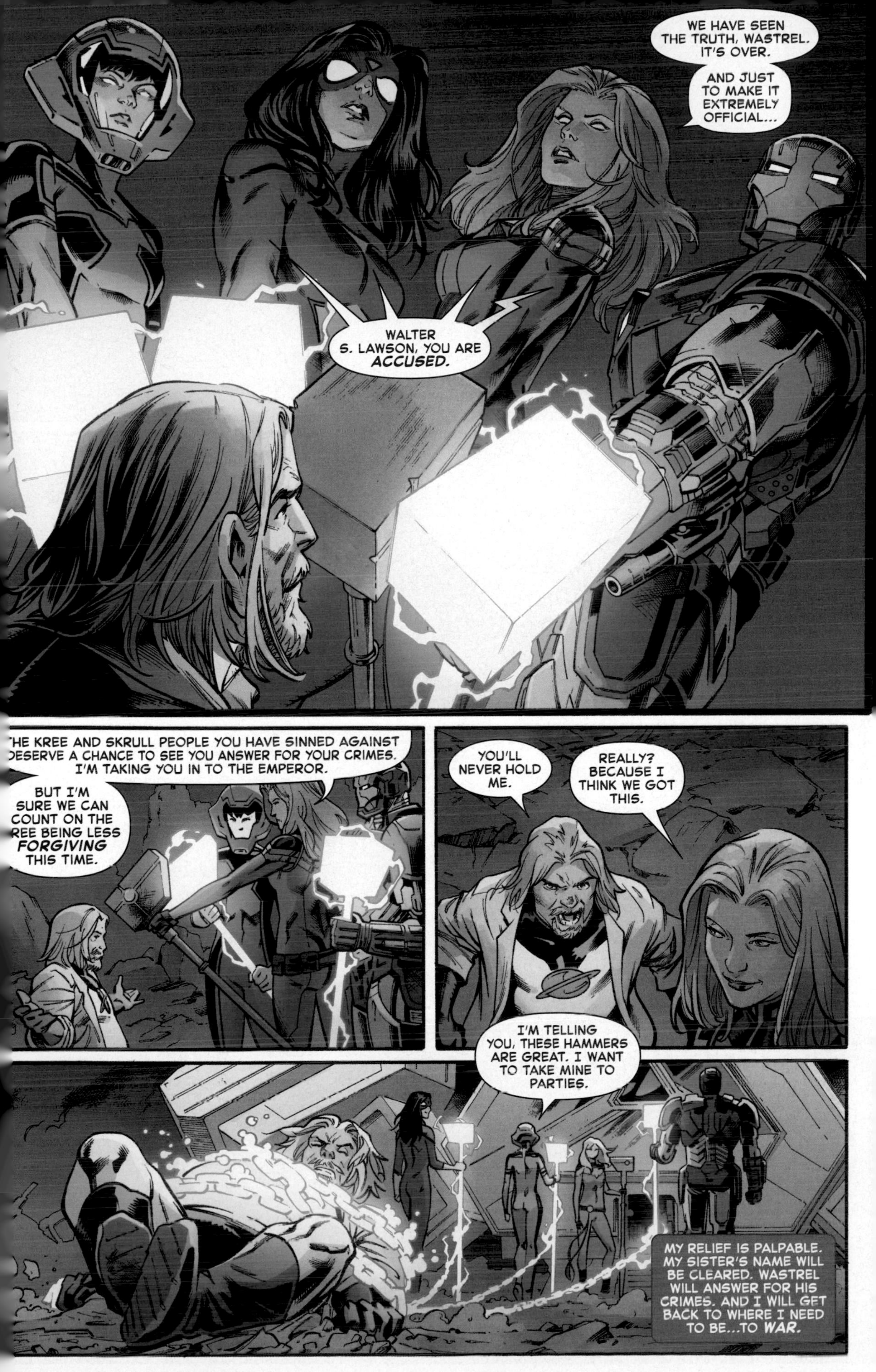
WE HAVE SEEN THE TRUTH, WASTREL. IT'S OVER.
AND JUST TO MAKE IT EXTREMELY OFFICIAL...
WALTER S. LAWSON, YOU ARE ACCUSED.
THE KREE AND SKRULL PEOPLE YOU HAVE SINNED AGAINST DESERVE A CHANCE TO SEE YOU ANSWER FOR YOUR CRIMES. I'M TAKING YOU IN TO THE EMPEROR.
BUT I'M SURE WE CAN COUNT ON THE KREE BEING LESS FORGIVING THIS TIME.
YOU'LL NEVER HOLD ME.
REALLY? BECAUSE I THINK WE GOT THIS.
I'M TELLING YOU, THESE HAMMERS ARE GREAT. I WANT TO TAKE MINE TO PARTIES.
MY RELIEF IS PALPABLE. MY SISTER'S NAME WILL BE CLEARED. WASTREL WILL ANSWER FOR HIS CRIMES. AND I WILL GET BACK TO WHERE I NEED TO BE...TO WAR.

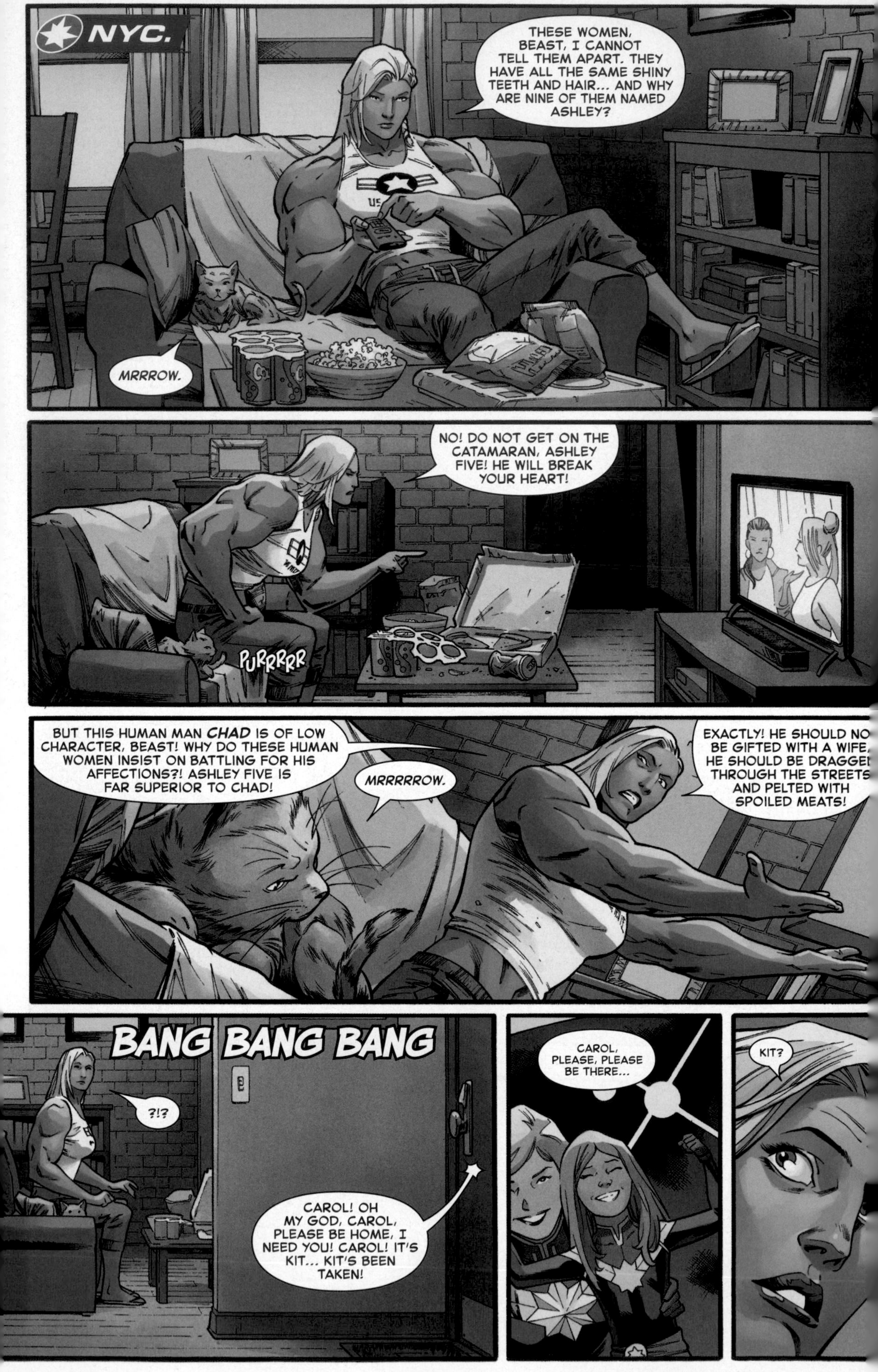
NYC.
THESE WOMEN, BEAST, I CANNOT TELL THEM APART. THEY HAVE ALL THE SAME SHINY TEETH AND HAIR... AND WHY ARE NINE OF THEM NAMED ASHLEY?
MRRROW.
NO! DO NOT GET ON THE CATAMARAN, ASHLEY FIVE! HE WILL BREAK YOUR HEART!
PURRRRR
BUT THIS HUMAN MAN CHAD IS OF LOW CHARACTER, BEAST! WHY DO THESE HUMAN WOMEN INSIST ON BATTLING FOR HIS AFFECTIONS?! ASHLEY FIVE IS FAR SUPERIOR TO CHAD!
MRRRRROW.
EXACTLY! HE SHOULD NO BE GIFTED WITH A WIFE, HE SHOULD BE DRAGGE THROUGH THE STREETS AND PELTED WITH SPOILED MEATS!
BANG BANG BANG
?!?
CAROL! OH MY GOD, CAROL, PLEASE BE HOME, I NEED YOU! CAROL! IT'S KIT... KIT'S BEEN TAKEN!
CAROL, PLEASE, PLEASE BE THERE...
KIT?

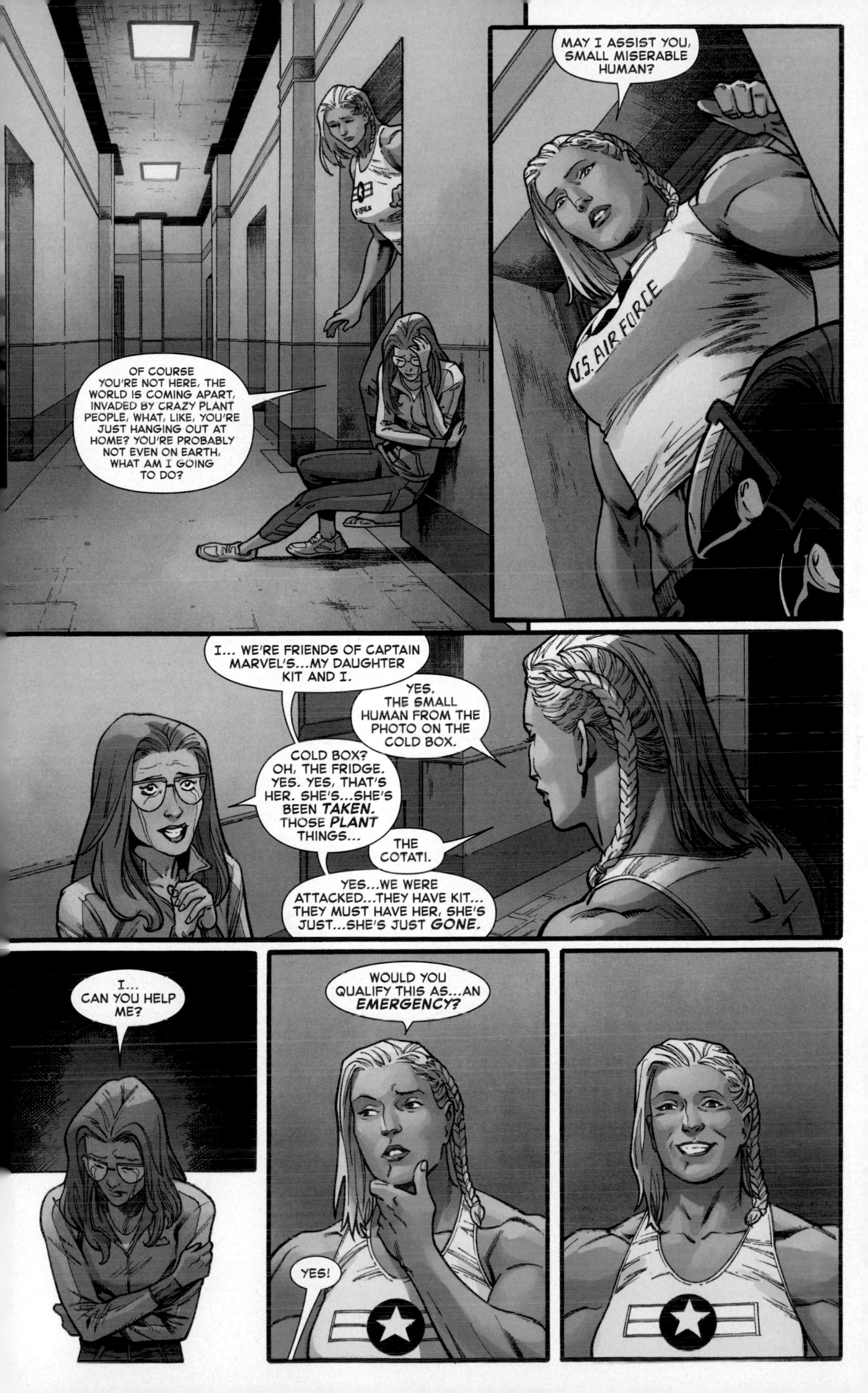
OF COURSE YOU'RE NOT HERE, THE WORLD IS COMING APART, INVADED BY CRAZY PLANT PEOPLE, WHAT, LIKE, YOU'RE JUST HANGING OUT AT HOME? YOU'RE PROBABLY NOT EVEN ON EARTH, WHAT AM I GOING TO DO?
MAY I ASSIST YOU, SMALL MISERABLE HUMAN?
U.S. AIR FORCE
I... WE'RE FRIENDS OF CAPTAIN MARVEL'S...MY DAUGHTER KIT AND I.
YES. THE SMALL HUMAN FROM THE PHOTO ON THE COLD BOX.
COLD BOX? OH, THE FRIDGE. YES. YES, THAT'S HER. SHE'S...SHE'S BEEN *TAKEN.* THOSE *PLANT* THINGS...
THE COTATI.
YES...WE WERE ATTACKED...THEY HAVE KIT... THEY MUST HAVE HER, SHE'S JUST...SHE'S JUST *GONE.*
I... CAN YOU HELP ME?
WOULD YOU QUALIFY THIS AS...AN *EMERGENCY?*
YES!

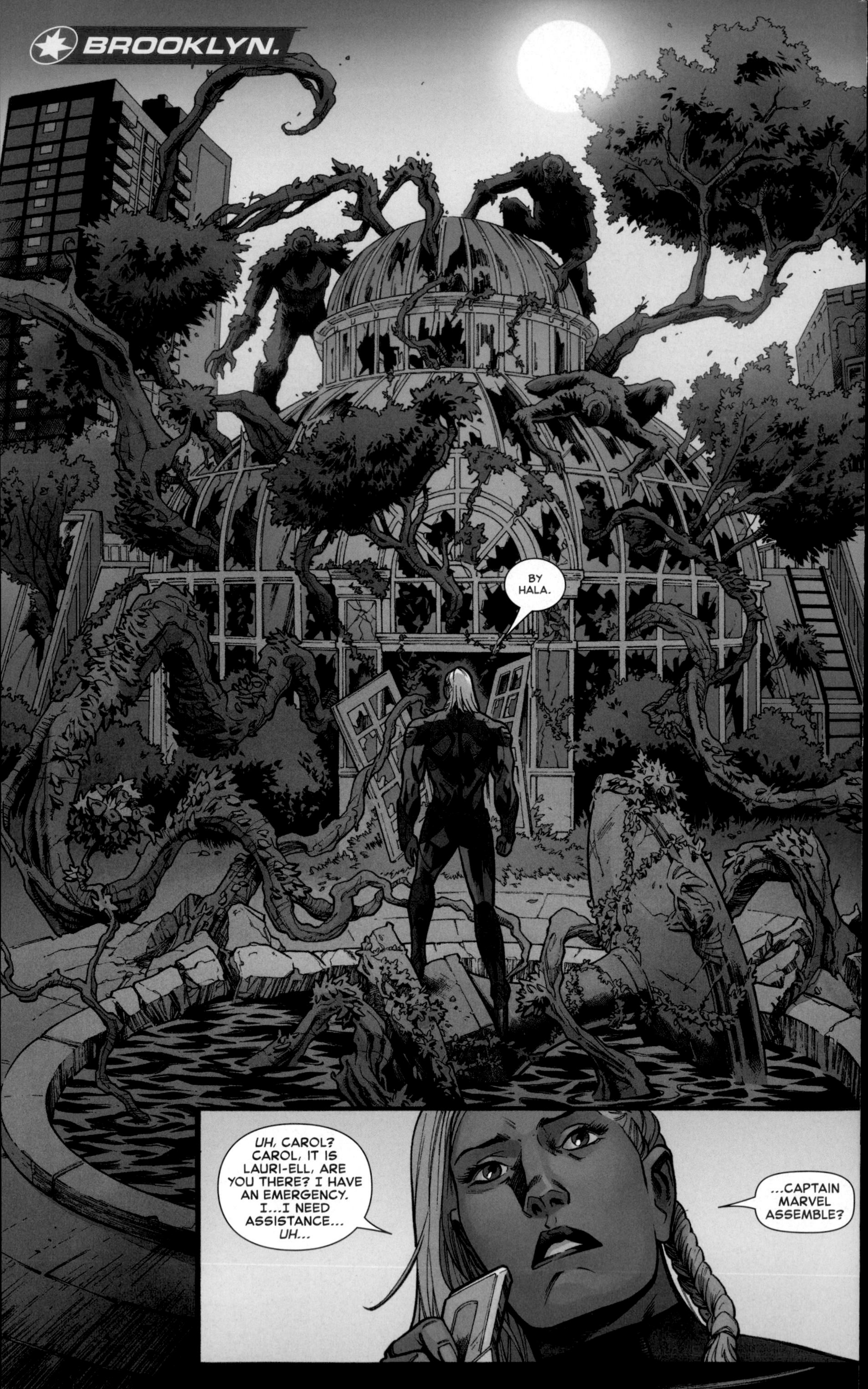
BROOKLYN.
BY HALA.
UH, CAROL? CAROL, IT IS LAURI-ELL, ARE YOU THERE? I HAVE AN EMERGENCY. I...I NEED ASSISTANCE... UH...
...CAPTAIN MARVEL ASSEMBLE?

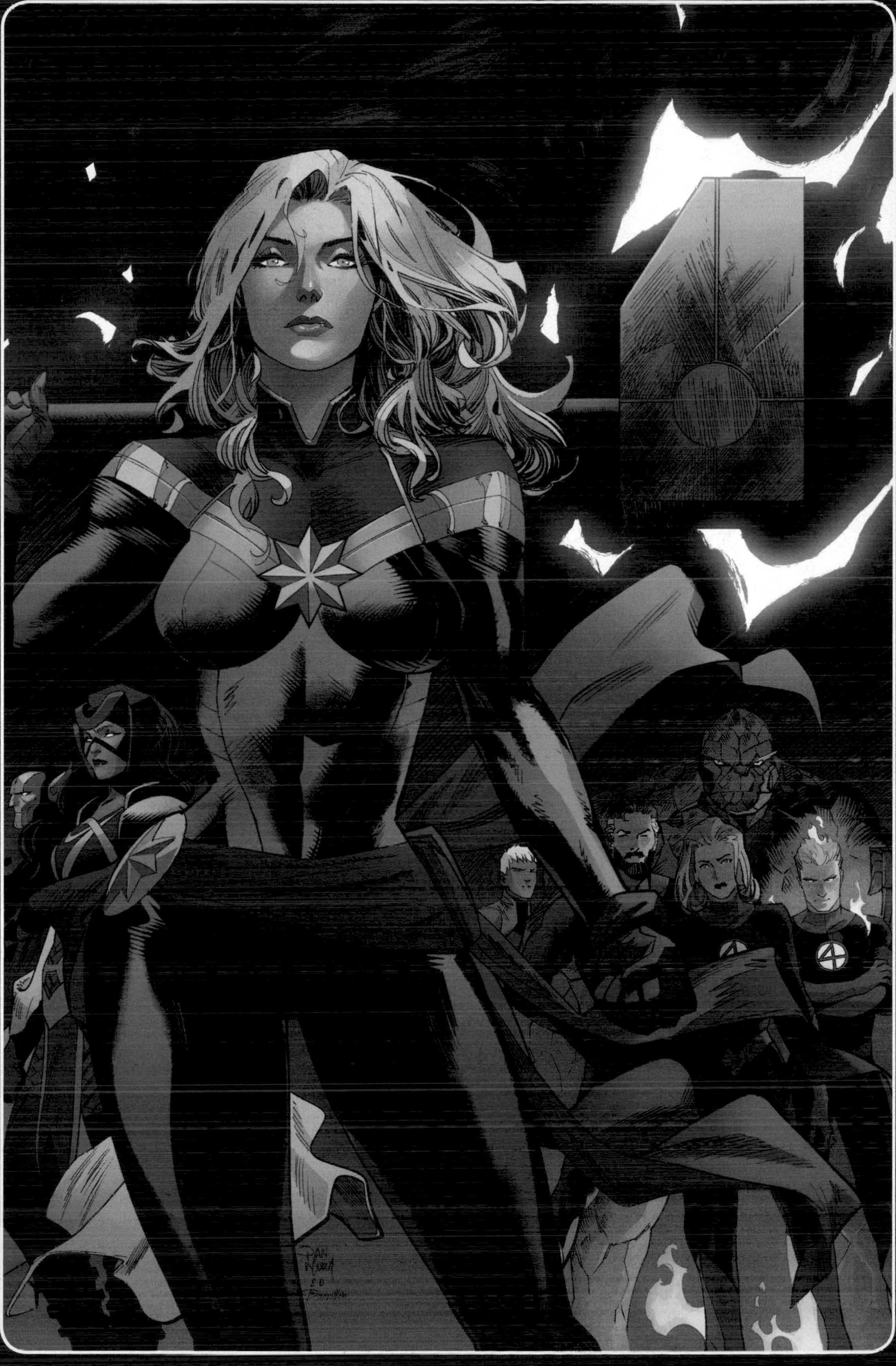

DAN MORA & TAMRA BONVILLAIN

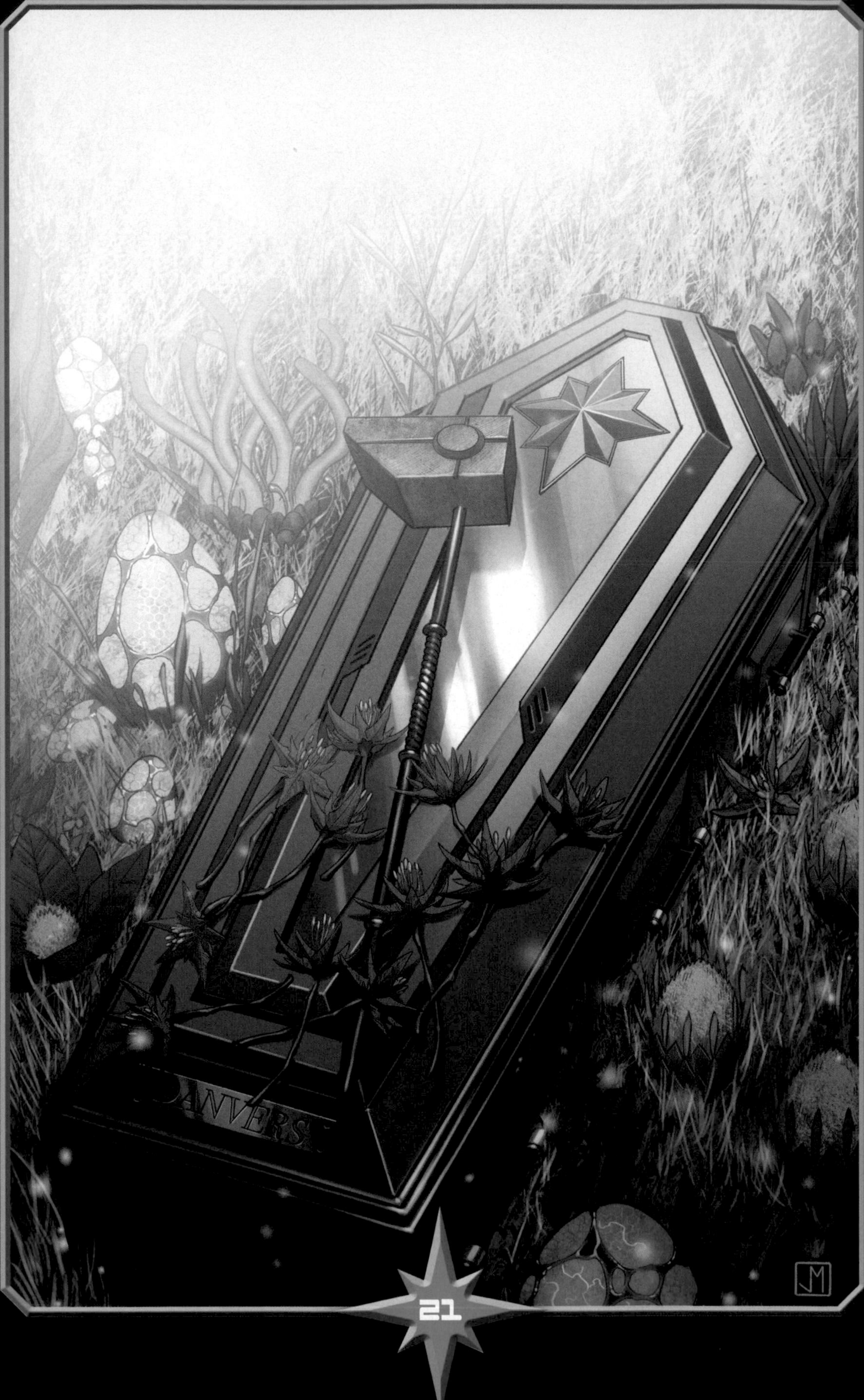
DANVERS
21

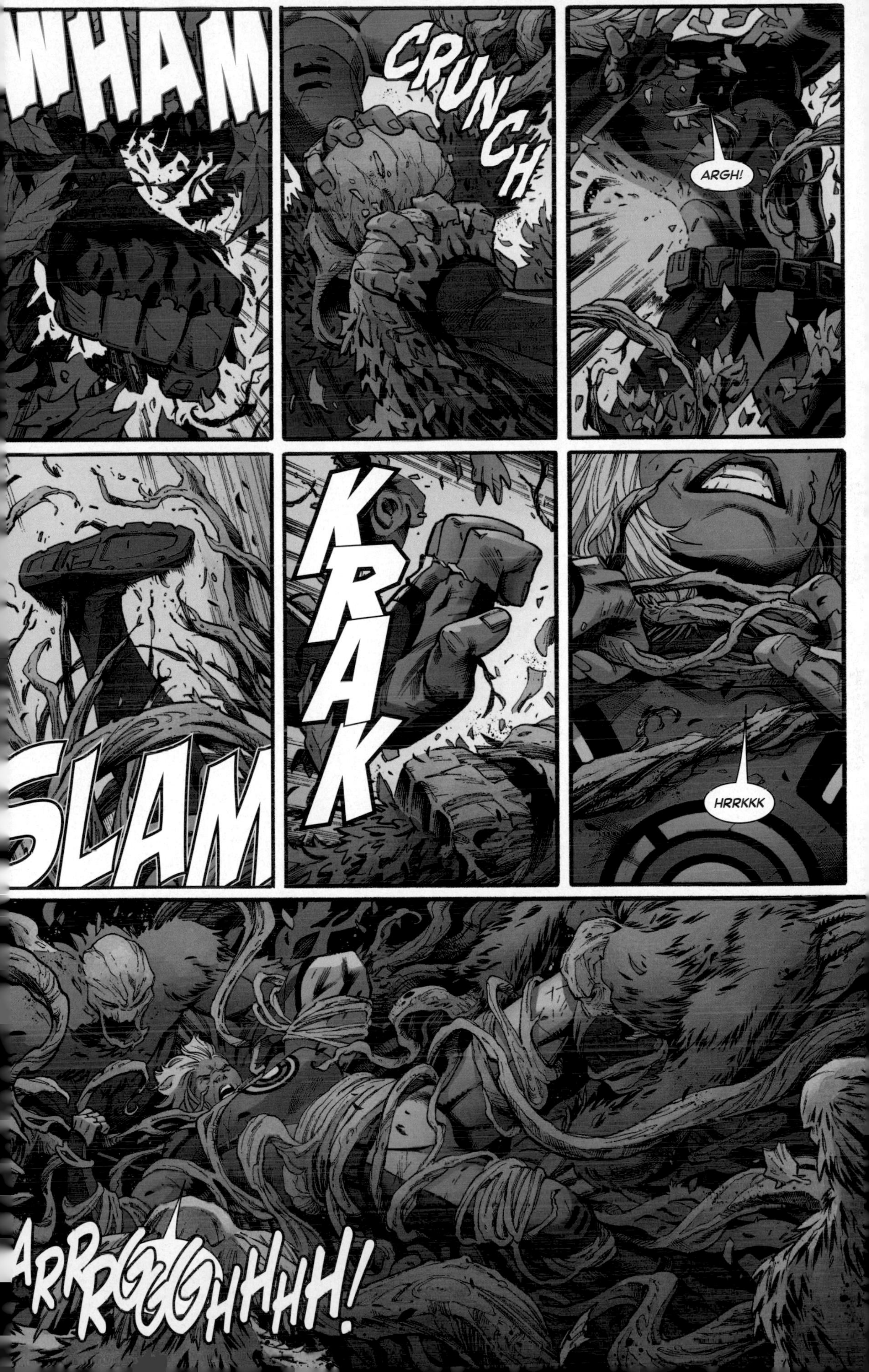
WHAM
CRUNCH
ARGH!
SLAM
KRAK
HRRKKK
ARRRGGGHHHH!

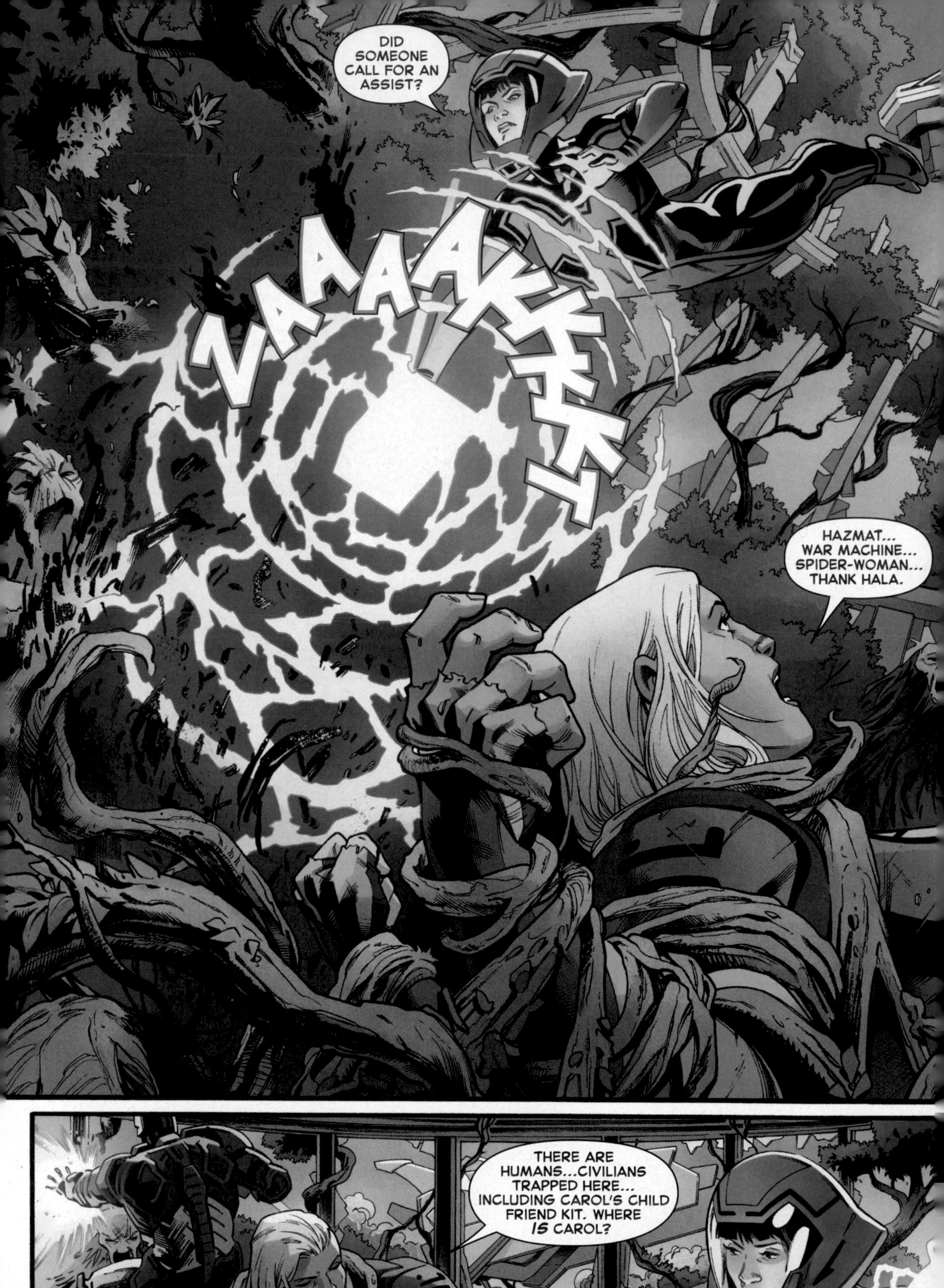
DID SOMEONE CALL FOR AN ASSIST?
ZAAAAKKKT
HAZMAT... WAR MACHINE... SPIDER-WOMAN... THANK HALA.
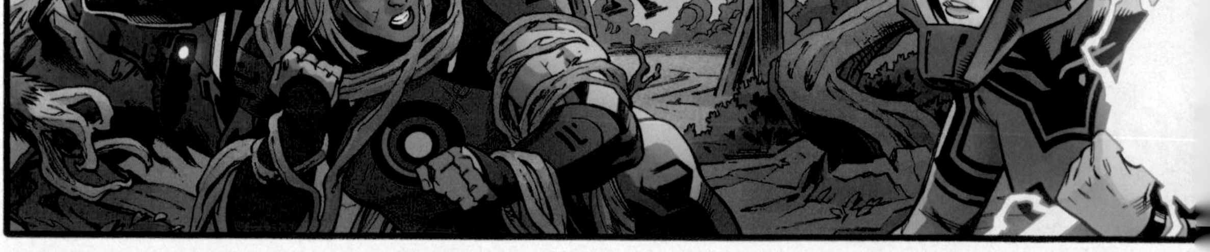
THERE ARE HUMANS...CIVILIANS TRAPPED HERE... INCLUDING CAROL'S CHILD FRIEND KIT. WHERE *IS* CAROL?

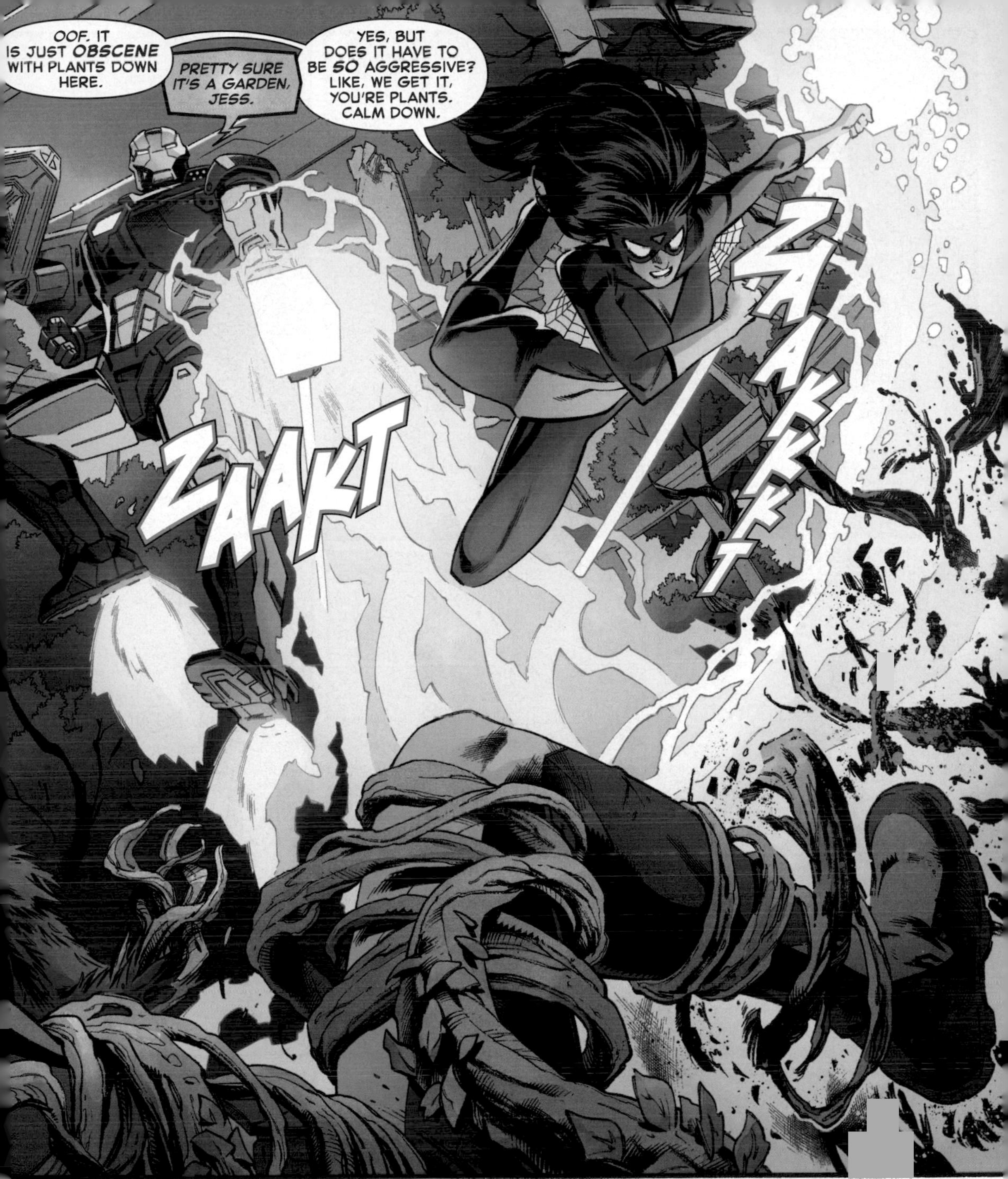
OOF. IT IS JUST OBSCENE WITH PLANTS DOWN HERE.
PRETTY SURE IT'S A GARDEN, JESS.
YES, BUT DOES IT HAVE TO BE SO AGGRESSIVE? LIKE, WE GET IT, YOU'RE PLANTS. CALM DOWN.
ZAAKT
ZAAKKKT

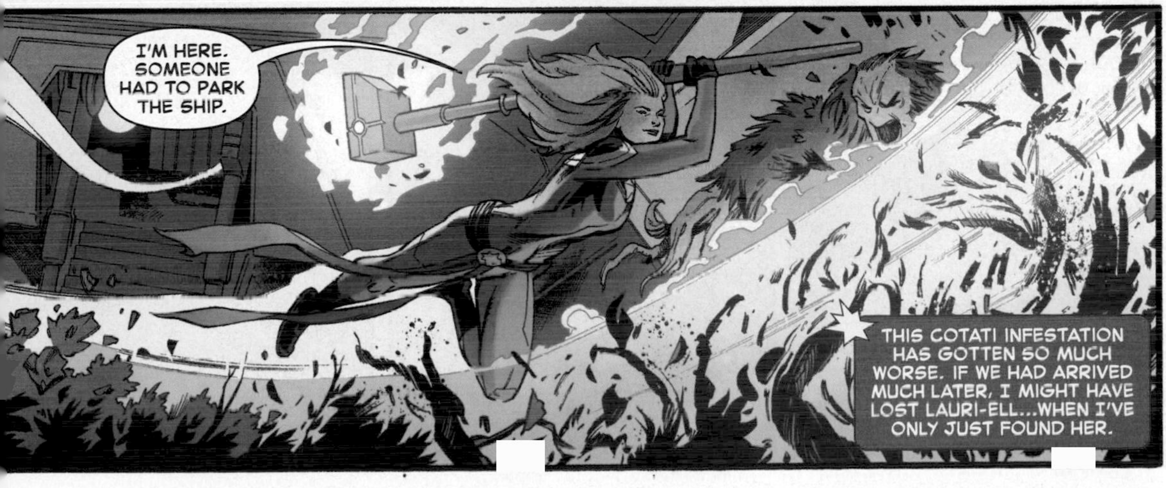
I'M HERE. SOMEONE HAD TO PARK THE SHIP.
THIS COTATI INFESTATION HAS GOTTEN SO MUCH WORSE. IF WE HAD ARRIVED MUCH LATER, I MIGHT HAVE LOST LAURI-ELL...WHEN I'VE ONLY JUST FOUND HER.

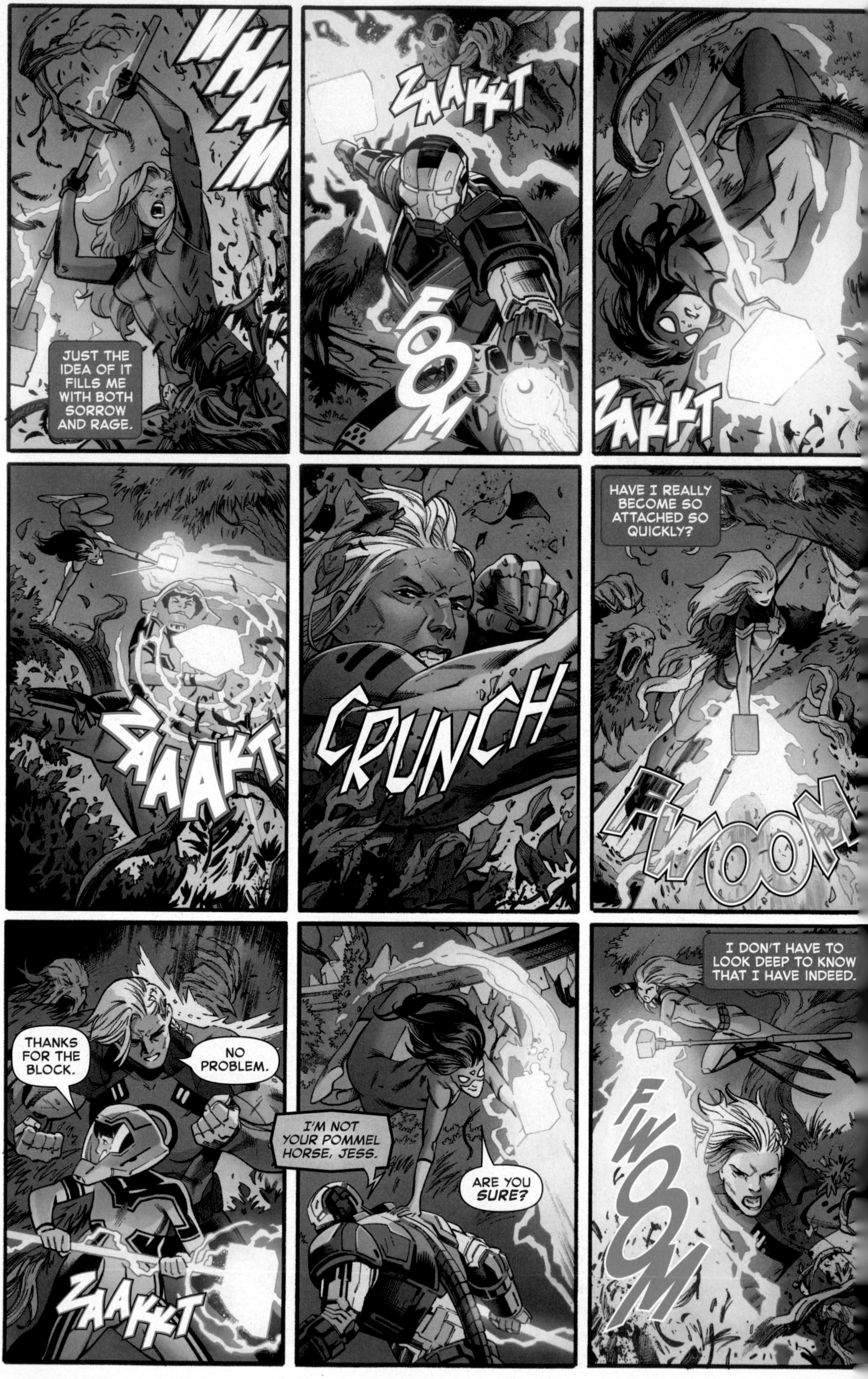
WHAM
JUST THE IDEA OF IT FILLS ME WITH BOTH SORROW AND RAGE.
ZAAKKT
FOOM
ZAAKKT
ZAAAKT
CRUNCH
HAVE I REALLY BECOME SO ATTACHED SO QUICKLY?
FWOOM
THANKS FOR THE BLOCK.
NO PROBLEM.
ZAAKKT
I'M NOT YOUR POMMEL HORSE, JESS.
ARE YOU SURE?
I DON'T HAVE TO LOOK DEEP TO KNOW THAT I HAVE INDEED.
FWOOM

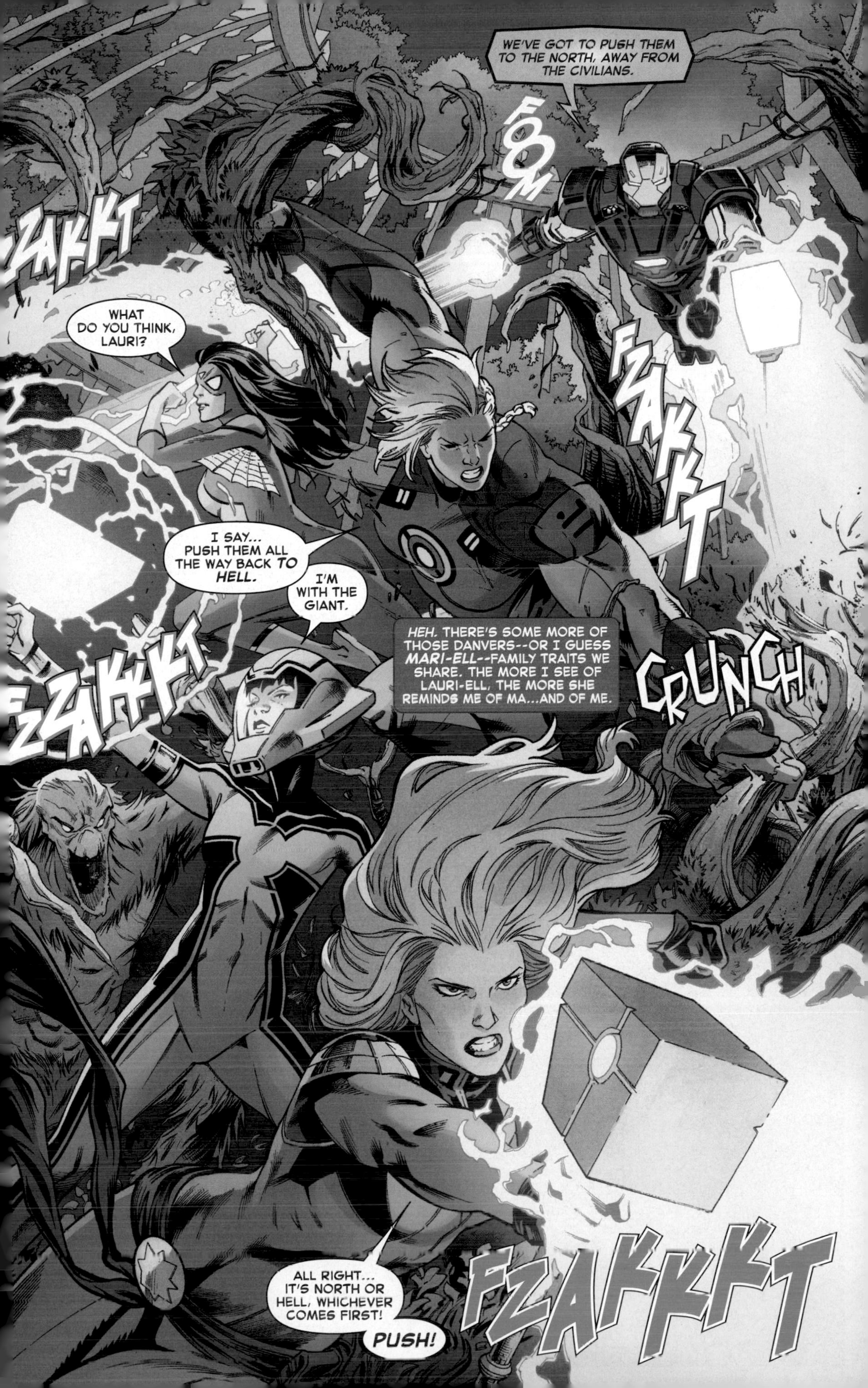
WE'VE GOT TO PUSH THEM TO THE NORTH, AWAY FROM THE CIVILIANS.
FOOM
FZAKKT
WHAT DO YOU THINK, LAURI?
FZAKKKT
I SAY... PUSH THEM ALL THE WAY BACK TO HELL.
I'M WITH THE GIANT.
HEH. THERE'S SOME MORE OF THOSE DANVERS--OR I GUESS MARI-ELL--FAMILY TRAITS WE SHARE. THE MORE I SEE OF LAURI-ELL, THE MORE SHE REMINDS ME OF MA...AND OF ME.
CRUNCH
FZZAKKKT
ALL RIGHT... IT'S NORTH OR HELL, WHICHEVER COMES FIRST!
PUSH!
FZAKKKKT

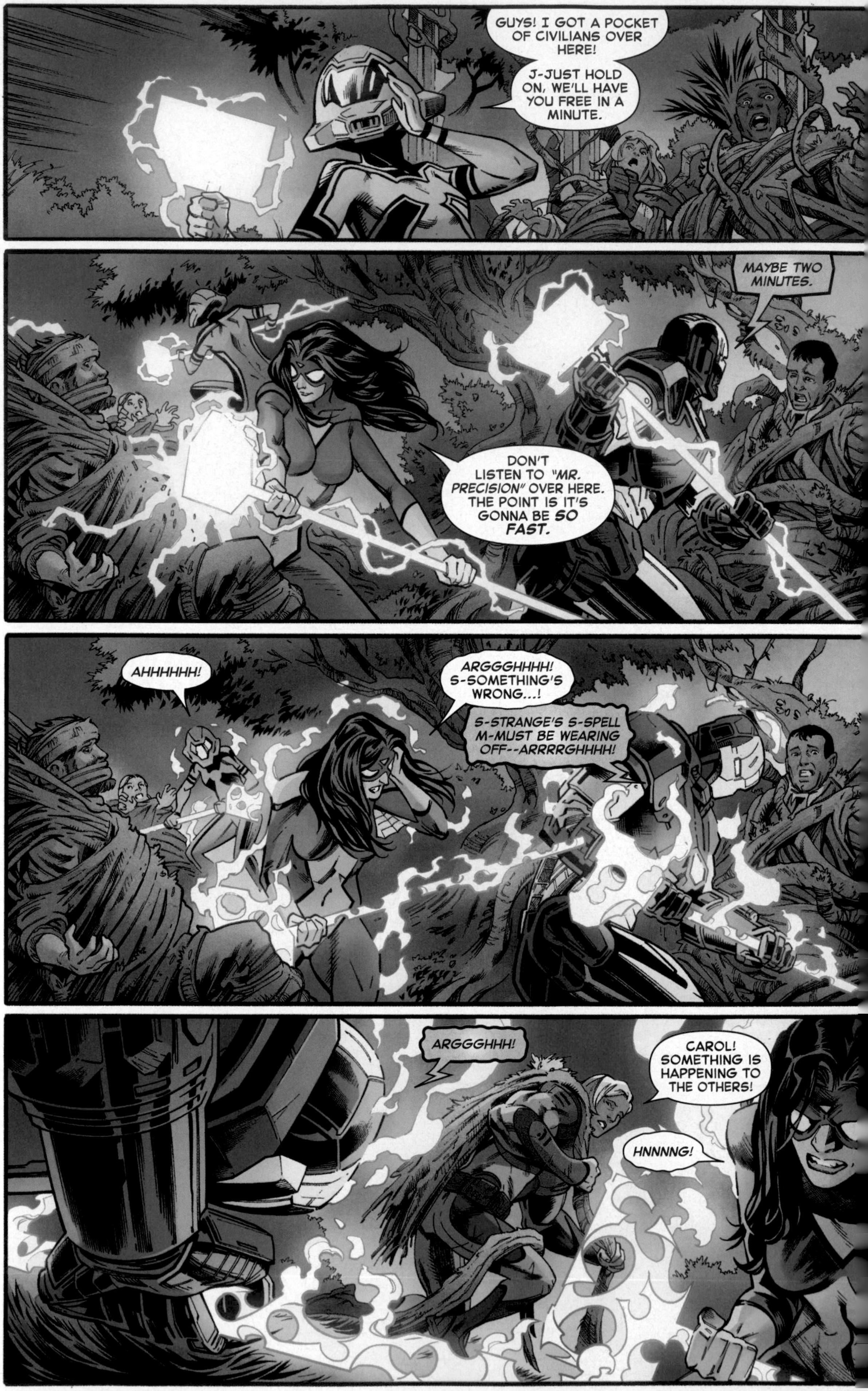
GUYS! I GOT A POCKET OF CIVILIANS OVER HERE!
J-JUST HOLD ON, WE'LL HAVE YOU FREE IN A MINUTE.
MAYBE TWO MINUTES.
DON'T LISTEN TO "MR. PRECISION" OVER HERE. THE POINT IS IT'S GONNA BE SO FAST.
AHHHHHH!
ARGGGHHHH! S-SOMETHING'S WRONG...!
S-STRANGE'S S-SPELL M-MUST BE WEARING OFF--ARRRRGHHHH!
ARGGGHHH!
CAROL! SOMETHING IS HAPPENING TO THE OTHERS!
HNNNNG!

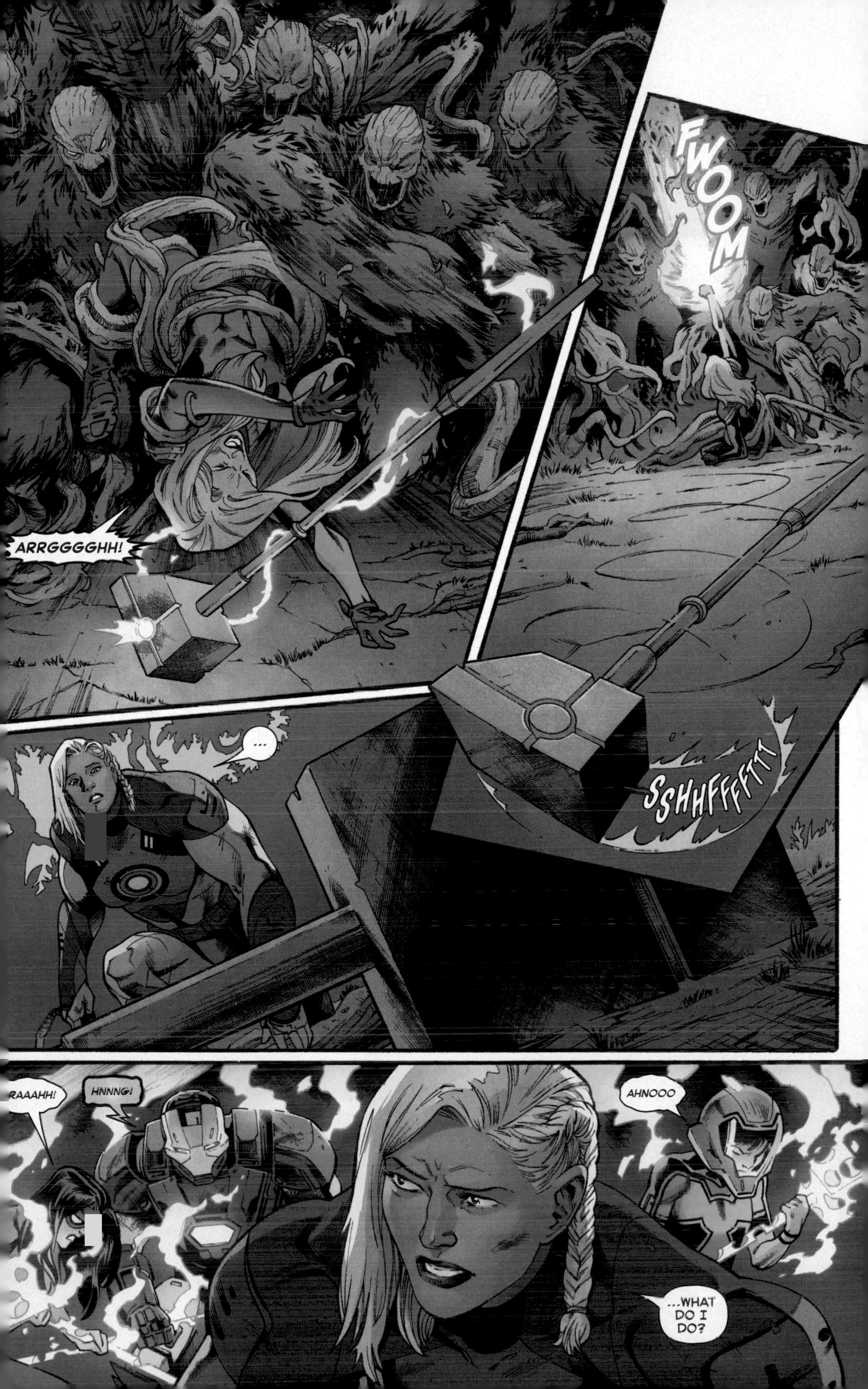
ARRGGGGHH!
FWOOM
...
SSHHFFFFTTT
RAAAHH!
HNNNG!
AHNOOO
...WHAT DO I DO?

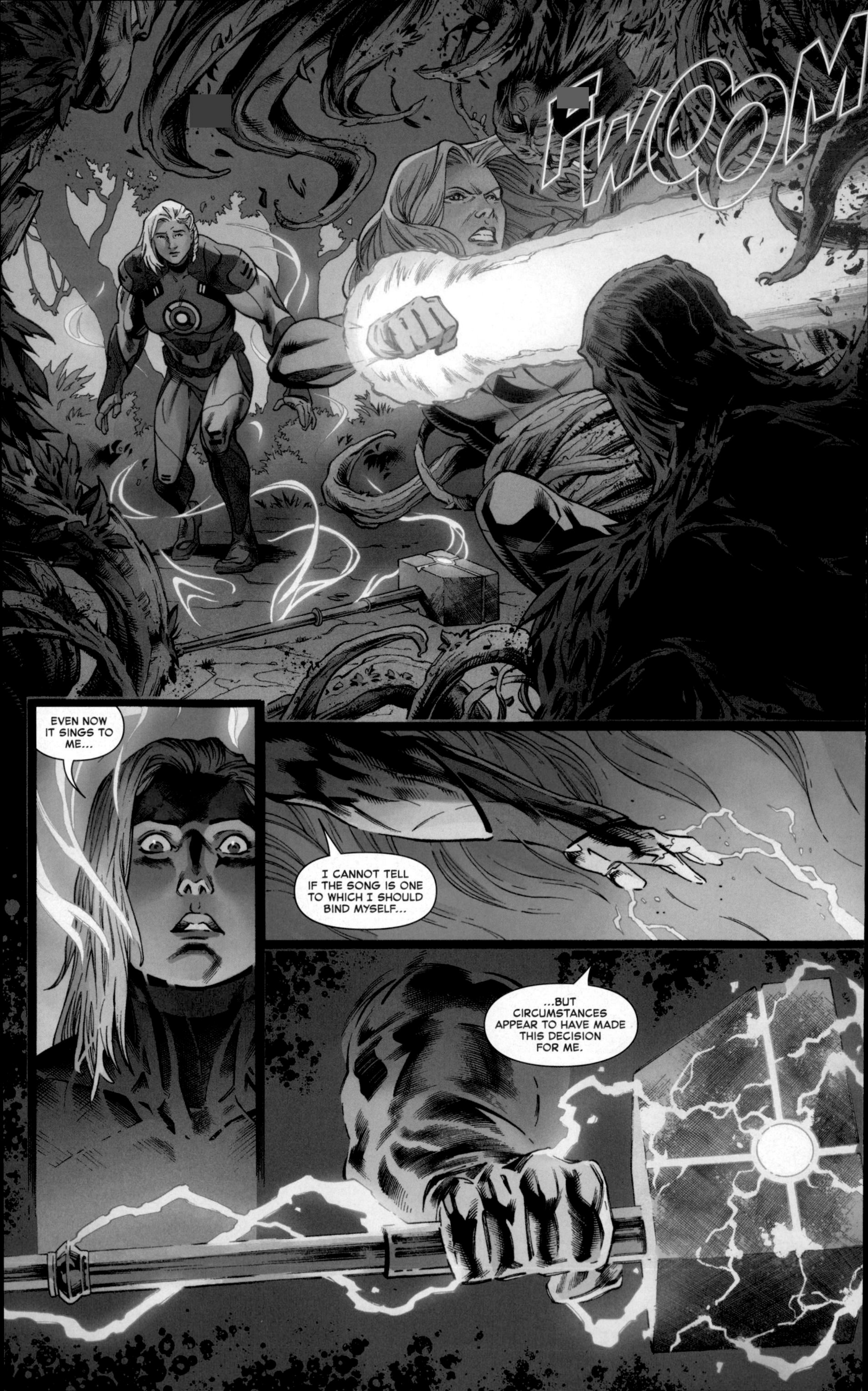
EVEN NOW IT SINGS TO ME...
I CANNOT TELL IF THE SONG IS ONE TO WHICH I SHOULD BIND MYSELF...
...BUT CIRCUMSTANCES APPEAR TO HAVE MADE THIS DECISION FOR ME.

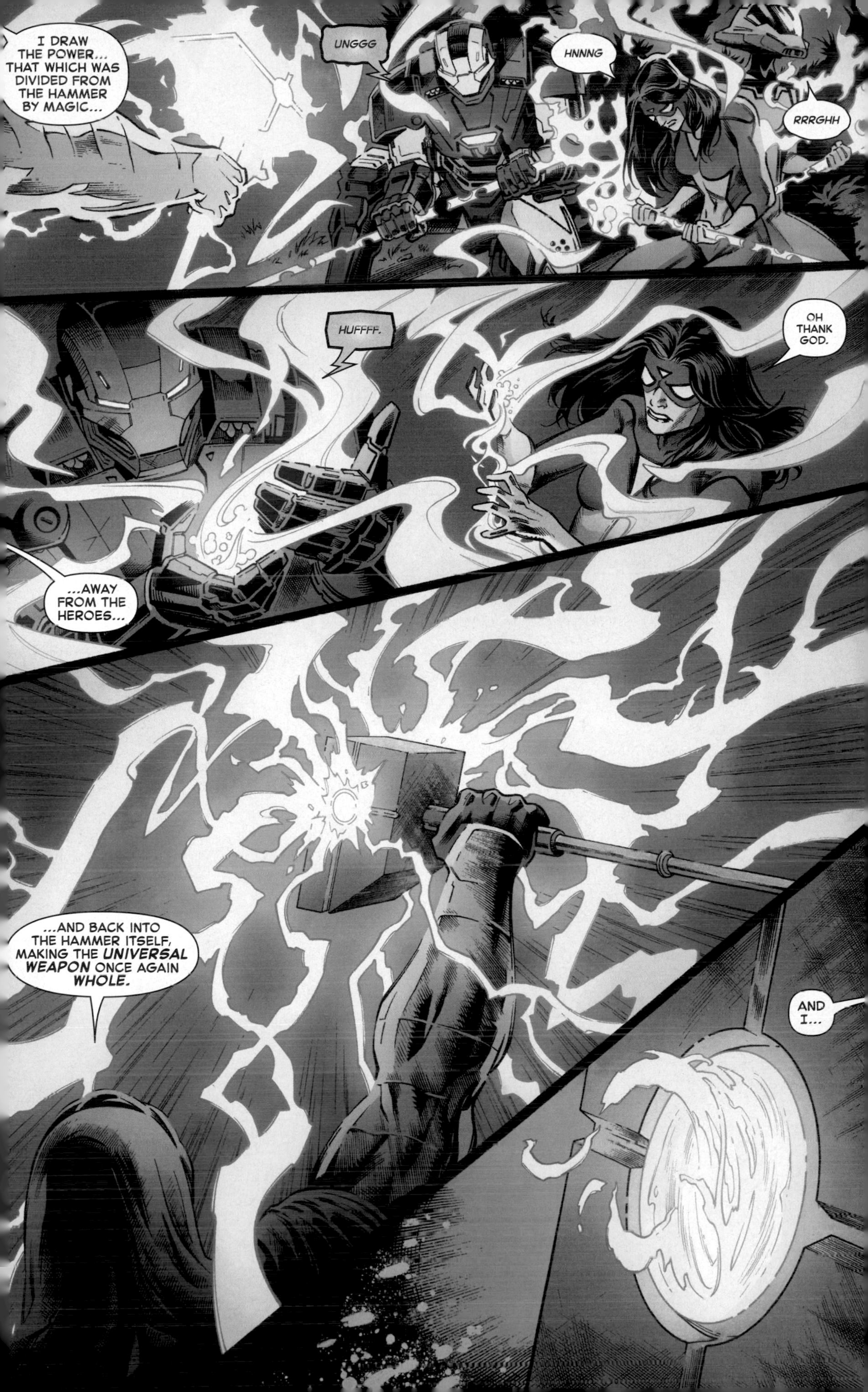

I DRAW THE POWER... THAT WHICH WAS DIVIDED FROM THE HAMMER BY MAGIC...
UNGGG
HNNNG
RRRGHH
HUFFFF.
OH THANK GOD.
...AWAY FROM THE HEROES...
...AND BACK INTO THE HAMMER ITSELF, MAKING THE UNIVERSAL WEAPON ONCE AGAIN WHOLE.
AND I...

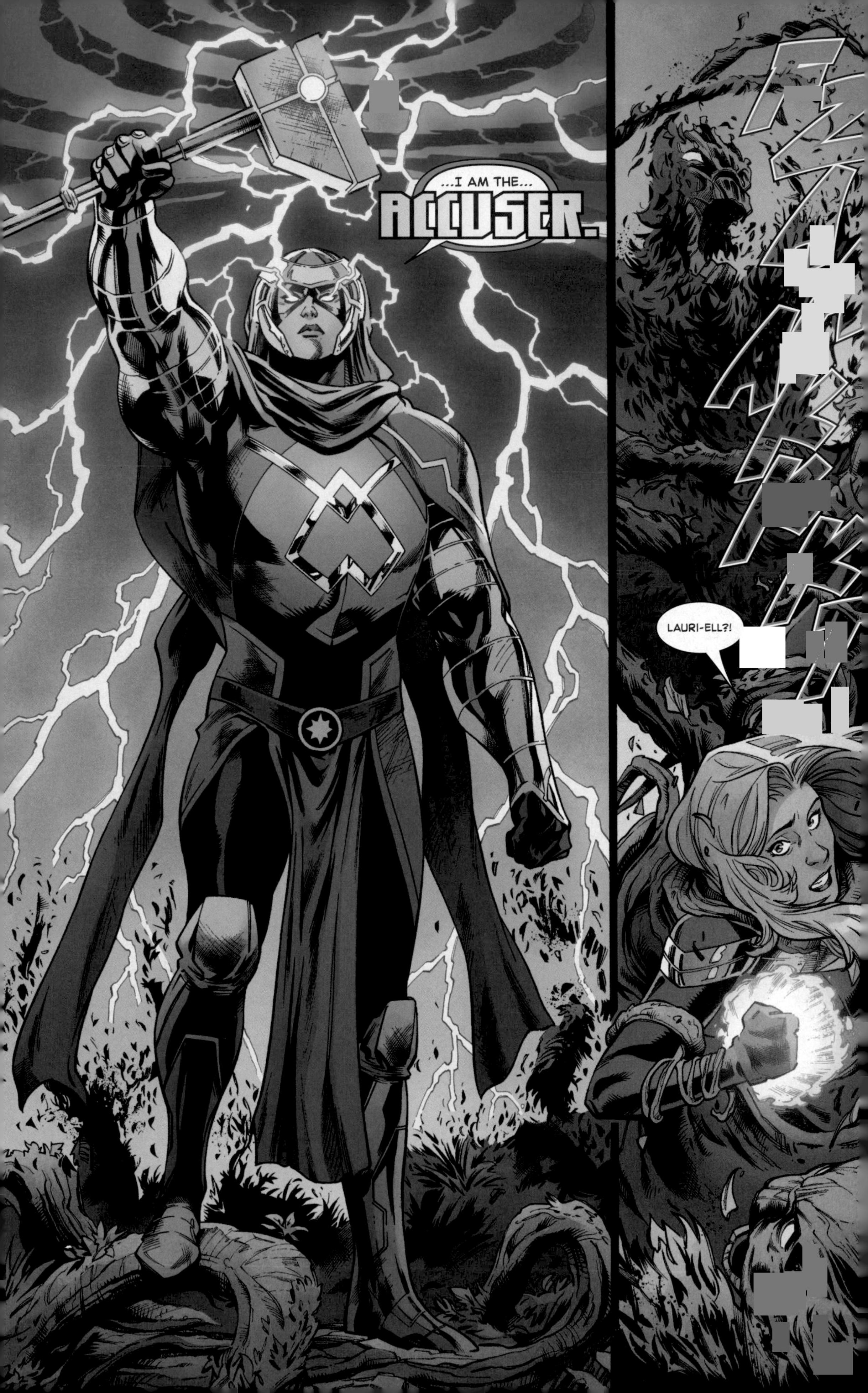
...I AM THE... ACCUSER.
LAURI-ELL?!

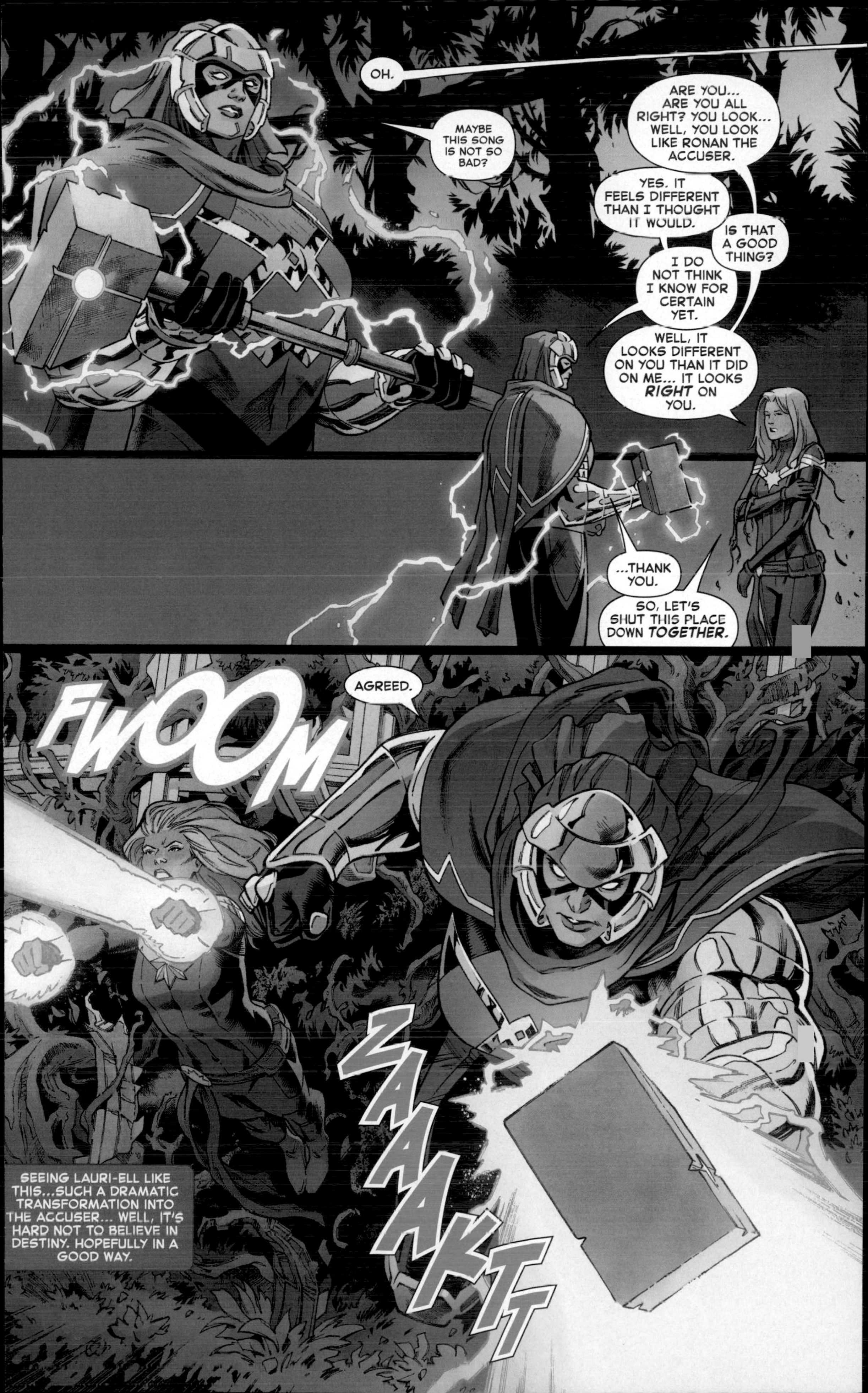
OH.
MAYBE THIS SONG IS NOT SO BAD?
ARE YOU... ARE YOU ALL RIGHT? YOU LOOK... WELL, YOU LOOK LIKE RONAN THE ACCUSER.
YES. IT FEELS DIFFERENT THAN I THOUGHT IT WOULD.
IS THAT A GOOD THING?
I DO NOT THINK I KNOW FOR CERTAIN YET.
WELL, IT LOOKS DIFFERENT ON YOU THAN IT DID ON ME... IT LOOKS RIGHT ON YOU.
...THANK YOU.
SO, LET'S SHUT THIS PLACE DOWN TOGETHER.
AGREED.
FWOOM
ZAAAKTT
SEEING LAURI-ELL LIKE THIS...SUCH A DRAMATIC TRANSFORMATION INTO THE ACCUSER... WELL, IT'S HARD NOT TO BELIEVE IN DESTINY. HOPEFULLY IN A GOOD WAY.

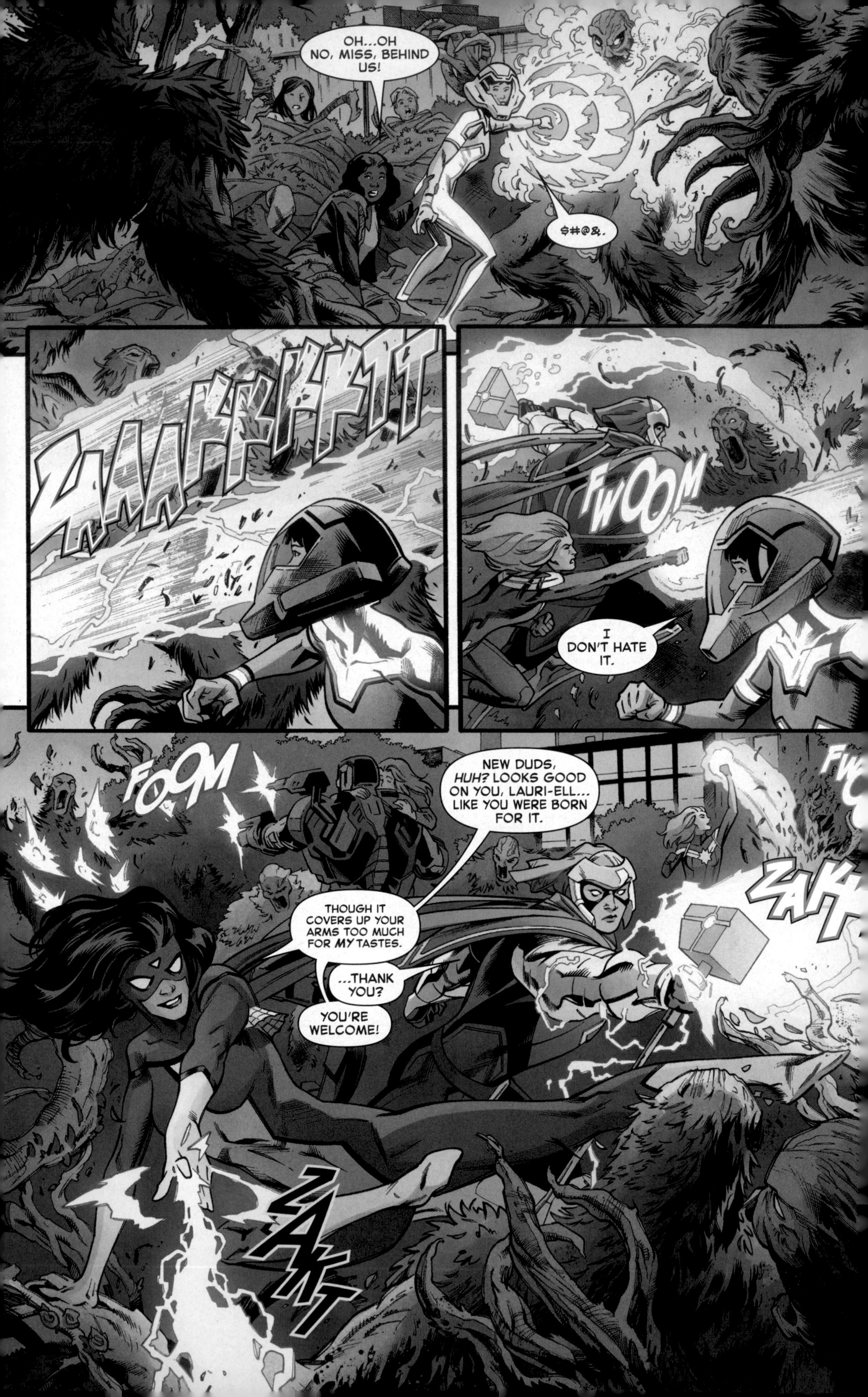

OH...OH NO, MISS, BEHIND US!
$#@&.
ZWAAKKKKKTTT
FWOOM
I DON'T HATE IT.
FOOM
NEW DUDS, HUH? LOOKS GOOD ON YOU, LAURI-ELL... LIKE YOU WERE BORN FOR IT.
THOUGH IT COVERS UP YOUR ARMS TOO MUCH FOR MY TASTES.
...THANK YOU?
YOU'RE WELCOME!
ZAKT

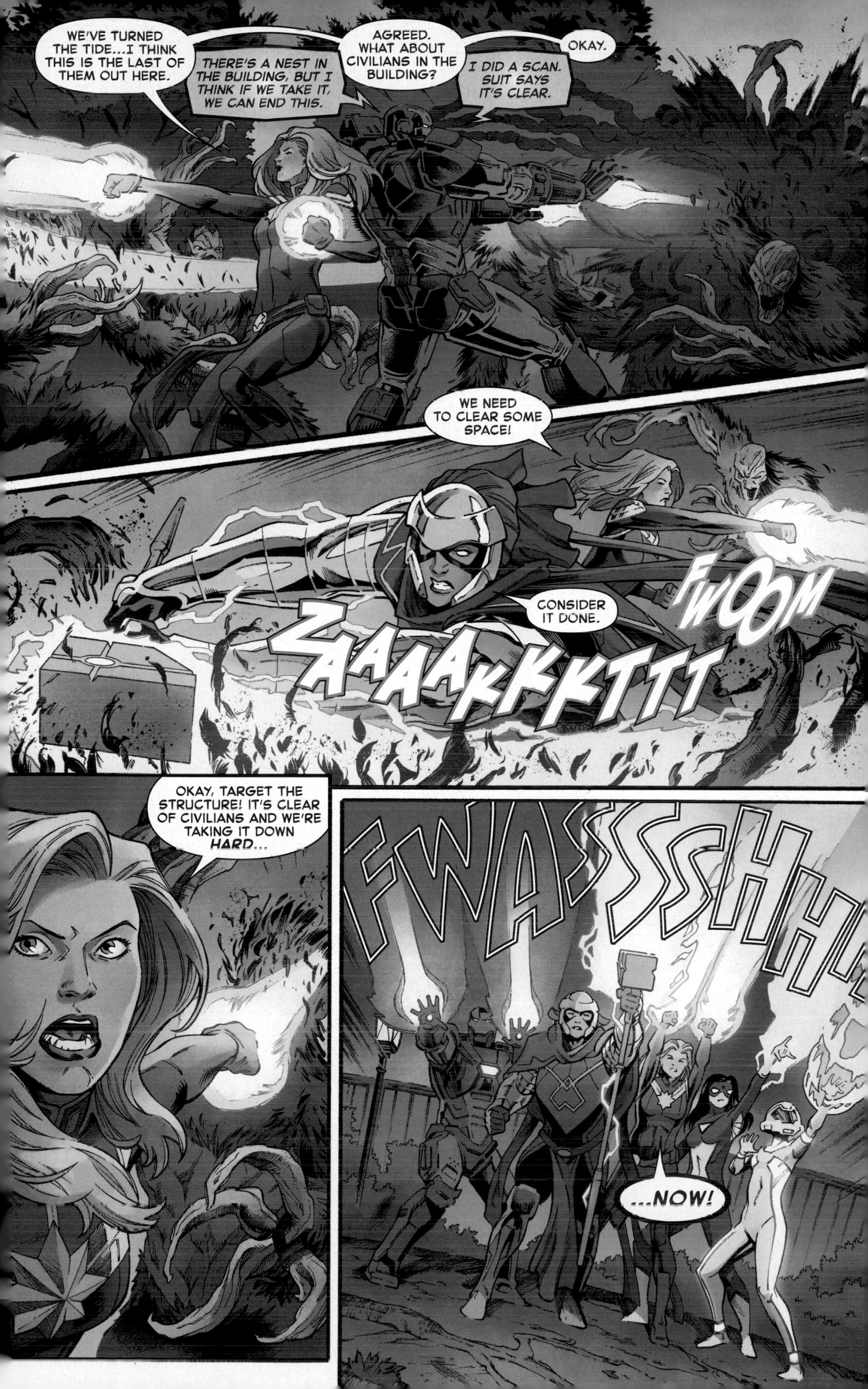
WE'VE TURNED THE TIDE...I THINK THIS IS THE LAST OF THEM OUT HERE.
THERE'S A NEST IN THE BUILDING, BUT I THINK IF WE TAKE IT, WE CAN END THIS.
AGREED. WHAT ABOUT CIVILIANS IN THE BUILDING?
I DID A SCAN. SUIT SAYS IT'S CLEAR.
OKAY.
WE NEED TO CLEAR SOME SPACE!
CONSIDER IT DONE.
ZAAAAKKKTTTT
FWOOOM
OKAY, TARGET THE STRUCTURE! IT'S CLEAR OF CIVILIANS AND WE'RE TAKING IT DOWN HARD...
FWASSSSHHH
...NOW!

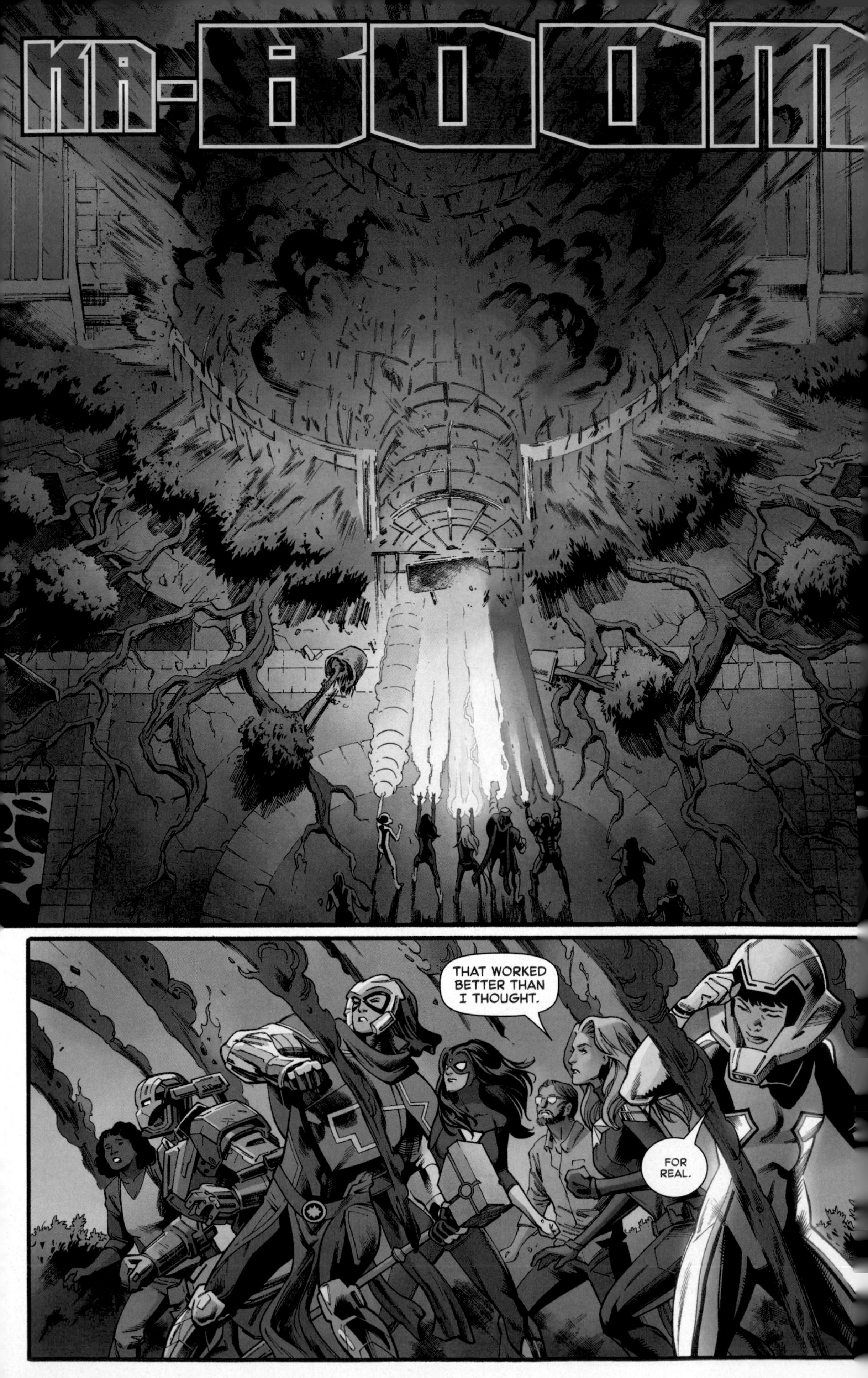
KA-BOOM
THAT WORKED BETTER THAN I THOUGHT.
FOR REAL.

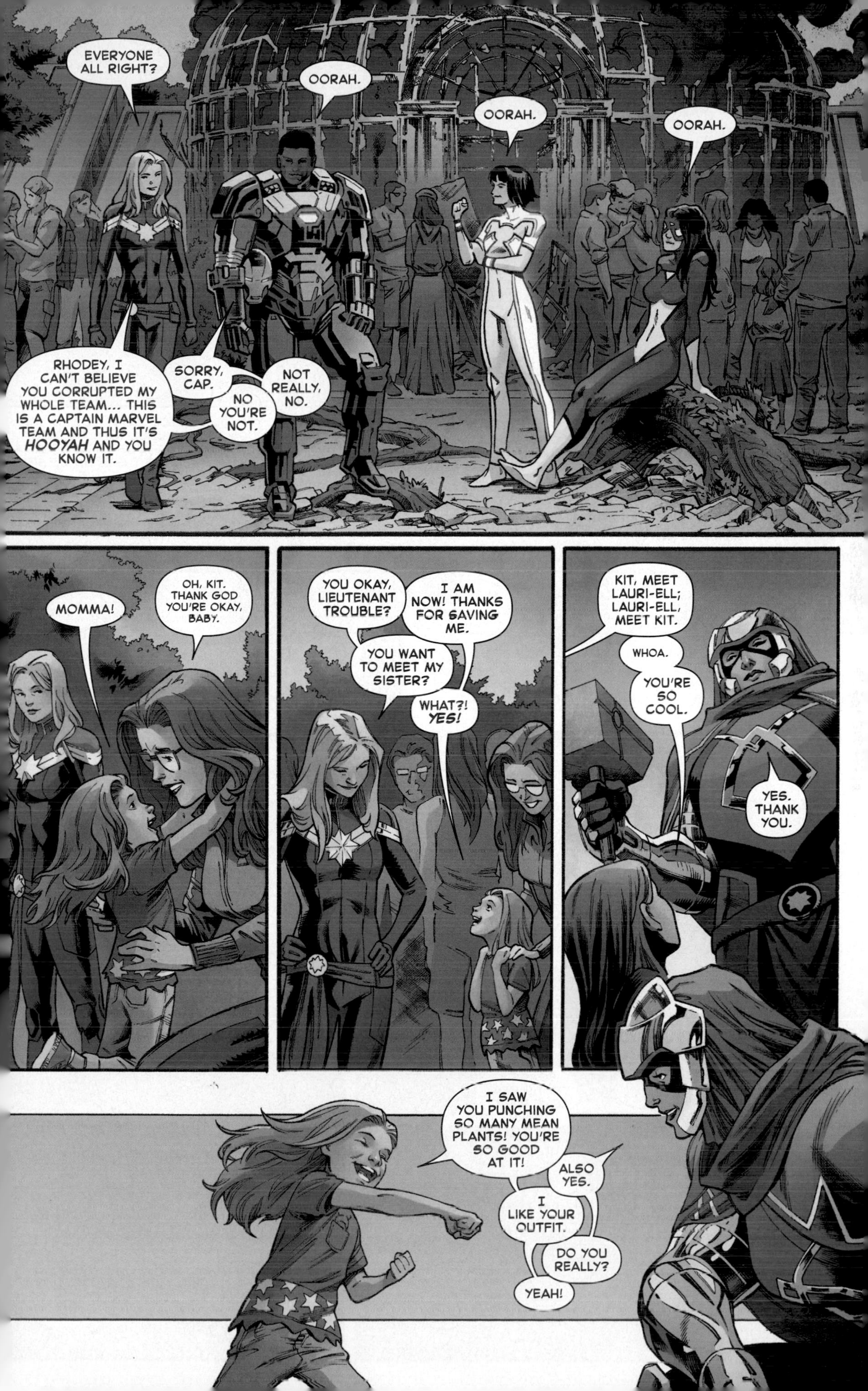
EVERYONE ALL RIGHT?
OORAH.
OORAH.
OORAH.
RHODEY, I CAN'T BELIEVE YOU CORRUPTED MY WHOLE TEAM... THIS IS A CAPTAIN MARVEL TEAM AND THUS IT'S *HOOYAH* AND YOU KNOW IT.
SORRY, CAP.
NO YOU'RE NOT.
NOT REALLY, NO.
MOMMA!
OH, KIT. THANK GOD YOU'RE OKAY, BABY.
YOU OKAY, LIEUTENANT TROUBLE?
I AM NOW! THANKS FOR SAVING ME.
YOU WANT TO MEET MY SISTER?
WHAT?! *YES!*
KIT, MEET LAURI-ELL; LAURI-ELL, MEET KIT.
WHOA.
YOU'RE SO COOL.
YES. THANK YOU.
I SAW YOU PUNCHING SO MANY MEAN PLANTS! YOU'RE SO GOOD AT IT!
ALSO YES.
I LIKE YOUR OUTFIT.
DO YOU REALLY?
YEAH!

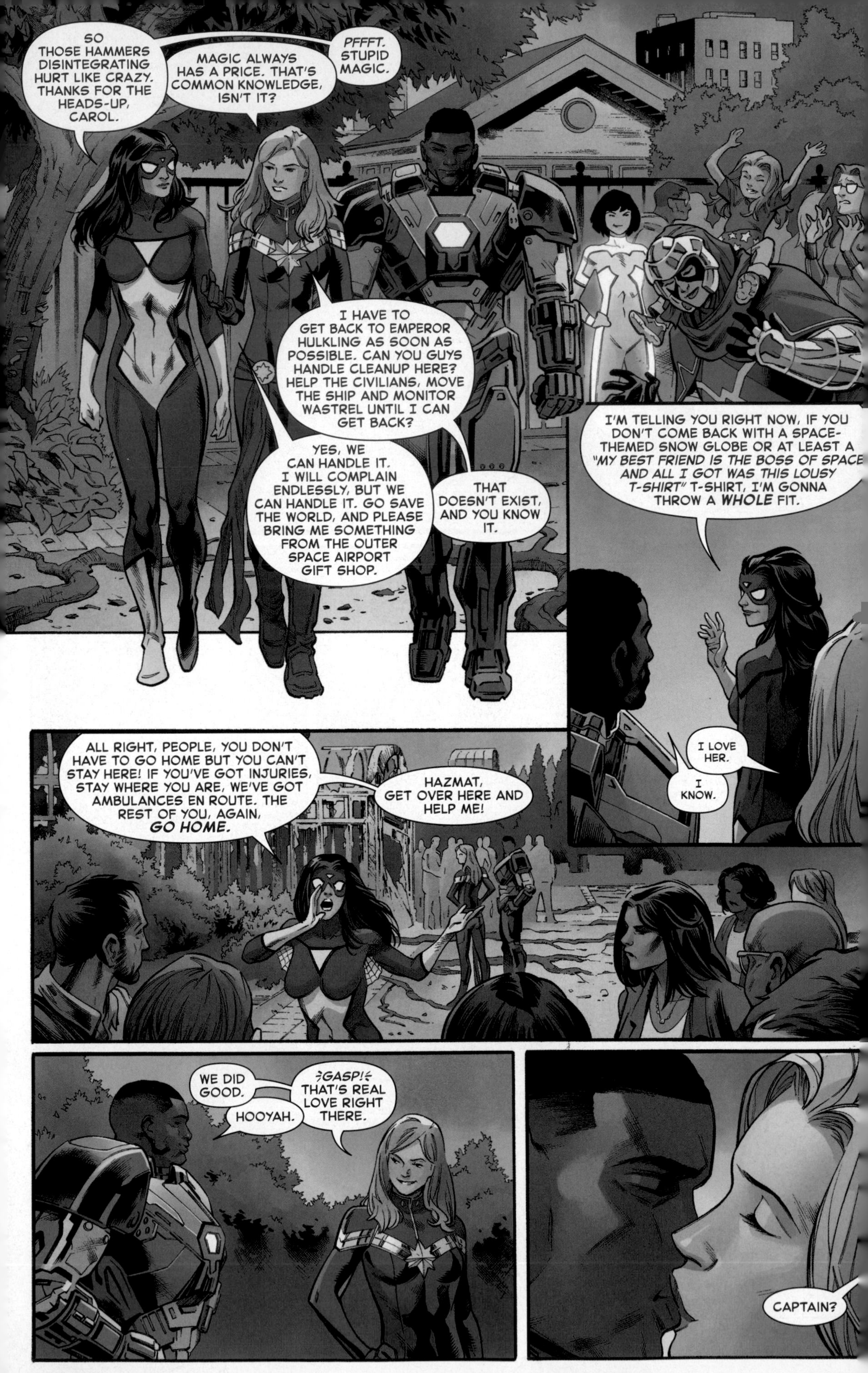
SO THOSE HAMMERS DISINTEGRATING HURT LIKE CRAZY. THANKS FOR THE HEADS-UP, CAROL.
MAGIC ALWAYS HAS A PRICE. THAT'S COMMON KNOWLEDGE, ISN'T IT?
PFFFT. STUPID MAGIC.
I HAVE TO GET BACK TO EMPEROR HULKLING AS SOON AS POSSIBLE. CAN YOU GUYS HANDLE CLEANUP HERE? HELP THE CIVILIANS, MOVE THE SHIP AND MONITOR WASTREL UNTIL I CAN GET BACK?
YES, WE CAN HANDLE IT. I WILL COMPLAIN ENDLESSLY, BUT WE CAN HANDLE IT. GO SAVE THE WORLD, AND PLEASE BRING ME SOMETHING FROM THE OUTER SPACE AIRPORT GIFT SHOP.
THAT DOESN'T EXIST, AND YOU KNOW IT.
I'M TELLING YOU RIGHT NOW, IF YOU DON'T COME BACK WITH A SPACE-THEMED SNOW GLOBE OR AT LEAST A "MY BEST FRIEND IS THE BOSS OF SPACE AND ALL I GOT WAS THIS LOUSY T-SHIRT" T-SHIRT, I'M GONNA THROW A WHOLE FIT.
I LOVE HER.
I KNOW.
ALL RIGHT, PEOPLE, YOU DON'T HAVE TO GO HOME BUT YOU CAN'T STAY HERE! IF YOU'VE GOT INJURIES, STAY WHERE YOU ARE, WE'VE GOT AMBULANCES EN ROUTE. THE REST OF YOU, AGAIN, GO HOME.
HAZMAT, GET OVER HERE AND HELP ME!
WE DID GOOD.
HOOYAH.
GASP! THAT'S REAL LOVE RIGHT THERE.
CAPTAIN?

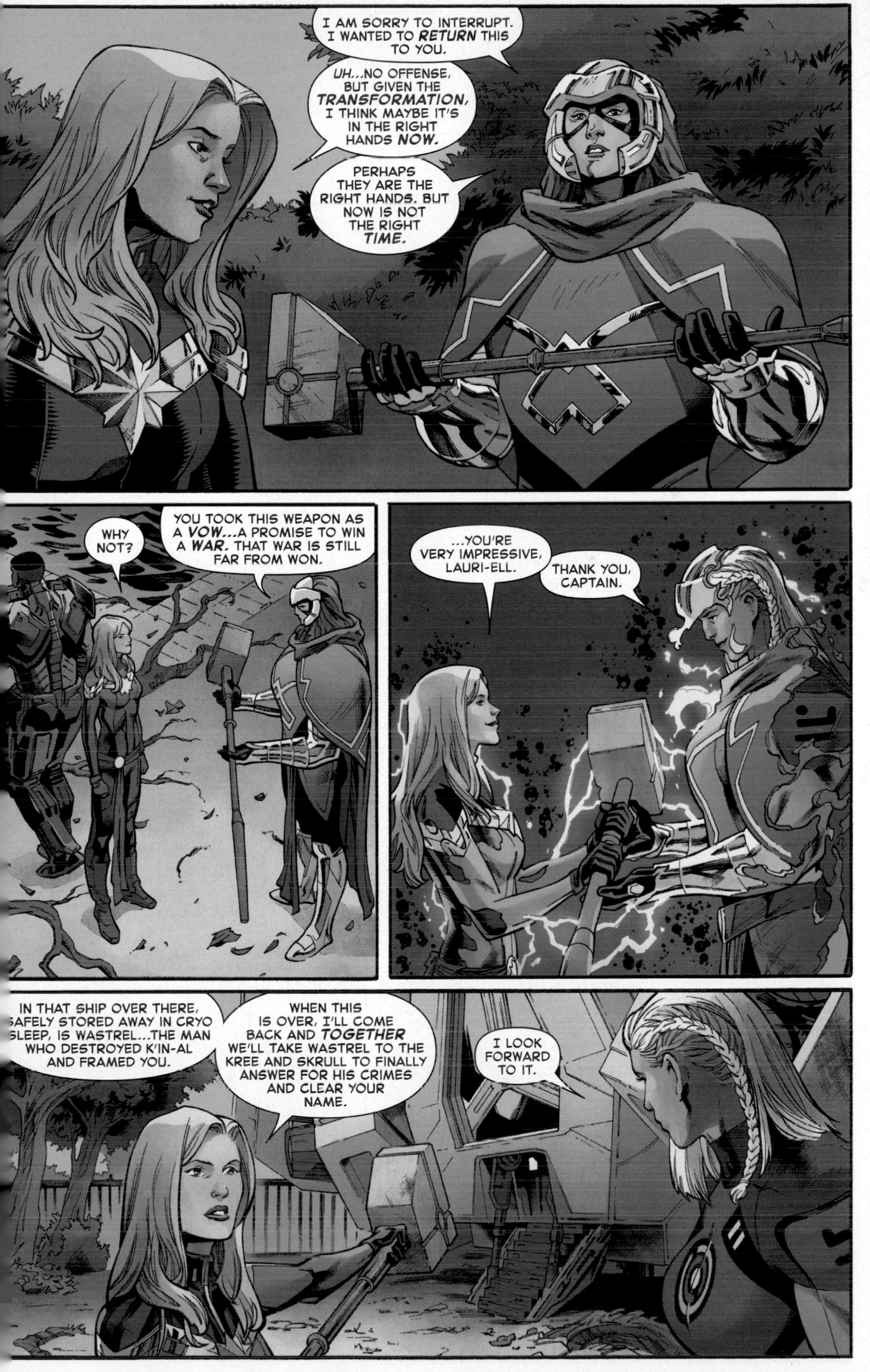
I AM SORRY TO INTERRUPT. I WANTED TO RETURN THIS TO YOU.
UH...NO OFFENSE, BUT GIVEN THE TRANSFORMATION, I THINK MAYBE IT'S IN THE RIGHT HANDS NOW.
PERHAPS THEY ARE THE RIGHT HANDS. BUT NOW IS NOT THE RIGHT TIME.
WHY NOT?
YOU TOOK THIS WEAPON AS A VOW...A PROMISE TO WIN A WAR. THAT WAR IS STILL FAR FROM WON.
...YOU'RE VERY IMPRESSIVE, LAURI-ELL.
THANK YOU, CAPTAIN.
IN THAT SHIP OVER THERE, SAFELY STORED AWAY IN CRYO SLEEP, IS WASTREL...THE MAN WHO DESTROYED K'IN-AL AND FRAMED YOU.
WHEN THIS IS OVER, I'LL COME BACK AND TOGETHER WE'LL TAKE WASTREL TO THE KREE AND SKRULL TO FINALLY ANSWER FOR HIS CRIMES AND CLEAR YOUR NAME.
I LOOK FORWARD TO IT.

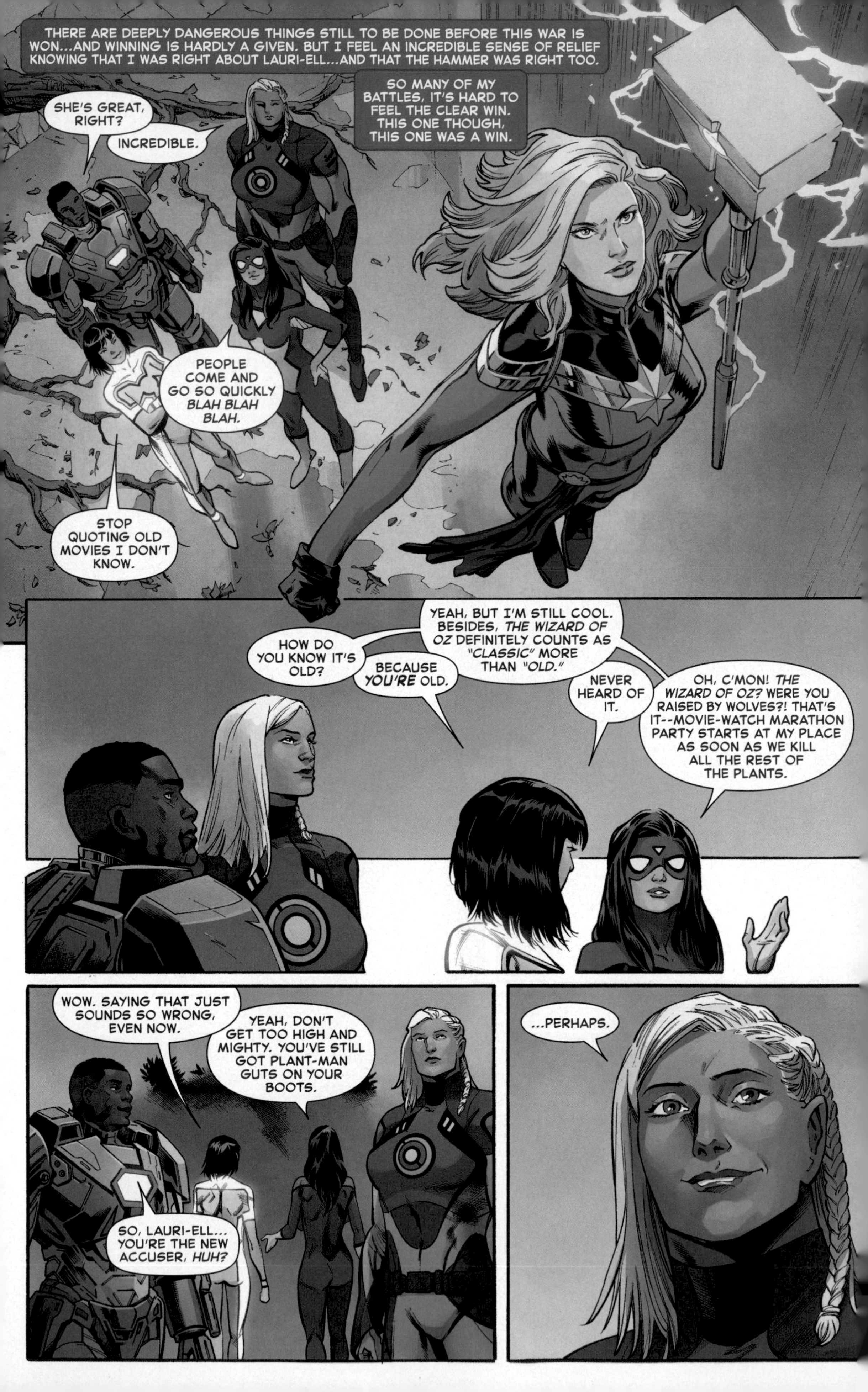

THERE ARE DEEPLY DANGEROUS THINGS STILL TO BE DONE BEFORE THIS WAR IS WON...AND WINNING IS HARDLY A GIVEN. BUT I FEEL AN INCREDIBLE SENSE OF RELIEF KNOWING THAT I WAS RIGHT ABOUT LAURI-ELL...AND THAT THE HAMMER WAS RIGHT TOO.
SO MANY OF MY BATTLES, IT'S HARD TO FEEL THE CLEAR WIN. THIS ONE THOUGH, THIS ONE WAS A WIN.
SHE'S GREAT, RIGHT?
INCREDIBLE.
PEOPLE COME AND GO SO QUICKLY *BLAH BLAH BLAH.*
STOP QUOTING OLD MOVIES I DON'T KNOW.
HOW DO YOU KNOW IT'S OLD?
BECAUSE *YOU'RE* OLD.
YEAH, BUT I'M STILL COOL. BESIDES, *THE WIZARD OF OZ* DEFINITELY COUNTS AS "*CLASSIC*" MORE THAN "*OLD.*"
NEVER HEARD OF IT.
OH, C'MON! *THE WIZARD OF OZ?* WERE YOU RAISED BY WOLVES?! THAT'S IT--MOVIE-WATCH MARATHON PARTY STARTS AT MY PLACE AS SOON AS WE KILL ALL THE REST OF THE PLANTS.
WOW. SAYING THAT JUST SOUNDS SO WRONG, EVEN NOW.
YEAH, DON'T GET TOO HIGH AND MIGHTY. YOU'VE STILL GOT PLANT-MAN GUTS ON YOUR BOOTS.
SO, LAURI-ELL... YOU'RE THE NEW ACCUSER, *HUH?*
...PERHAPS.

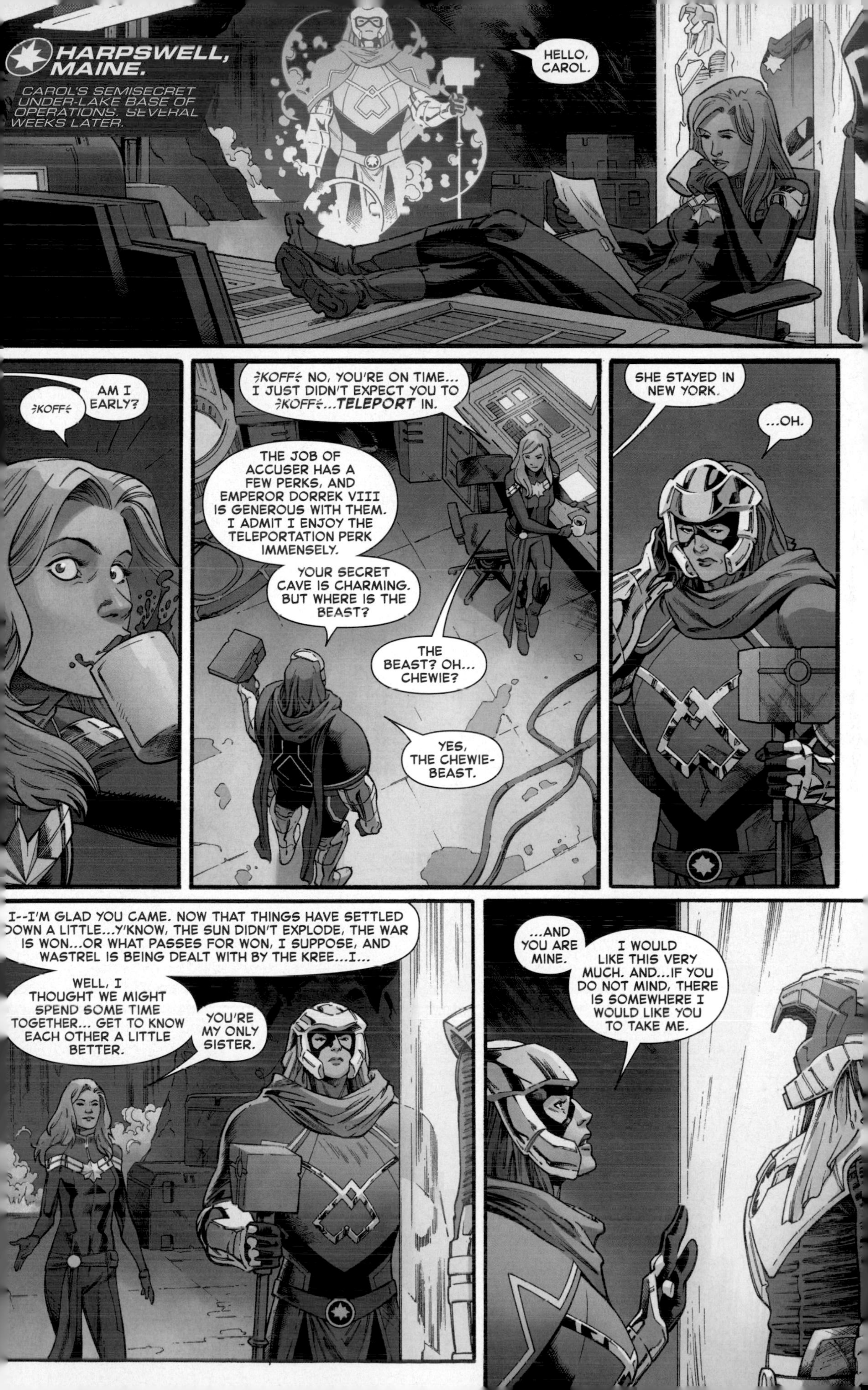
HARPSWELL, MAINE.
CAROL'S SEMISECRET UNDER-LAKE BASE OF OPERATIONS. SEVERAL WEEKS LATER.
HELLO, CAROL.
AM I EARLY?
⚡KOFF⚡
⚡KOFF⚡ NO, YOU'RE ON TIME... I JUST DIDN'T EXPECT YOU TO ⚡KOFF⚡...TELEPORT IN.
THE JOB OF ACCUSER HAS A FEW PERKS, AND EMPEROR DORREK VIII IS GENEROUS WITH THEM. I ADMIT I ENJOY THE TELEPORTATION PERK IMMENSELY.
YOUR SECRET CAVE IS CHARMING. BUT WHERE IS THE BEAST?
THE BEAST? OH... CHEWIE?
YES, THE CHEWIE-BEAST.
SHE STAYED IN NEW YORK.
...OH.
I--I'M GLAD YOU CAME. NOW THAT THINGS HAVE SETTLED DOWN A LITTLE...Y'KNOW, THE SUN DIDN'T EXPLODE, THE WAR IS WON...OR WHAT PASSES FOR WON, I SUPPOSE, AND WASTREL IS BEING DEALT WITH BY THE KREE...I...
WELL, I THOUGHT WE MIGHT SPEND SOME TIME TOGETHER... GET TO KNOW EACH OTHER A LITTLE BETTER.
YOU'RE MY ONLY SISTER.
...AND YOU ARE MINE.
I WOULD LIKE THIS VERY MUCH. AND...IF YOU DO NOT MIND, THERE IS SOMEWHERE I WOULD LIKE YOU TO TAKE ME.

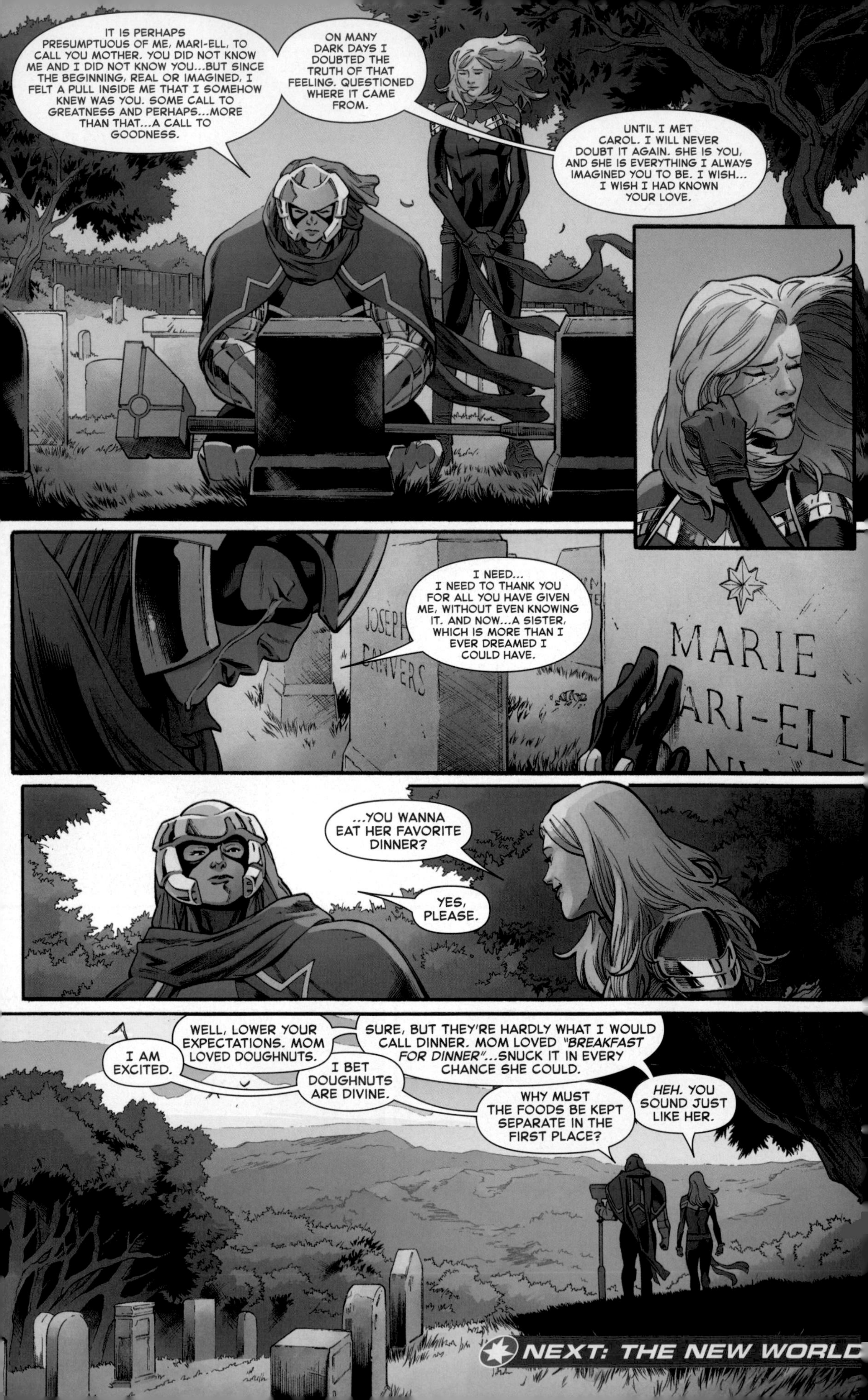
IT IS PERHAPS PRESUMPTUOUS OF ME, MARI-ELL, TO CALL YOU MOTHER. YOU DID NOT KNOW ME AND I DID NOT KNOW YOU...BUT SINCE THE BEGINNING, REAL OR IMAGINED, I FELT A PULL INSIDE ME THAT I SOMEHOW KNEW WAS YOU. SOME CALL TO GREATNESS AND PERHAPS...MORE THAN THAT...A CALL TO GOODNESS.
ON MANY DARK DAYS I DOUBTED THE TRUTH OF THAT FEELING. QUESTIONED WHERE IT CAME FROM.
UNTIL I MET CAROL. I WILL NEVER DOUBT IT AGAIN. SHE IS YOU, AND SHE IS EVERYTHING I ALWAYS IMAGINED YOU TO BE. I WISH... I WISH I HAD KNOWN YOUR LOVE.
I NEED... I NEED TO THANK YOU FOR ALL YOU HAVE GIVEN ME, WITHOUT EVEN KNOWING IT. AND NOW...A SISTER, WHICH IS MORE THAN I EVER DREAMED I COULD HAVE.
MARIE
...YOU WANNA EAT HER FAVORITE DINNER?
YES, PLEASE.
I AM EXCITED.
WELL, LOWER YOUR EXPECTATIONS. MOM LOVED DOUGHNUTS.
I BET DOUGHNUTS ARE DIVINE.
SURE, BUT THEY'RE HARDLY WHAT I WOULD CALL DINNER. MOM LOVED *"BREAKFAST FOR DINNER"*...SNUCK IT IN EVERY CHANCE SHE COULD.
WHY MUST THE FOODS BE KEPT SEPARATE IN THE FIRST PLACE?
HEH. YOU SOUND JUST LIKE HER.
NEXT: THE NEW WORLD

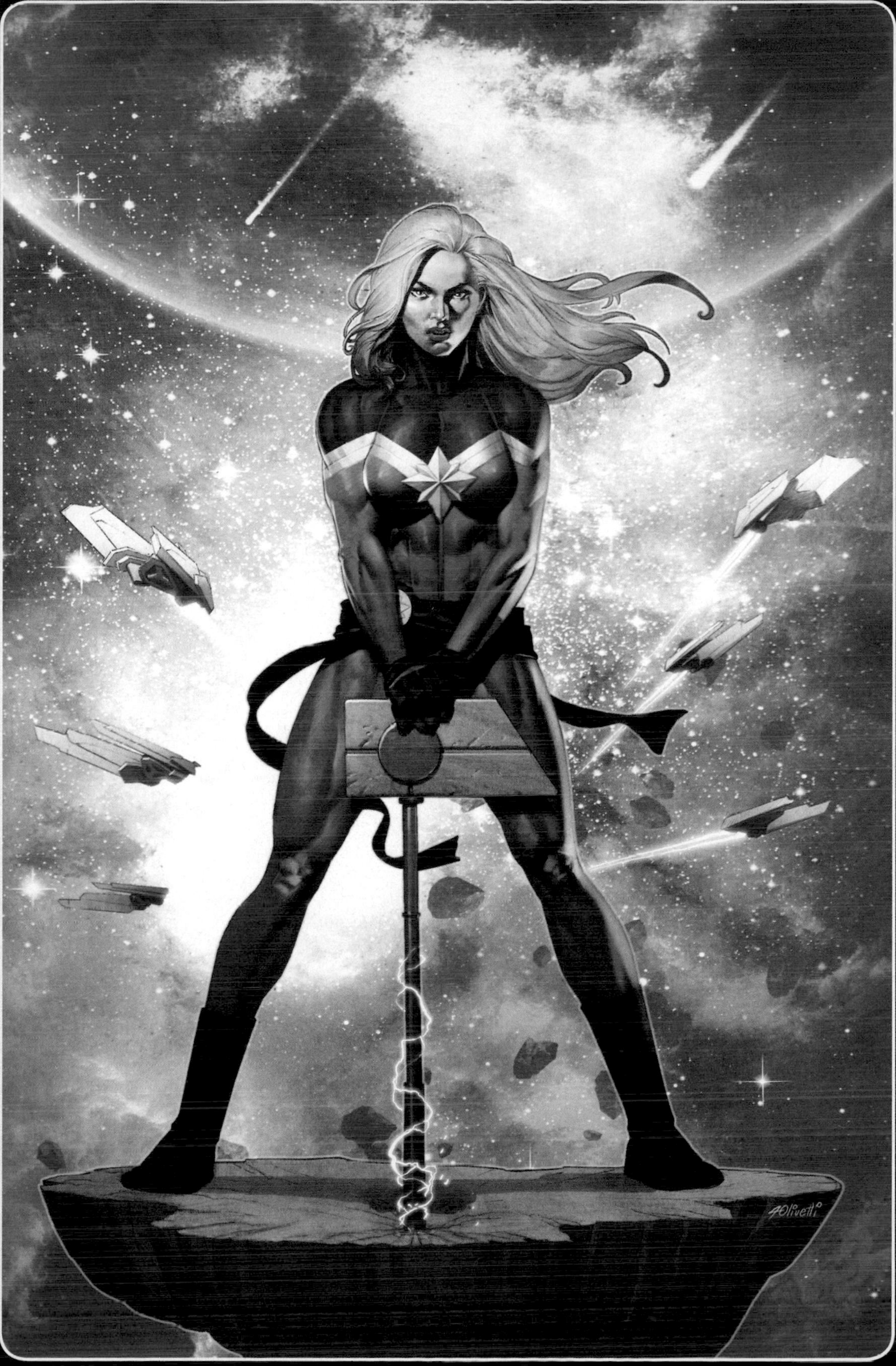
AOlivetti

ARIEL OLIVETTI
19 VARIANT

THE KREE AND THE SKRULLS HAVE UNITED UNDER A NEW EMPEROR – AND THEIR WAR FLEET IS HEADING TOWARD EARTH! AS THE EVENTS OF *EMPYRE* UNFOLD, CAROL DANVERS ONCE AGAIN TAKES THE INTERGALACTIC STAGE.

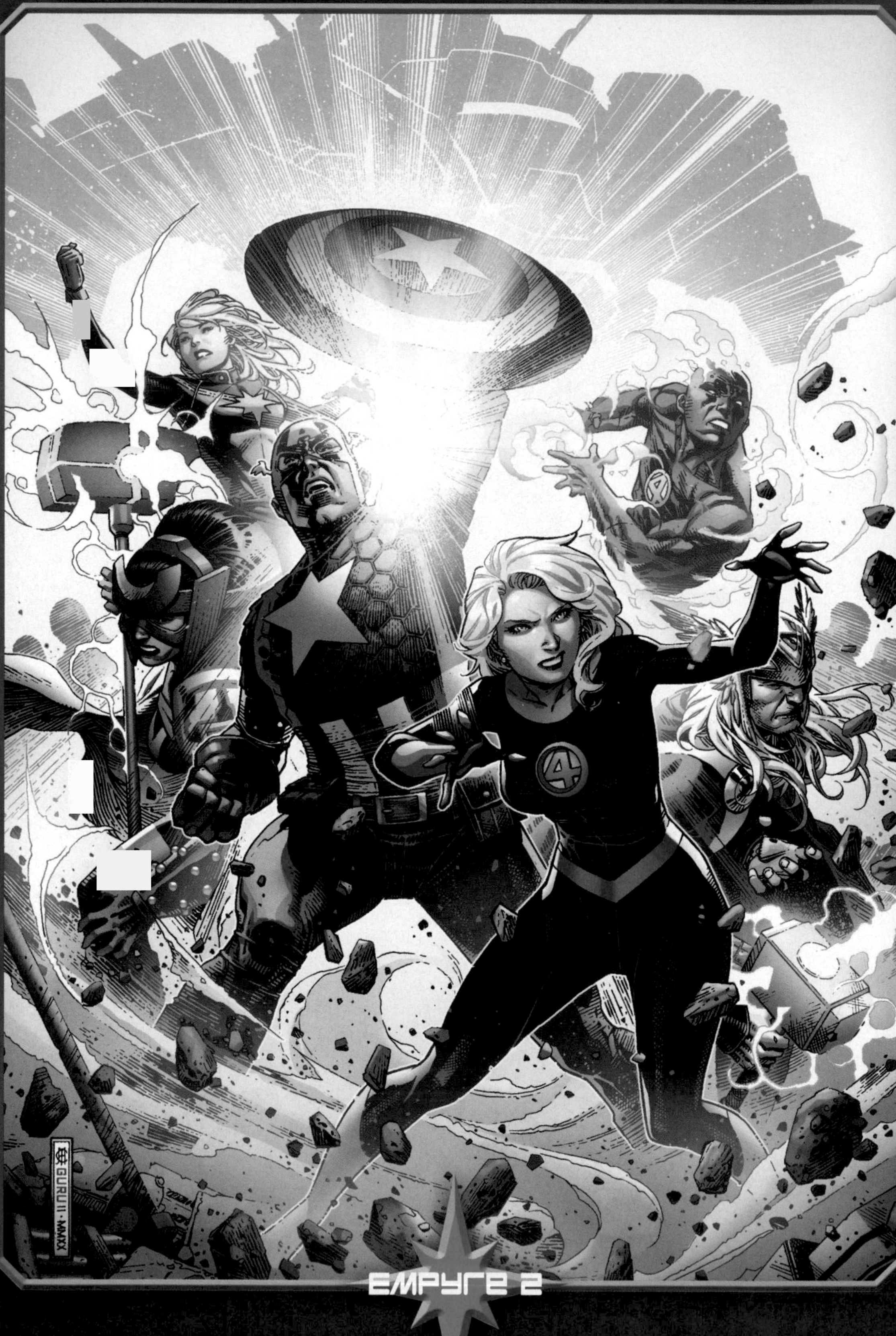

EMPYRE 2

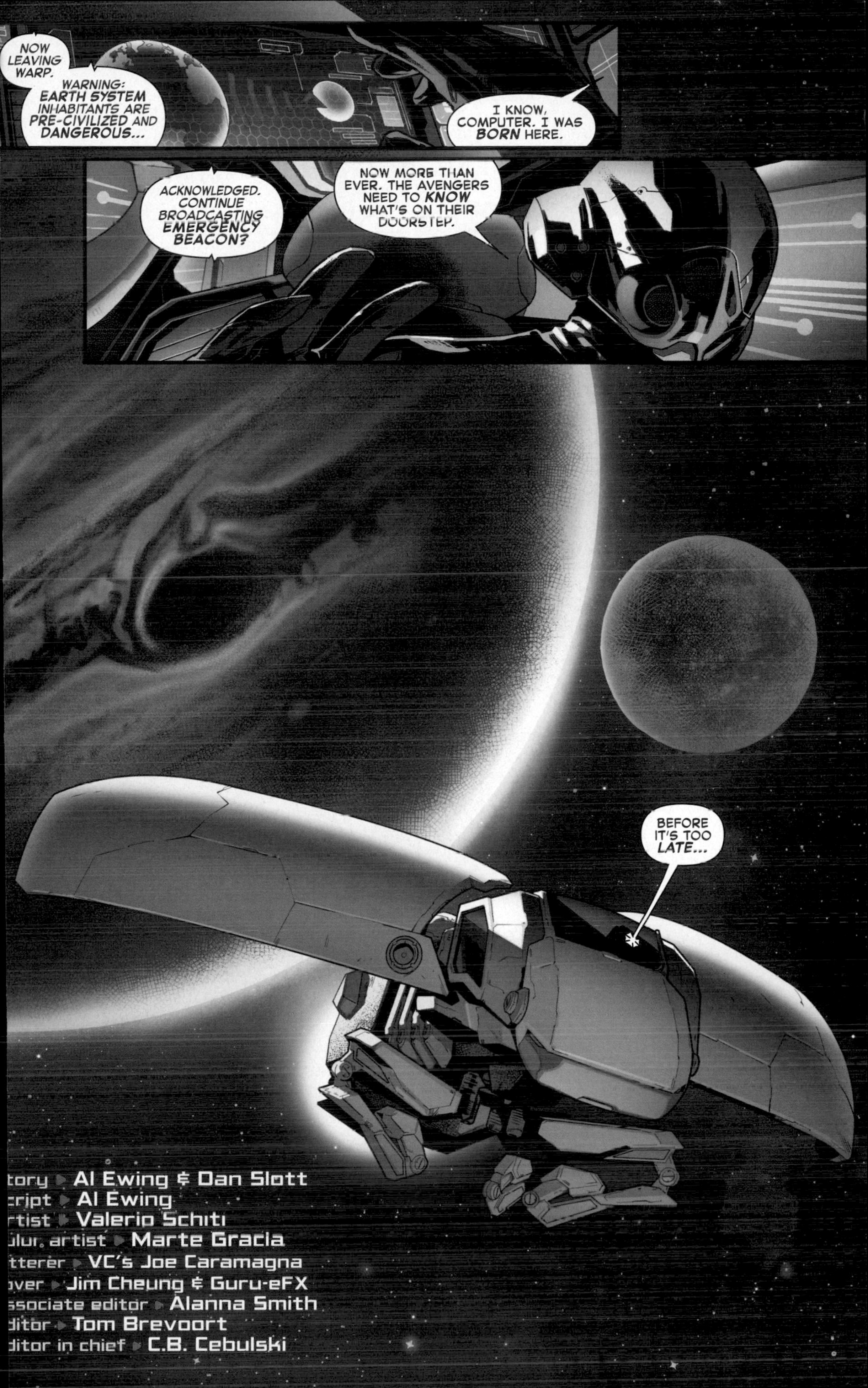
NOW LEAVING WARP.
WARNING: EARTH SYSTEM INHABITANTS ARE PRE-CIVILIZED AND DANGEROUS...
I KNOW, COMPUTER. I WAS BORN HERE.
ACKNOWLEDGED. CONTINUE BROADCASTING EMERGENCY BEACON?
NOW MORE THAN EVER. THE AVENGERS NEED TO KNOW WHAT'S ON THEIR DOORSTEP.
BEFORE IT'S TOO LATE...
tory ▸ Al Ewing & Dan Slott
cript ▸ Al Ewing
rtist ▸ Valerio Schiti
olor artist ▸ Marte Gracia
tterer ▸ VC's Joe Caramagna
over ▸ Jim Cheung & Guru-eFX
ssociate editor ▸ Alanna Smith
ditor ▸ Tom Brevoort
ditor in chief ▸ C.B. Cebulski

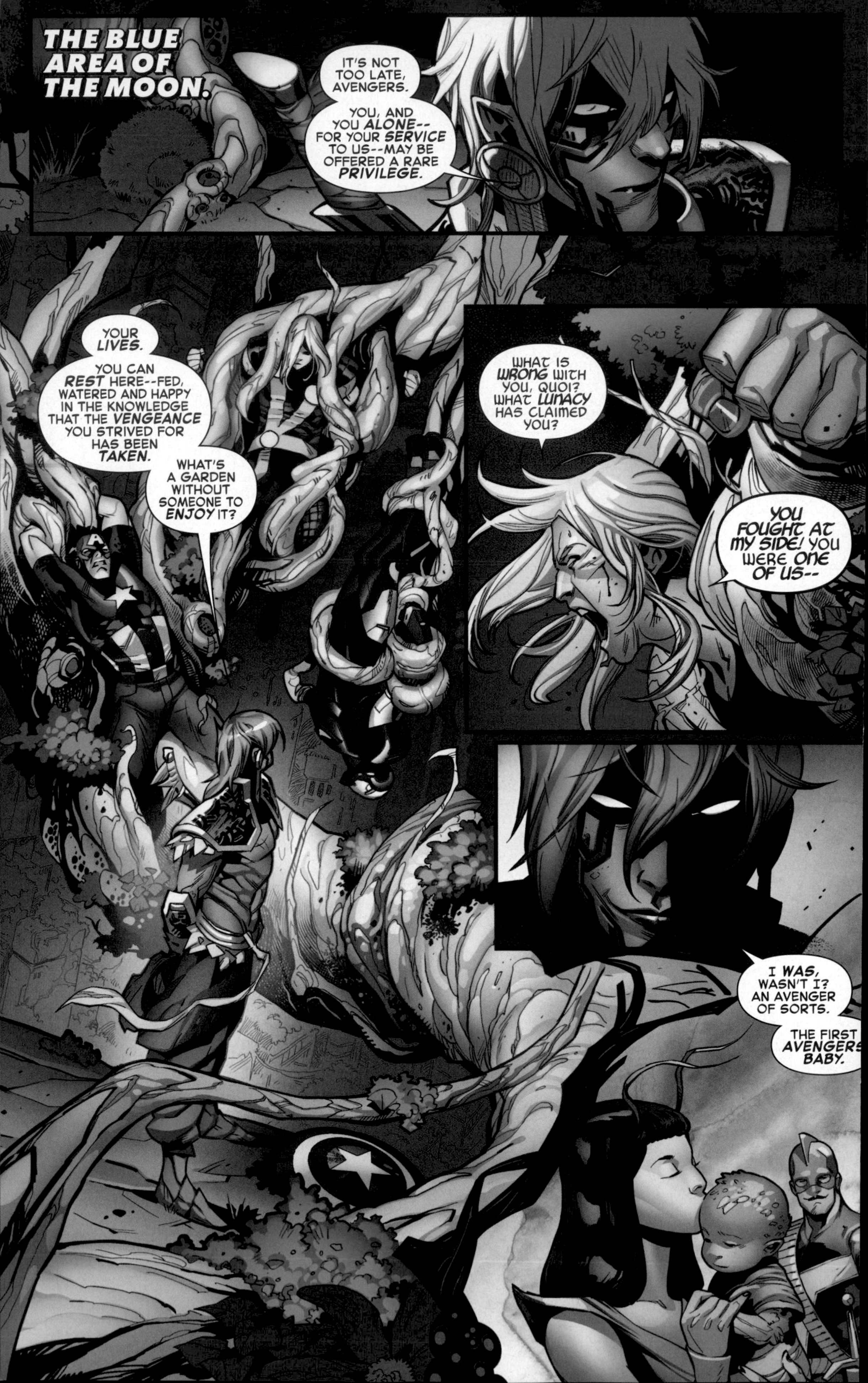
THE BLUE AREA OF THE MOON.
IT'S NOT TOO LATE, AVENGERS.
YOU, AND YOU ALONE-- FOR YOUR SERVICE TO US--MAY BE OFFERED A RARE PRIVILEGE.
YOUR LIVES.
YOU CAN REST HERE--FED, WATERED AND HAPPY IN THE KNOWLEDGE THAT THE VENGEANCE YOU STRIVED FOR HAS BEEN TAKEN.
WHAT'S A GARDEN WITHOUT SOMEONE TO ENJOY IT?
WHAT IS WRONG WITH YOU, QUOI? WHAT LUNACY HAS CLAIMED YOU?
YOU FOUGHT AT MY SIDE! YOU WERE ONE OF US--
I WAS, WASN'T I? AN AVENGER OF SORTS.
THE FIRST AVENGERS BABY.

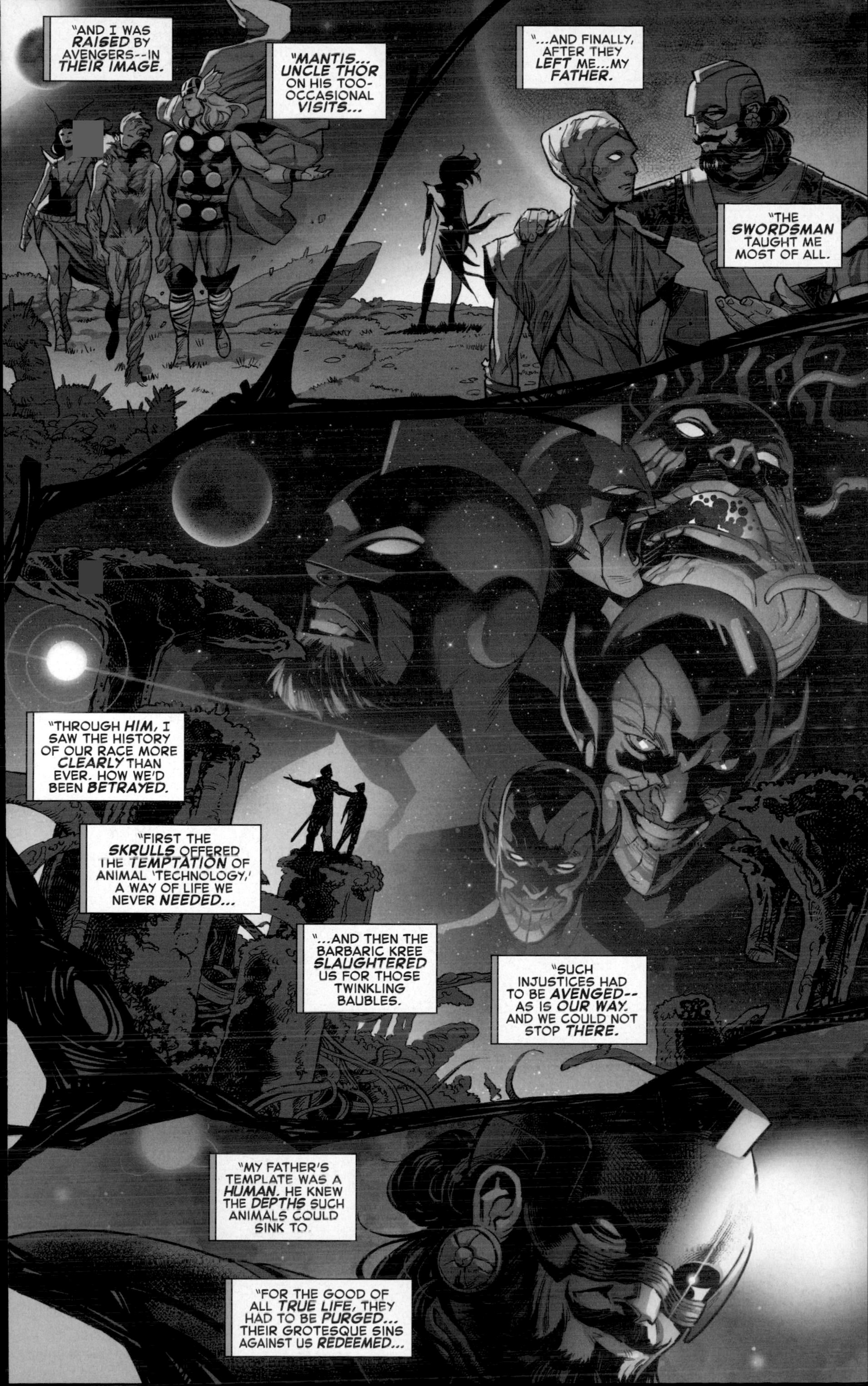
"AND I WAS RAISED BY AVENGERS--IN THEIR IMAGE.
"MANTIS... UNCLE THOR ON HIS TOO-OCCASIONAL VISITS...
"...AND FINALLY, AFTER THEY LEFT ME...MY FATHER.
"THE SWORDSMAN TAUGHT ME MOST OF ALL.
"THROUGH HIM, I SAW THE HISTORY OF OUR RACE MORE CLEARLY THAN EVER. HOW WE'D BEEN BETRAYED.
"FIRST THE SKRULLS OFFERED THE TEMPTATION OF ANIMAL 'TECHNOLOGY,' A WAY OF LIFE WE NEVER NEEDED...
"...AND THEN THE BARBARIC KREE SLAUGHTERED US FOR THOSE TWINKLING BAUBLES.
"SUCH INJUSTICES HAD TO BE AVENGED--AS IS OUR WAY. AND WE COULD NOT STOP THERE.
"MY FATHER'S TEMPLATE WAS A HUMAN. HE KNEW THE DEPTHS SUCH ANIMALS COULD SINK TO.
"FOR THE GOOD OF ALL TRUE LIFE, THEY HAD TO BE PURGED... THEIR GROTESQUE SINS AGAINST US REDEEMED...

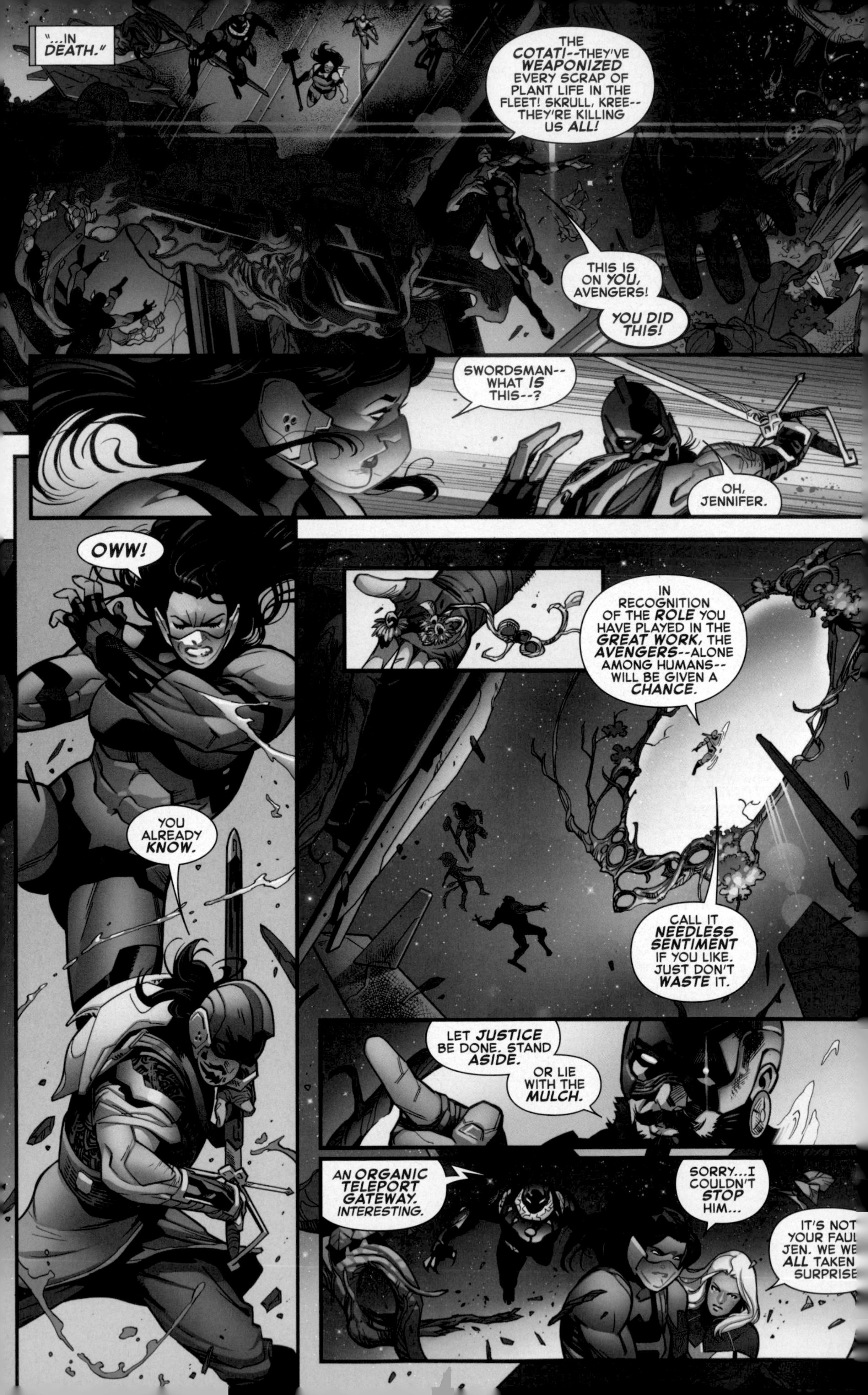
"...IN DEATH."
THE COTATI--THEY'VE WEAPONIZED EVERY SCRAP OF PLANT LIFE IN THE FLEET! SKRULL, KREE--THEY'RE KILLING US ALL!
THIS IS ON YOU, AVENGERS!
YOU DID THIS!
SWORDSMAN--WHAT IS THIS--?
OH, JENNIFER.
OWW!
YOU ALREADY KNOW.
IN RECOGNITION OF THE ROLE YOU HAVE PLAYED IN THE GREAT WORK, THE AVENGERS--ALONE AMONG HUMANS--WILL BE GIVEN A CHANCE.
CALL IT NEEDLESS SENTIMENT IF YOU LIKE. JUST DON'T WASTE IT.
LET JUSTICE BE DONE. STAND ASIDE.
OR LIE WITH THE MULCH.
AN ORGANIC TELEPORT GATEWAY. INTERESTING.
SORRY...I COULDN'T STOP HIM...
IT'S NOT YOUR FAUL JEN. WE WE ALL TAKEN SURPRISE

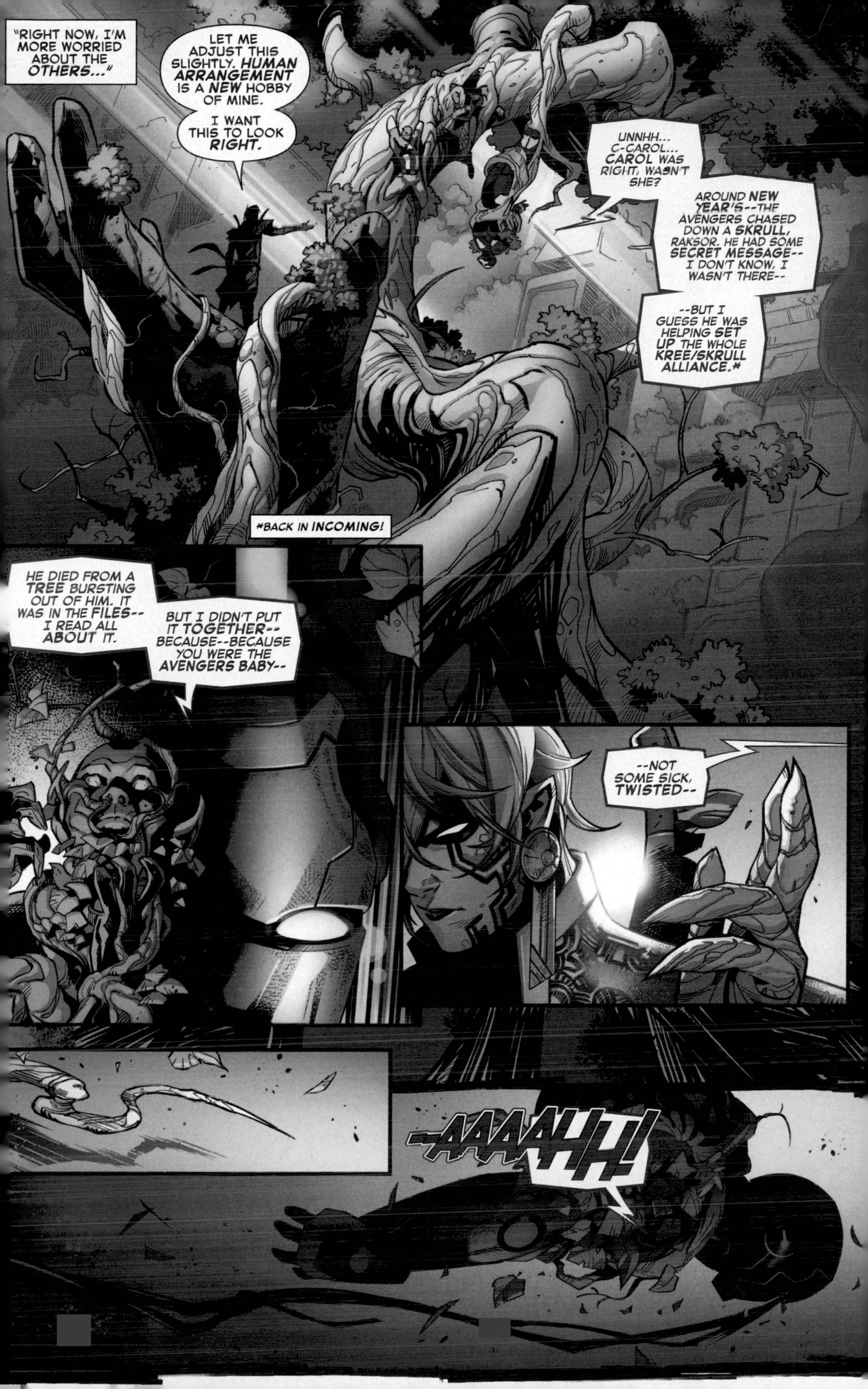
"RIGHT NOW, I'M MORE WORRIED ABOUT THE OTHERS..."
LET ME ADJUST THIS SLIGHTLY. HUMAN ARRANGEMENT IS A NEW HOBBY OF MINE.
I WANT THIS TO LOOK RIGHT.
UNNHH... C-CAROL... CAROL WAS RIGHT, WASN'T SHE?
AROUND NEW YEAR'S--THE AVENGERS CHASED DOWN A SKRULL, RAKSOR. HE HAD SOME SECRET MESSAGE--I DON'T KNOW, I WASN'T THERE--
--BUT I GUESS HE WAS HELPING SET UP THE WHOLE KREE/SKRULL ALLIANCE.*
*BACK IN INCOMING!
HE DIED FROM A TREE BURSTING OUT OF HIM. IT WAS IN THE FILES--I READ ALL ABOUT IT.
BUT I DIDN'T PUT IT TOGETHER--BECAUSE--BECAUSE YOU WERE THE AVENGERS BABY--
--NOT SOME SICK, TWISTED--
-AAAAHH!

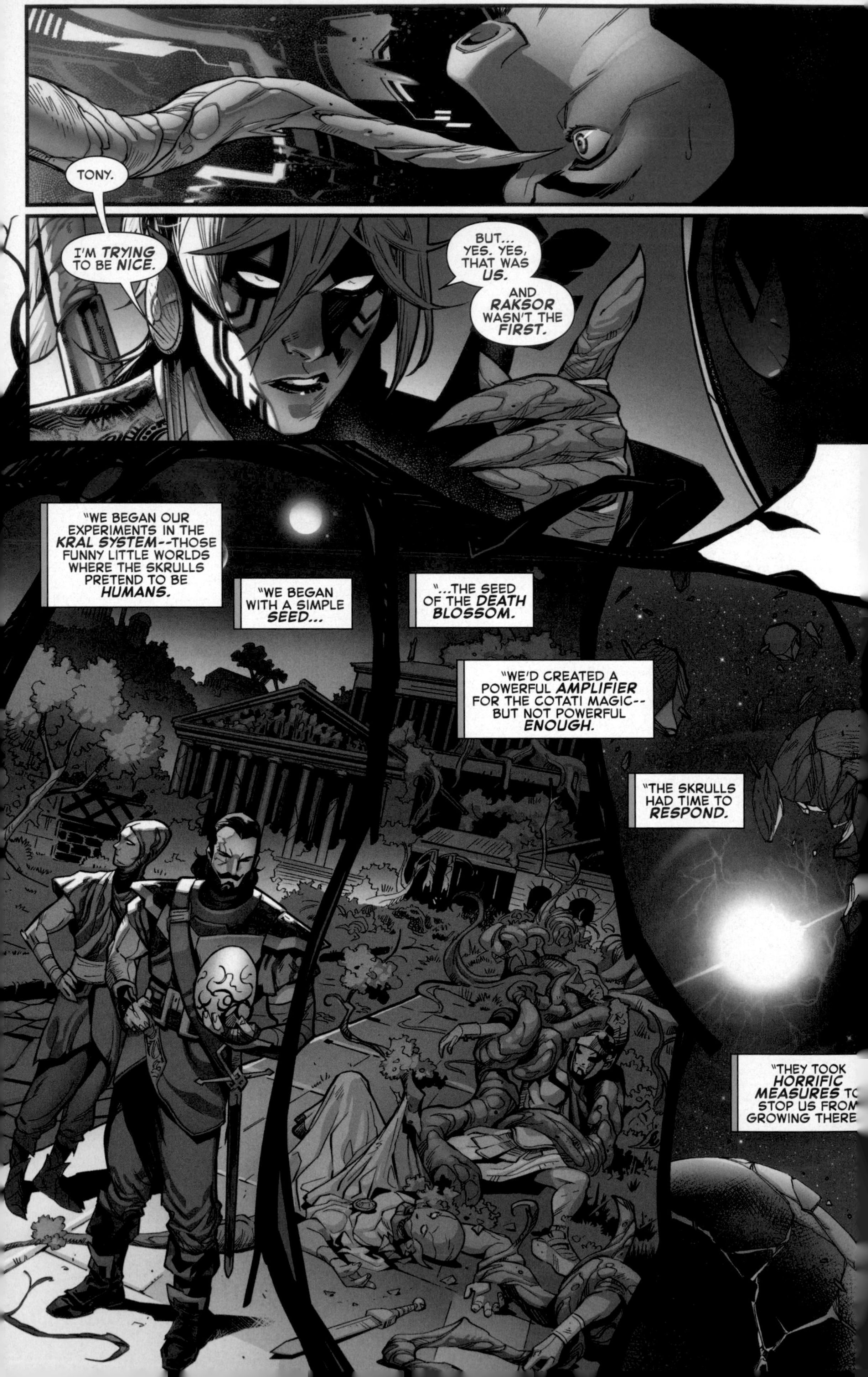

TONY.
I'M TRYING TO BE NICE.
BUT... YES. YES, THAT WAS US.
AND RAKSOR WASN'T THE FIRST.
"WE BEGAN OUR EXPERIMENTS IN THE KRAL SYSTEM--THOSE FUNNY LITTLE WORLDS WHERE THE SKRULLS PRETEND TO BE HUMANS.
"WE BEGAN WITH A SIMPLE SEED...
"...THE SEED OF THE DEATH BLOSSOM.
"WE'D CREATED A POWERFUL AMPLIFIER FOR THE COTATI MAGIC--BUT NOT POWERFUL ENOUGH.
"THE SKRULLS HAD TIME TO RESPOND.
"THEY TOOK HORRIFIC MEASURES TO STOP US FROM GROWING THERE

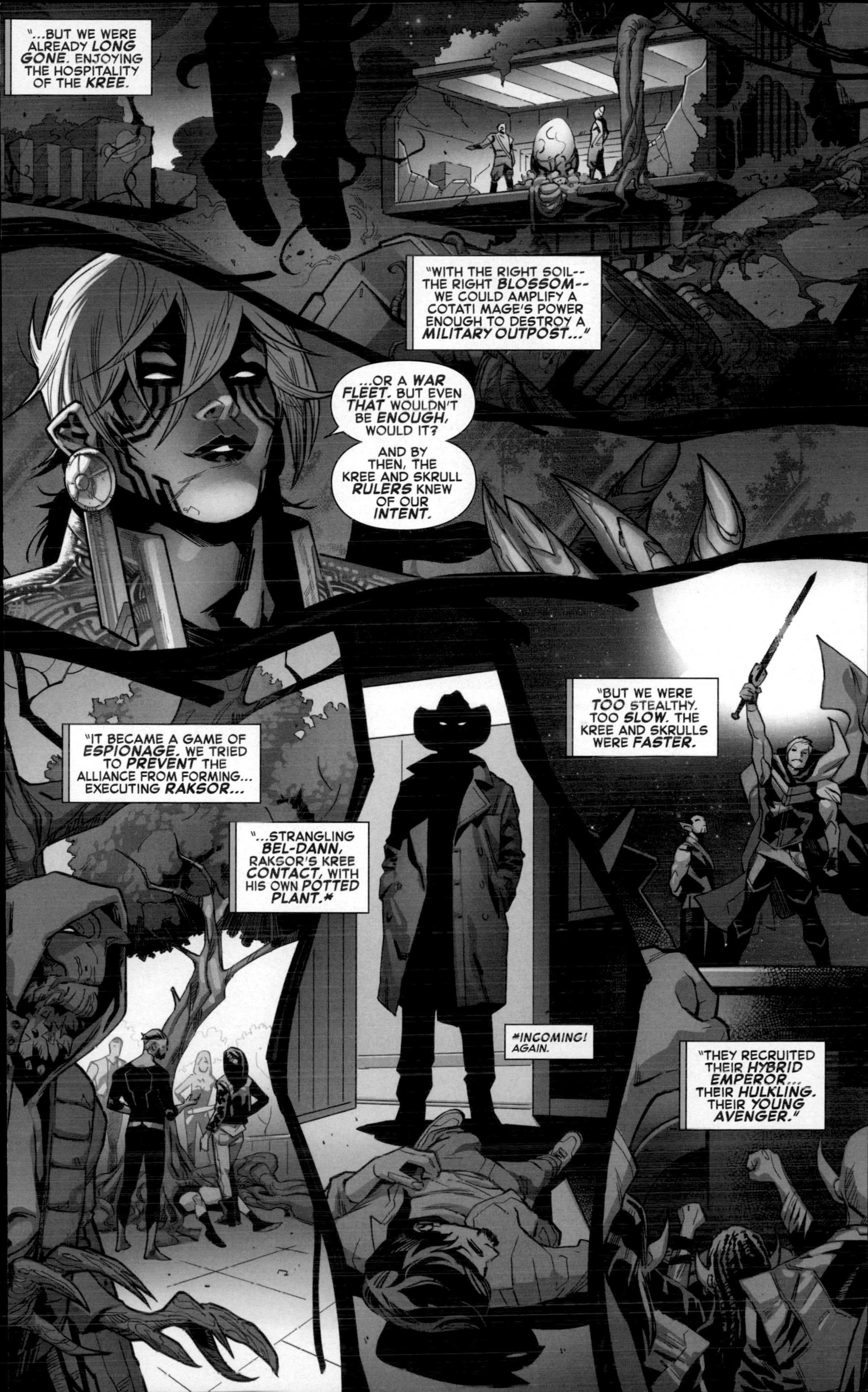
"...BUT WE WERE ALREADY LONG GONE. ENJOYING THE HOSPITALITY OF THE KREE.
"WITH THE RIGHT SOIL-- THE RIGHT BLOSSOM-- WE COULD AMPLIFY A COTATI MAGE'S POWER ENOUGH TO DESTROY A MILITARY OUTPOST..."
...OR A WAR FLEET. BUT EVEN THAT WOULDN'T BE ENOUGH, WOULD IT?
AND BY THEN, THE KREE AND SKRULL RULERS KNEW OF OUR INTENT.
"IT BECAME A GAME OF ESPIONAGE. WE TRIED TO PREVENT THE ALLIANCE FROM FORMING... EXECUTING RAKSOR...
"...STRANGLING BEL-DANN, RAKSOR'S KREE CONTACT, WITH HIS OWN POTTED PLANT.*
*INCOMING! AGAIN.
"BUT WE WERE TOO STEALTHY. TOO SLOW. THE KREE AND SKRULLS WERE FASTER.
"THEY RECRUITED THEIR HYBRID EMPEROR... THEIR HULKLING. THEIR YOUNG AVENGER."

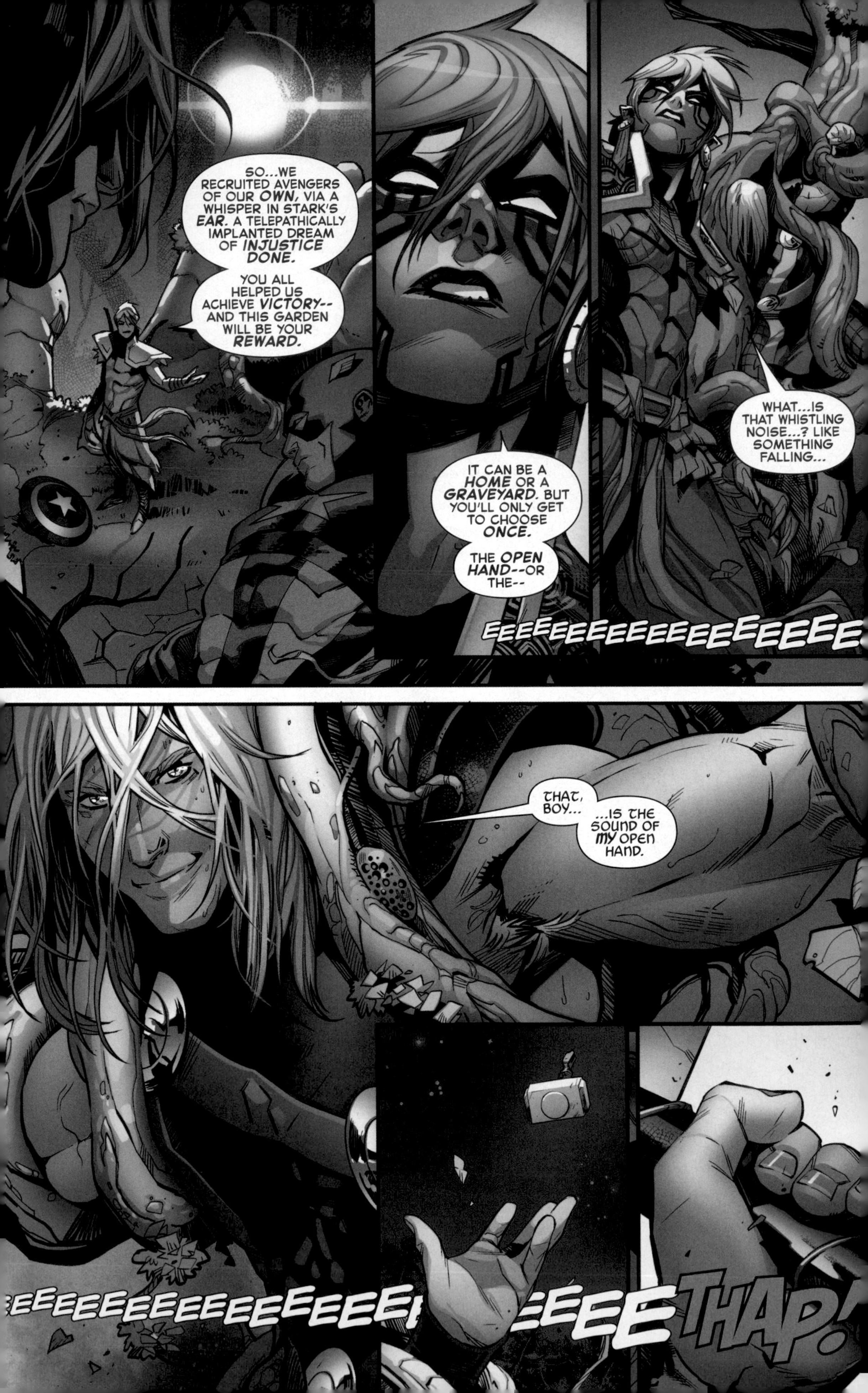
SO...WE RECRUITED AVENGERS OF OUR OWN, VIA A WHISPER IN STARK'S EAR. A TELEPATHICALLY IMPLANTED DREAM OF INJUSTICE DONE.
YOU ALL HELPED US ACHIEVE VICTORY-- AND THIS GARDEN WILL BE YOUR REWARD.
IT CAN BE A HOME OR A GRAVEYARD. BUT YOU'LL ONLY GET TO CHOOSE ONCE.
THE OPEN HAND--OR THE--
WHAT...IS THAT WHISTLING NOISE...? LIKE SOMETHING FALLING...
EEEEEEEEEEEEEEEEEEE
THAT, BOY...
...IS THE SOUND OF MY OPEN HAND.
EEEEEEEEEEEEEEEEEEE
EEEEEE
THAP!

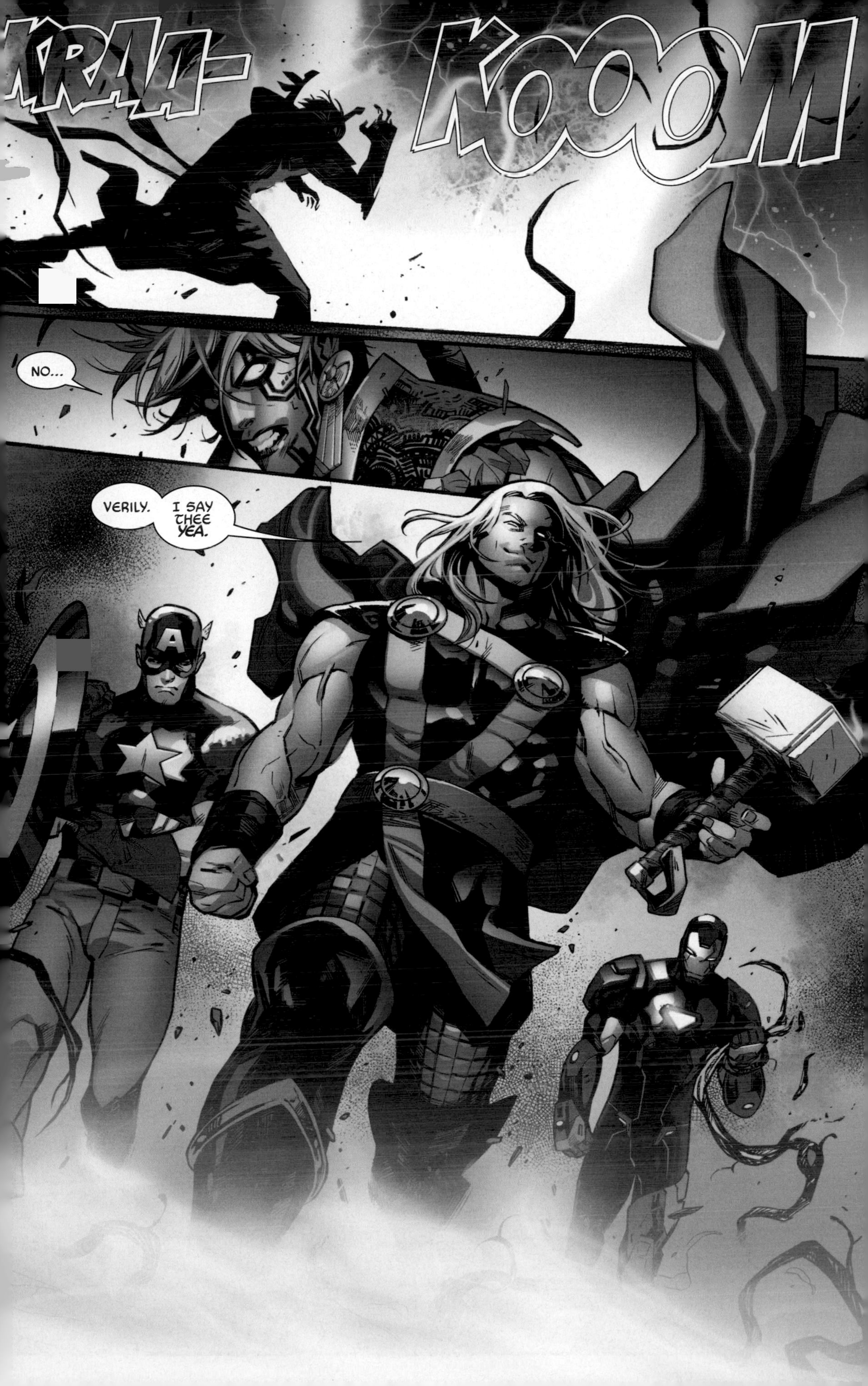
KRAA-
KOOOM
NO...
VERILY.
I SAY THEE YEA.

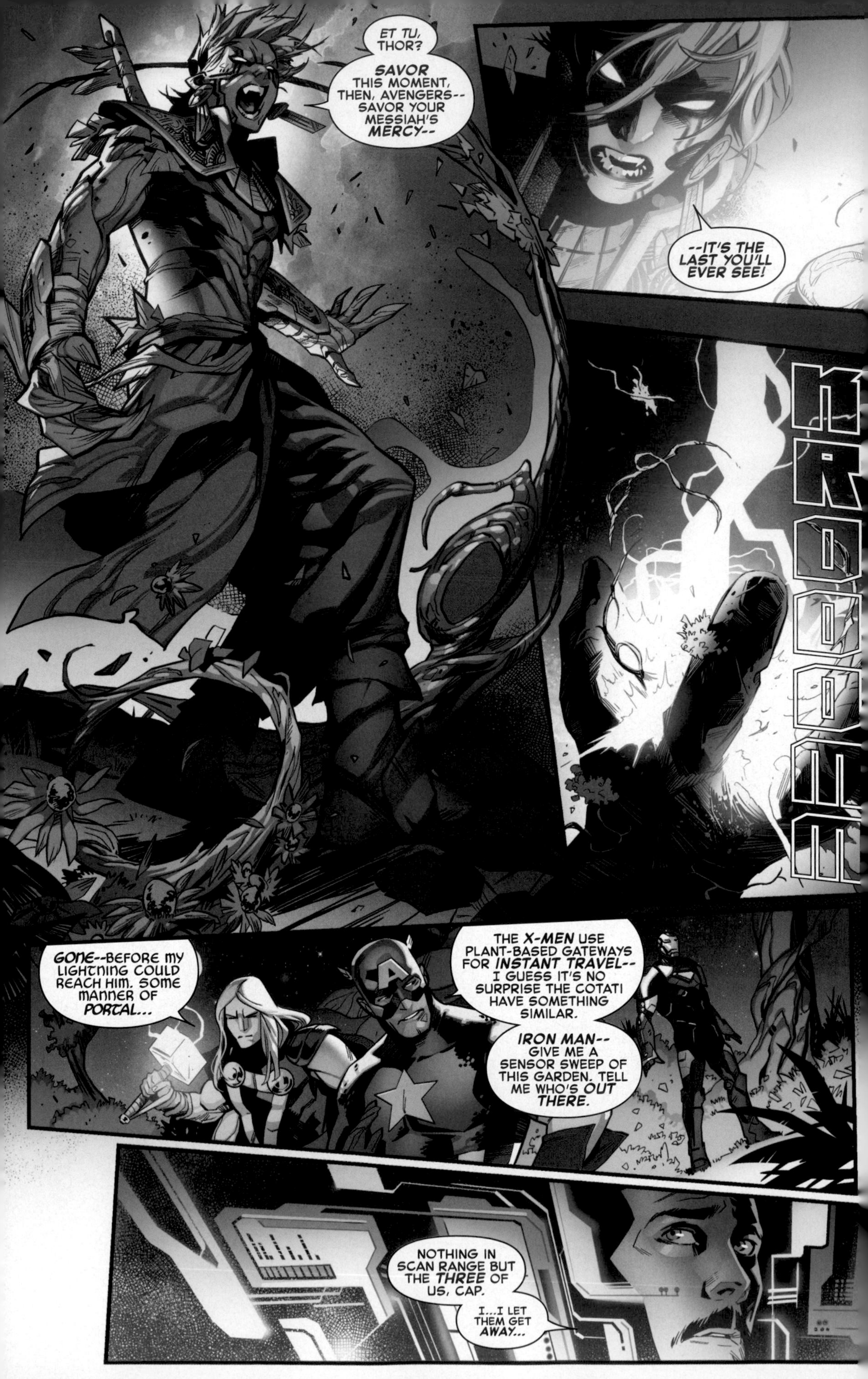
ET TU, THOR?
SAVOR THIS MOMENT, THEN, AVENGERS-- SAVOR YOUR MESSIAH'S MERCY--
--IT'S THE LAST YOU'LL EVER SEE!
GONE--BEFORE MY LIGHTNING COULD REACH HIM. SOME MANNER OF PORTAL...
THE X-MEN USE PLANT-BASED GATEWAYS FOR INSTANT TRAVEL-- I GUESS IT'S NO SURPRISE THE COTATI HAVE SOMETHING SIMILAR.
IRON MAN-- GIVE ME A SENSOR SWEEP OF THIS GARDEN. TELL ME WHO'S OUT THERE.
NOTHING IN SCAN RANGE BUT THE THREE OF US, CAP.
I...I LET THEM GET AWAY...

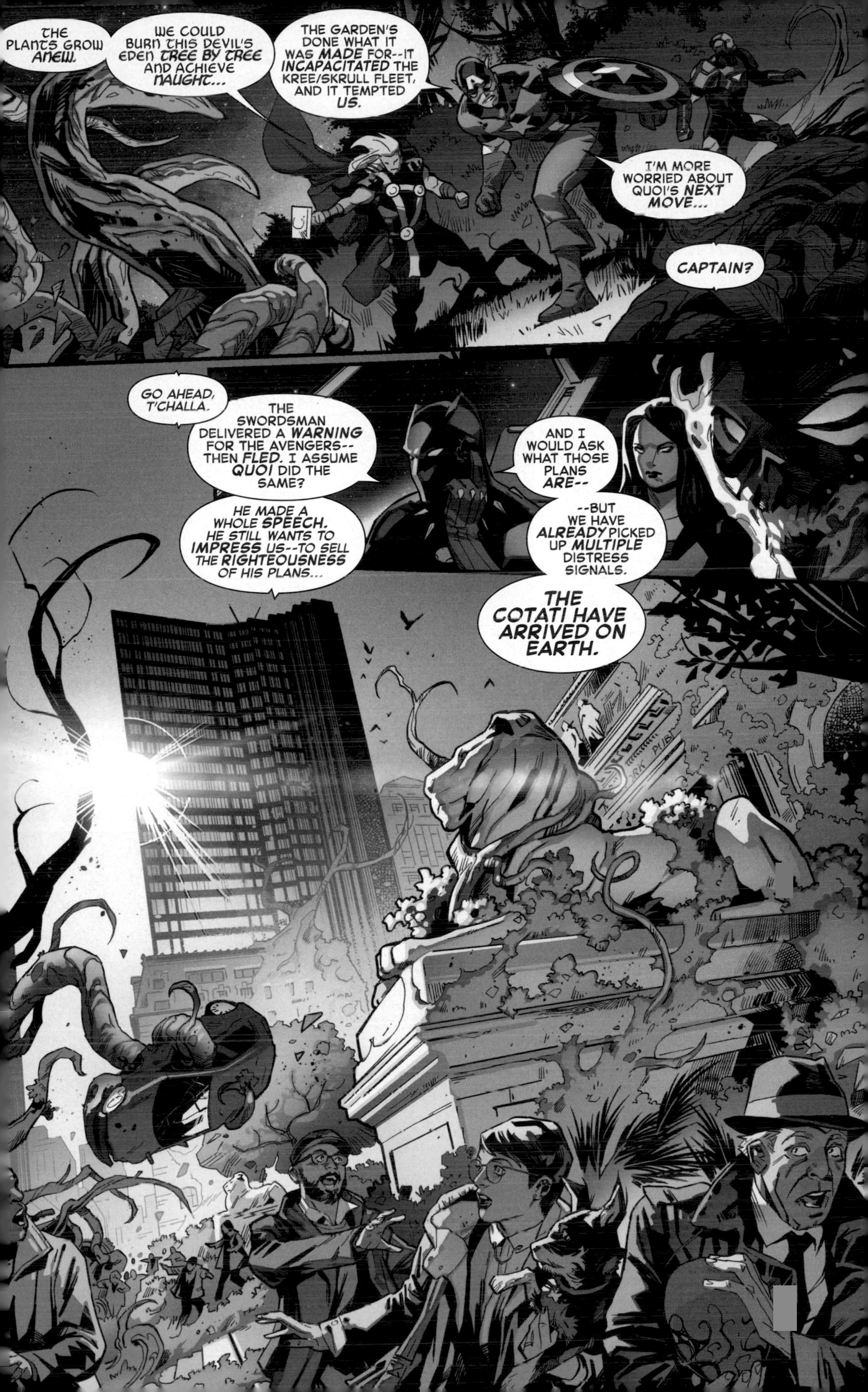
THE PLANTS GROW ANEW.
WE COULD BURN THIS DEVIL'S EDEN TREE BY TREE AND ACHIEVE NAUGHT...
THE GARDEN'S DONE WHAT IT WAS MADE FOR--IT INCAPACITATED THE KREE/SKRULL FLEET, AND IT TEMPTED US.
I'M MORE WORRIED ABOUT QUOI'S NEXT MOVE...
CAPTAIN?
GO AHEAD, T'CHALLA.
THE SWORDSMAN DELIVERED A WARNING FOR THE AVENGERS--THEN FLED. I ASSUME QUOI DID THE SAME?
HE MADE A WHOLE SPEECH. HE STILL WANTS TO IMPRESS US--TO SELL THE RIGHTEOUSNESS OF HIS PLANS...
AND I WOULD ASK WHAT THOSE PLANS ARE--
--BUT WE HAVE ALREADY PICKED UP MULTIPLE DISTRESS SIGNALS.
THE COTATI HAVE ARRIVED ON EARTH.

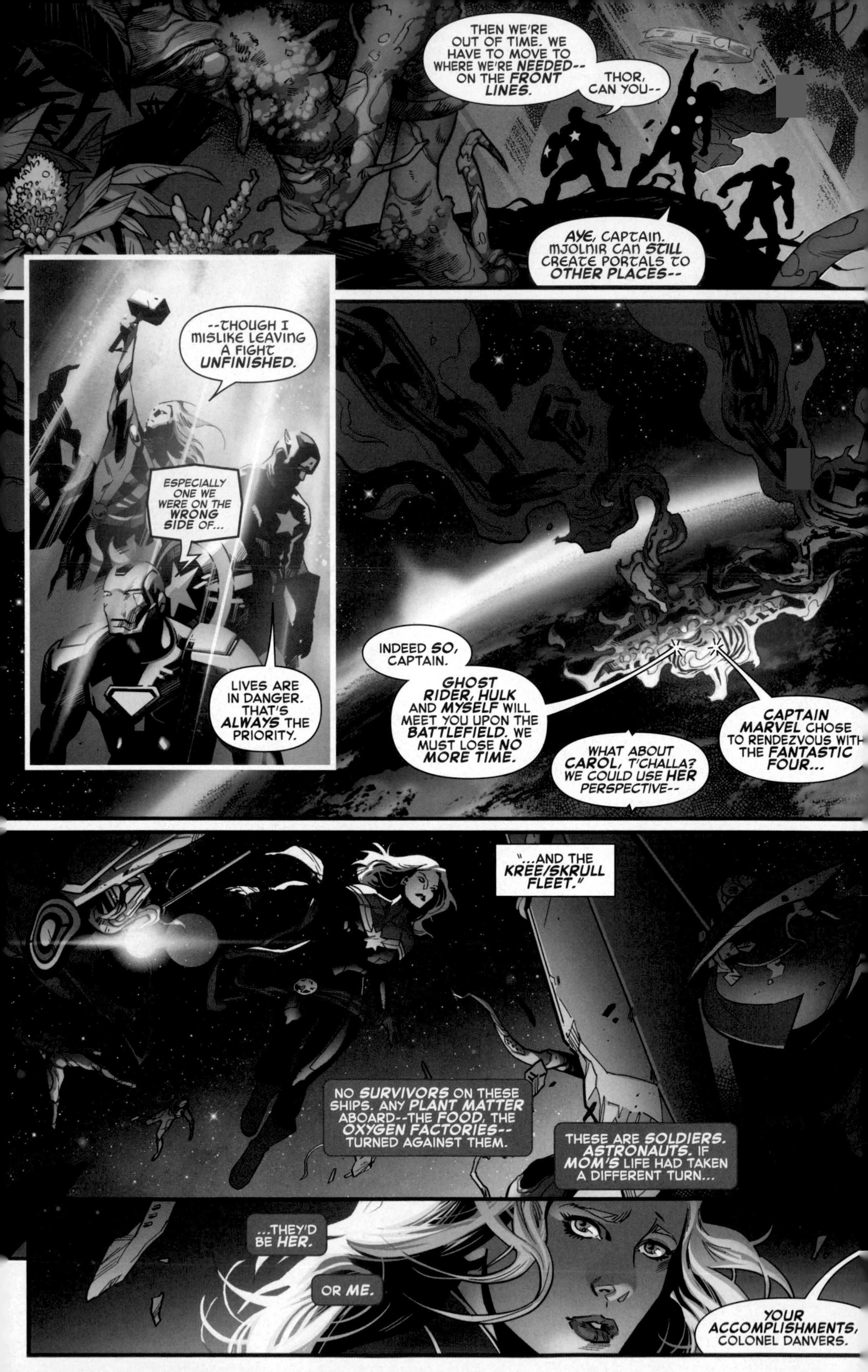
THEN WE'RE OUT OF TIME. WE HAVE TO MOVE TO WHERE WE'RE NEEDED-- ON THE FRONT LINES.
THOR, CAN YOU--
AYE, CAPTAIN. MJOLNIR CAN STILL CREATE PORTALS TO OTHER PLACES--
--THOUGH I MISLIKE LEAVING A FIGHT UNFINISHED.
ESPECIALLY ONE WE WERE ON THE WRONG SIDE OF...
LIVES ARE IN DANGER. THAT'S ALWAYS THE PRIORITY.
INDEED SO, CAPTAIN.
GHOST RIDER, HULK AND MYSELF WILL MEET YOU UPON THE BATTLEFIELD. WE MUST LOSE NO MORE TIME.
WHAT ABOUT CAROL, T'CHALLA? WE COULD USE HER PERSPECTIVE--
CAPTAIN MARVEL CHOSE TO RENDEZVOUS WITH THE FANTASTIC FOUR...
"...AND THE KREE/SKRULL FLEET."
NO SURVIVORS ON THESE SHIPS. ANY PLANT MATTER ABOARD--THE FOOD, THE OXYGEN FACTORIES-- TURNED AGAINST THEM.
THESE ARE SOLDIERS. ASTRONAUTS. IF MOM'S LIFE HAD TAKEN A DIFFERENT TURN...
...THEY'D BE HER.
OR ME.
YOUR ACCOMPLISHMENTS, COLONEL DANVERS.

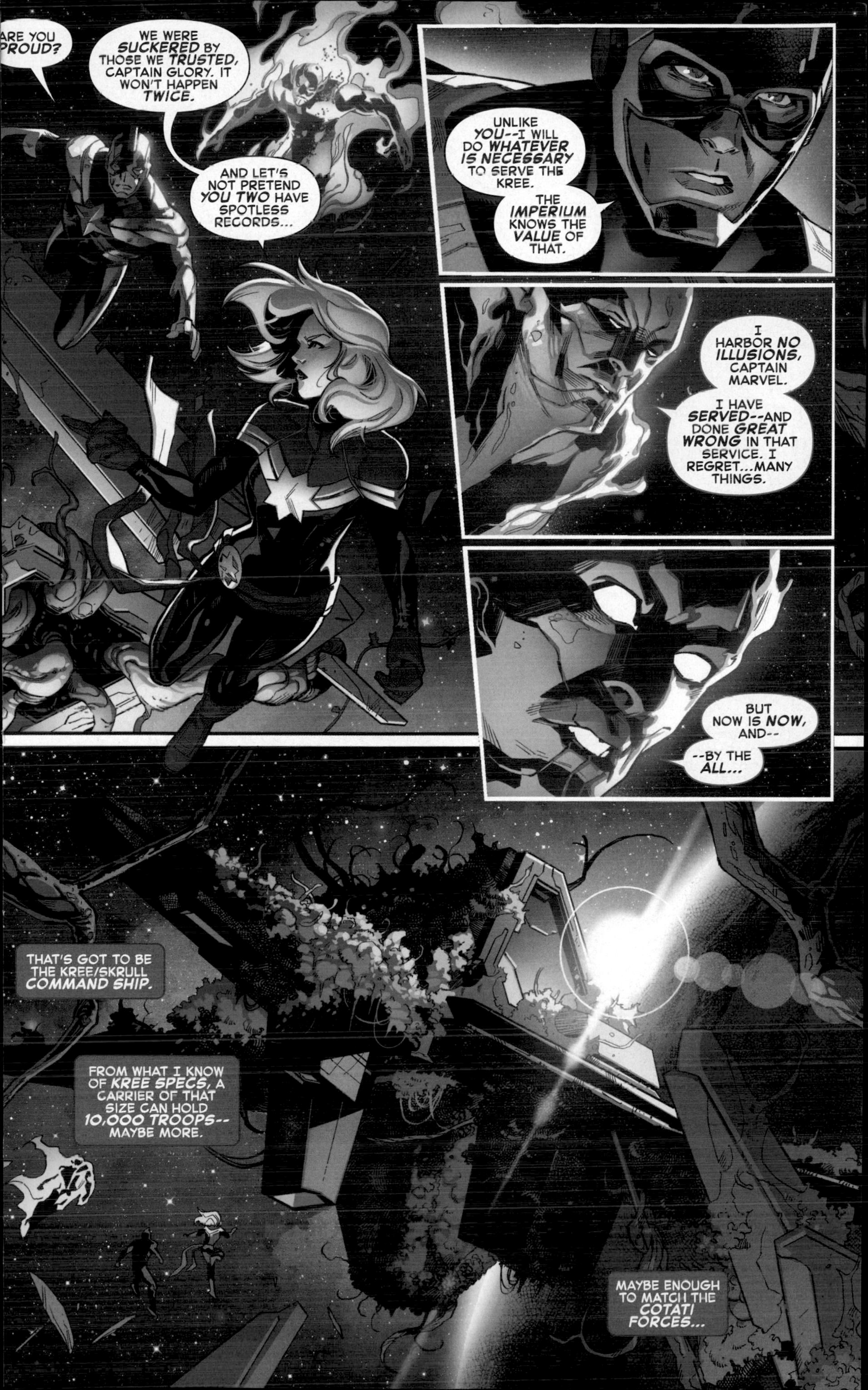

ARE YOU PROUD?
WE WERE SUCKERED BY THOSE WE TRUSTED, CAPTAIN GLORY. IT WON'T HAPPEN TWICE.
AND LET'S NOT PRETEND YOU TWO HAVE SPOTLESS RECORDS...
UNLIKE YOU--I WILL DO WHATEVER IS NECESSARY TO SERVE THE KREE.
THE IMPERIUM KNOWS THE VALUE OF THAT.
I HARBOR NO ILLUSIONS, CAPTAIN MARVEL.
I HAVE SERVED--AND DONE GREAT WRONG IN THAT SERVICE. I REGRET...MANY THINGS.
BUT NOW IS NOW, AND--
--BY THE ALL...
THAT'S GOT TO BE THE KREE/SKRULL COMMAND SHIP.
FROM WHAT I KNOW OF KREE SPECS, A CARRIER OF THAT SIZE CAN HOLD 10,000 TROOPS--MAYBE MORE.
MAYBE ENOUGH TO MATCH THE COTATI FORCES...

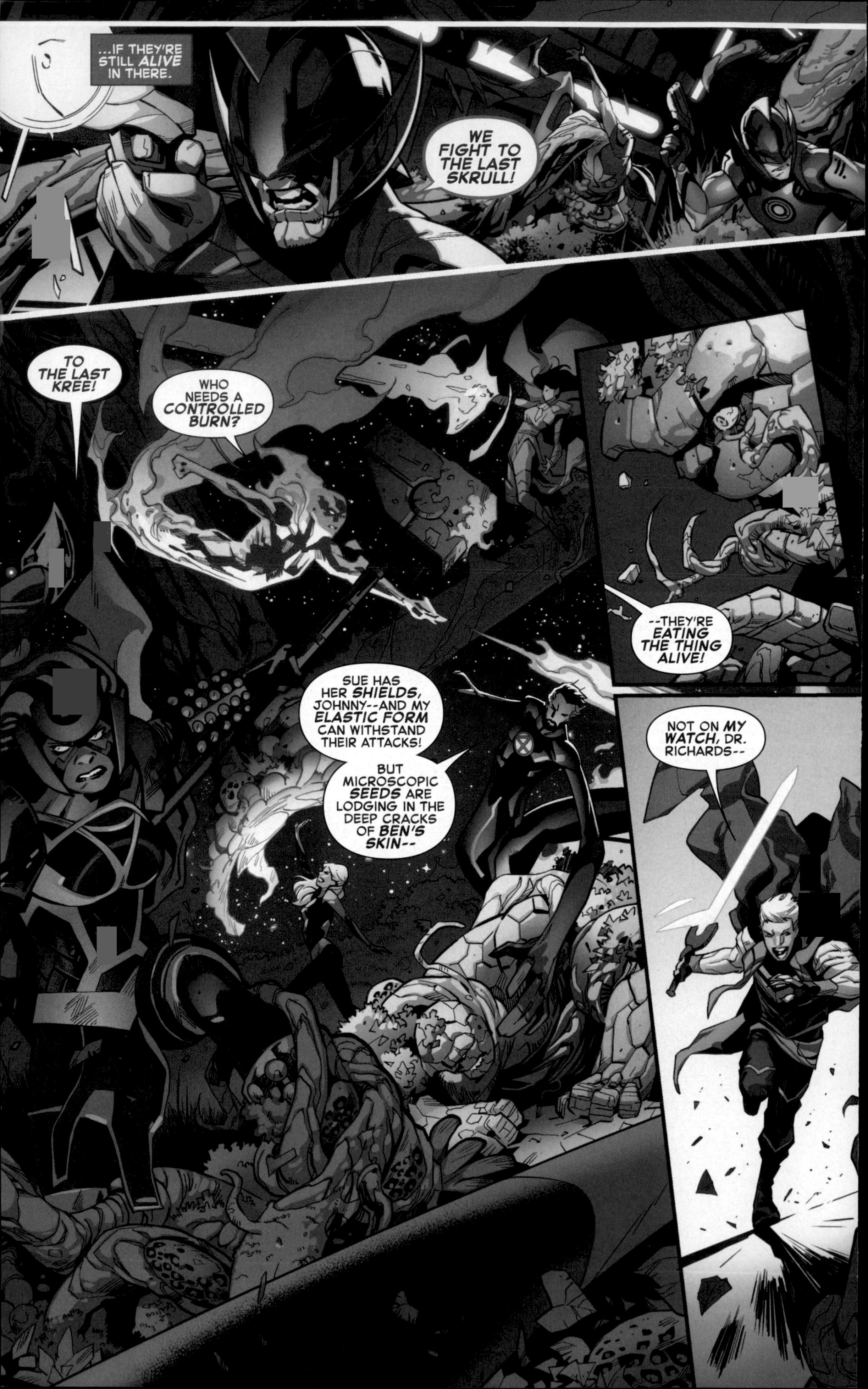
...IF THEY'RE STILL ALIVE IN THERE.
WE FIGHT TO THE LAST SKRULL!
TO THE LAST KREE!
WHO NEEDS A CONTROLLED BURN?
--THEY'RE EATING THE THING ALIVE!
SUE HAS HER SHIELDS, JOHNNY--AND MY ELASTIC FORM CAN WITHSTAND THEIR ATTACKS!
BUT MICROSCOPIC SEEDS ARE LODGING IN THE DEEP CRACKS OF BEN'S SKIN--
NOT ON MY WATCH, DR. RICHARDS--

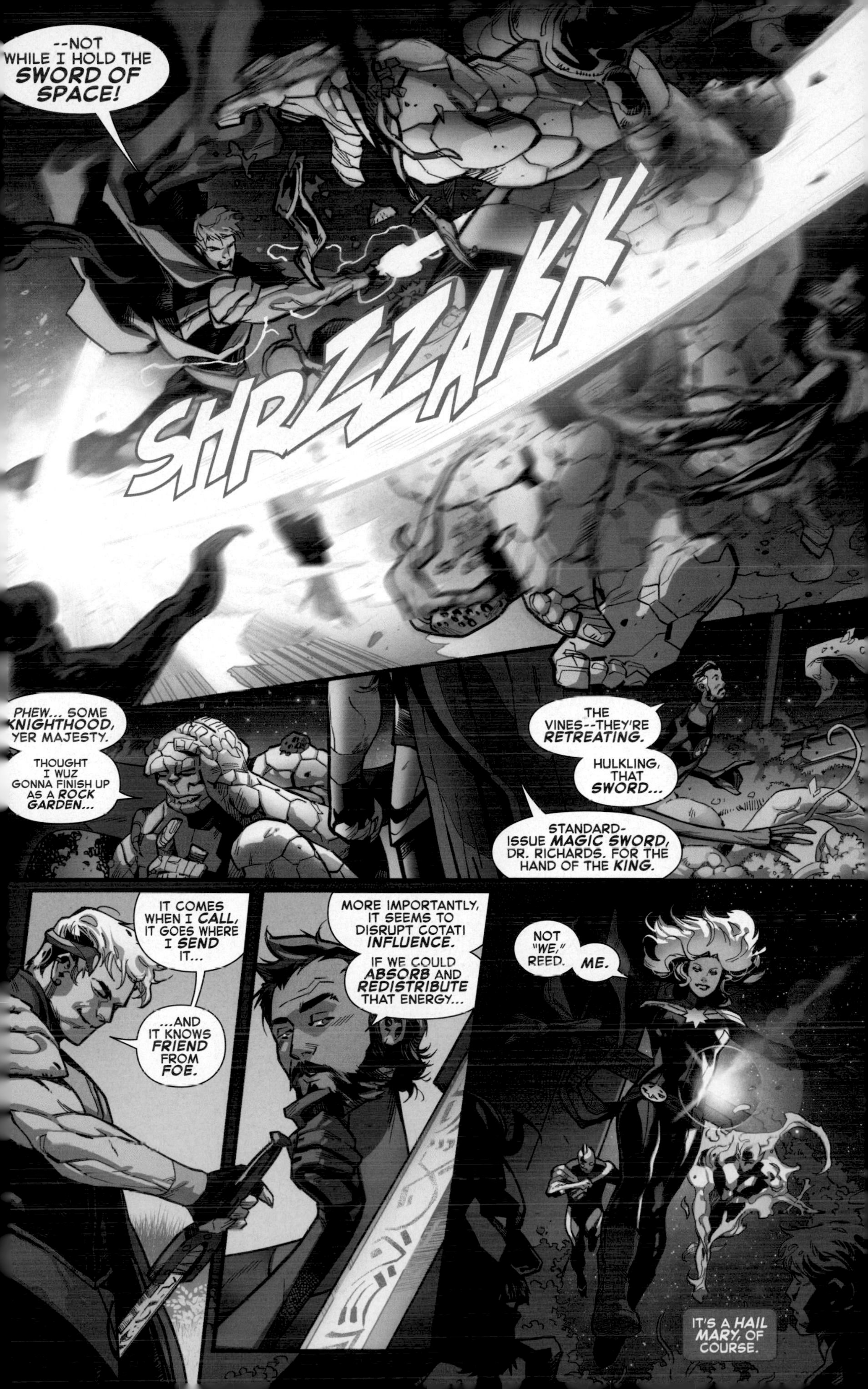
--NOT WHILE I HOLD THE SWORD OF SPACE!
SHRZZZAKK
PHEW... SOME KNIGHTHOOD, YER MAJESTY.
THOUGHT I WUZ GONNA FINISH UP AS A ROCK GARDEN...
THE VINES--THEY'RE RETREATING.
HULKLING, THAT SWORD...
STANDARD-ISSUE MAGIC SWORD, DR. RICHARDS. FOR THE HAND OF THE KING.
IT COMES WHEN I CALL, IT GOES WHERE I SEND IT...
...AND IT KNOWS FRIEND FROM FOE.
MORE IMPORTANTLY, IT SEEMS TO DISRUPT COTATI INFLUENCE.
IF WE COULD ABSORB AND REDISTRIBUTE THAT ENERGY...
NOT "WE," REED.
ME.
IT'S A HAIL MARY, OF COURSE.

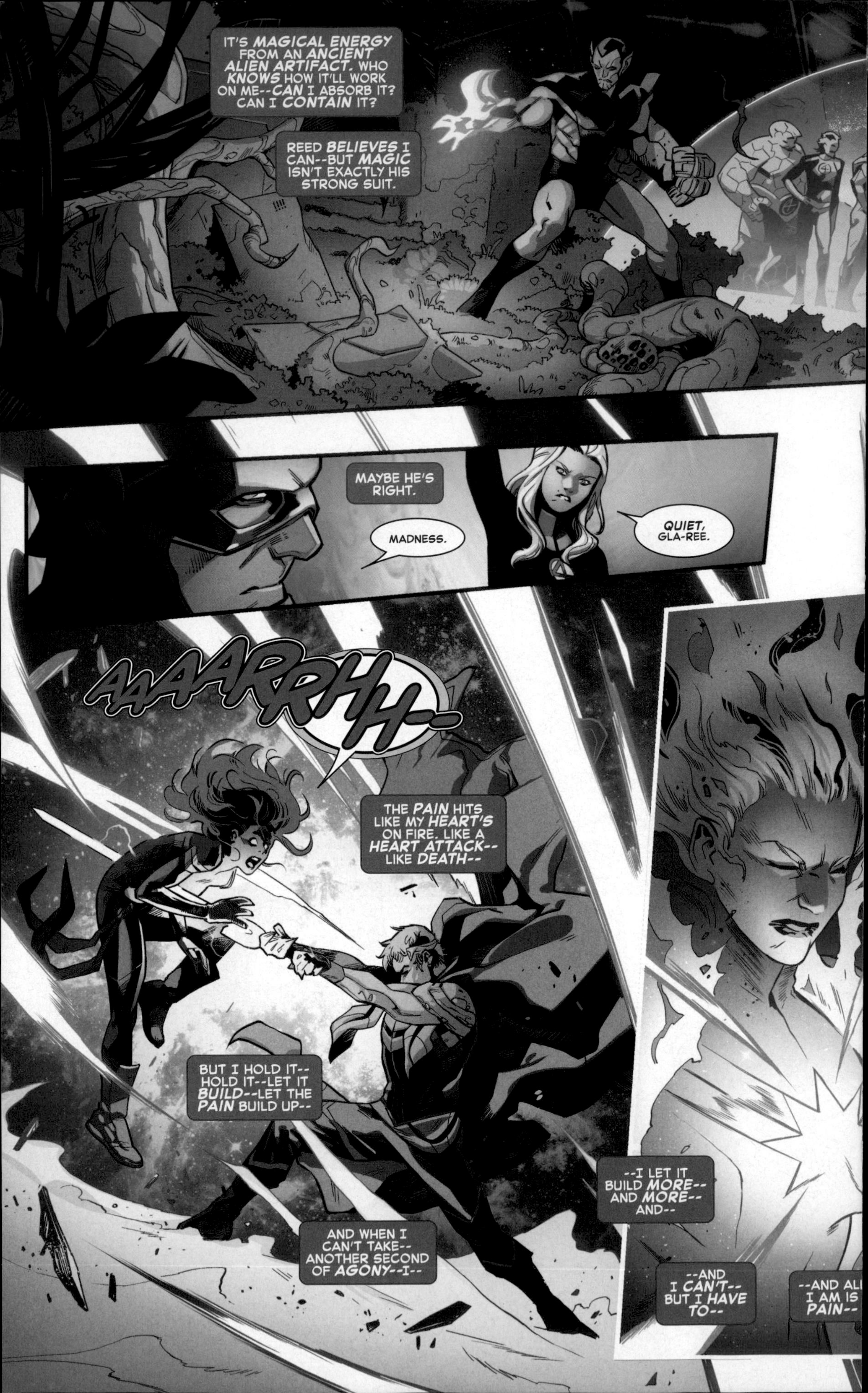
IT'S MAGICAL ENERGY FROM AN ANCIENT ALIEN ARTIFACT. WHO KNOWS HOW IT'LL WORK ON ME--CAN I ABSORB IT? CAN I CONTAIN IT?
REED BELIEVES I CAN--BUT MAGIC ISN'T EXACTLY HIS STRONG SUIT.
MAYBE HE'S RIGHT.
MADNESS.
QUIET, GLA-REE.
AAAARRHH--
THE PAIN HITS LIKE MY HEART'S ON FIRE. LIKE A HEART ATTACK-- LIKE DEATH--
BUT I HOLD IT-- HOLD IT--LET IT BUILD--LET THE PAIN BUILD UP--
AND WHEN I CAN'T TAKE-- ANOTHER SECOND OF AGONY--I--
--I LET IT BUILD MORE-- AND MORE-- AND--
--AND I CAN'T-- BUT I HAVE TO--
--AND AL I AM IS PAIN--

...READY?
HULKLING, ON THE OTHER HAND, KNOWS THE SWORD--AND THE MAGIC--BETTER THAN ANYONE ALIVE.
HE LOOKS WORRIED.
AND THEN
THE PAIN
EXPLODES
AND I'M DEAD.

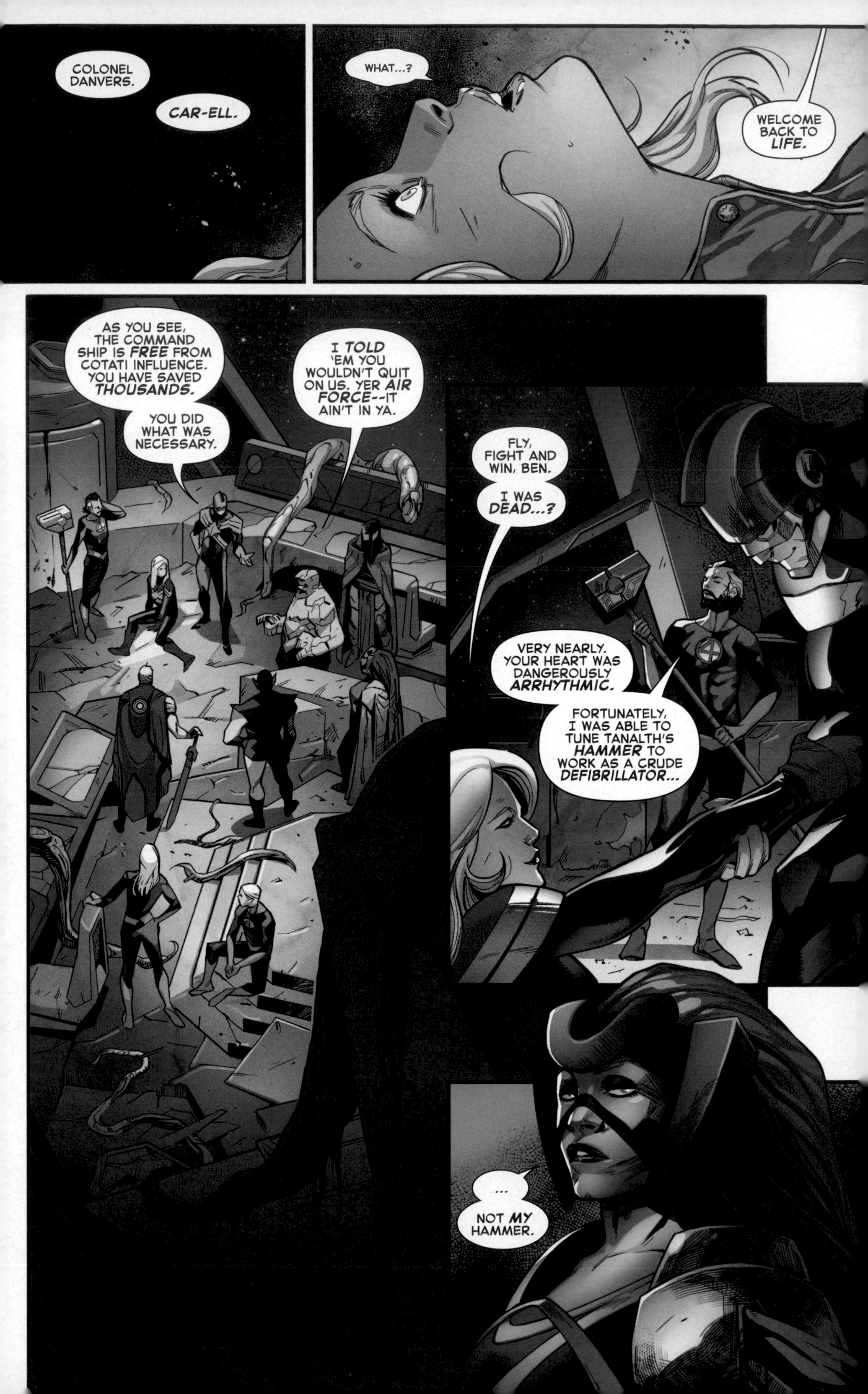
COLONEL DANVERS.
CAR-ELL.
WHAT...?
WELCOME BACK TO LIFE.
AS YOU SEE, THE COMMAND SHIP IS FREE FROM COTATI INFLUENCE. YOU HAVE SAVED THOUSANDS.
YOU DID WHAT WAS NECESSARY.
I TOLD 'EM YOU WOULDN'T QUIT ON US. YER AIR FORCE--IT AIN'T IN YA.
FLY, FIGHT AND WIN, BEN.
I WAS DEAD...?
VERY NEARLY. YOUR HEART WAS DANGEROUSLY ARRHYTHMIC.
FORTUNATELY, I WAS ABLE TO TUNE TANALTH'S HAMMER TO WORK AS A CRUDE DEFIBRILLATOR...
...
NOT MY HAMMER.

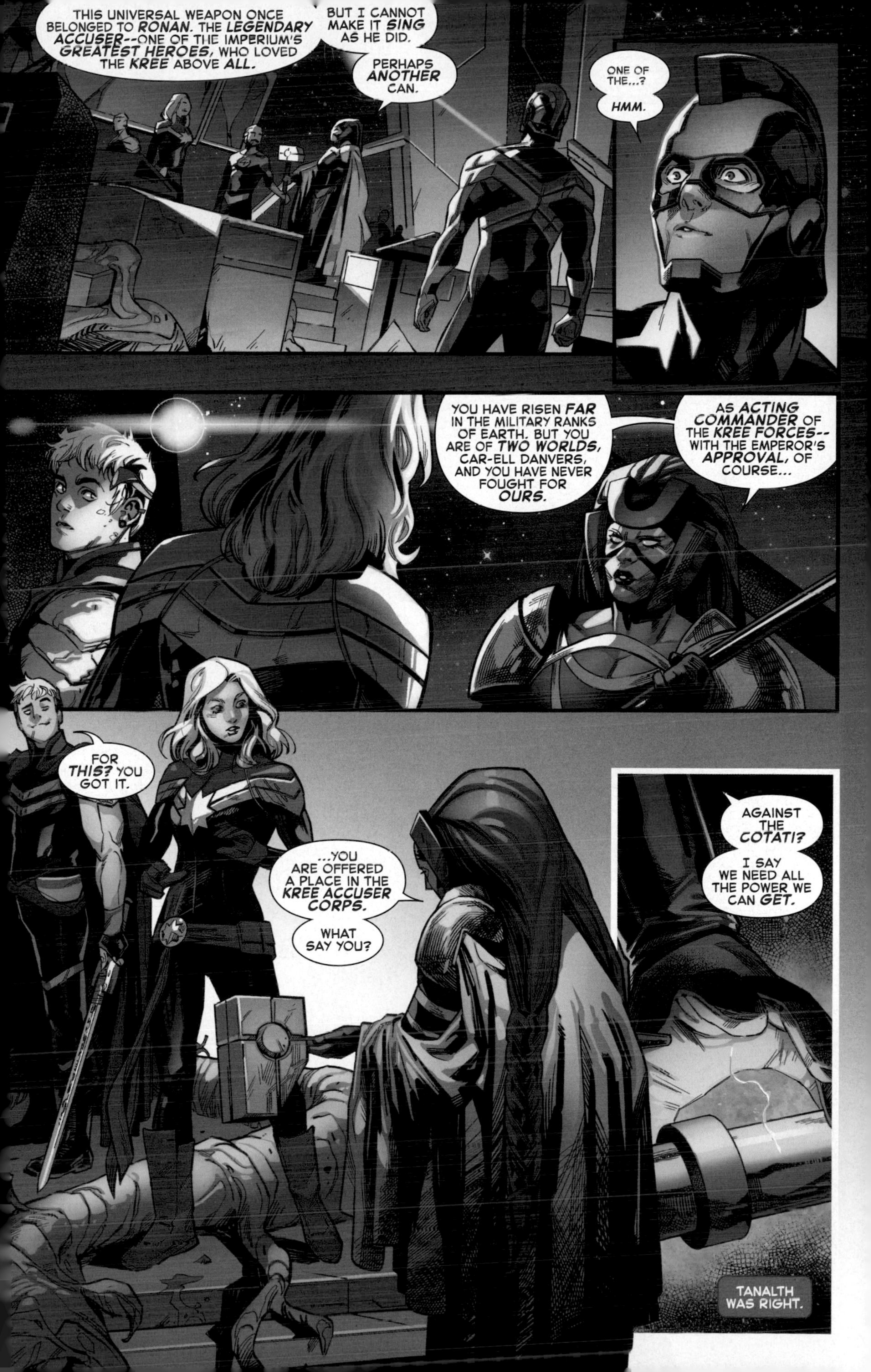
THIS UNIVERSAL WEAPON ONCE BELONGED TO RONAN. THE LEGENDARY ACCUSER--ONE OF THE IMPERIUM'S GREATEST HEROES, WHO LOVED THE KREE ABOVE ALL.
BUT I CANNOT MAKE IT SING AS HE DID.
PERHAPS ANOTHER CAN.
ONE OF THE...?
HMM.
YOU HAVE RISEN FAR IN THE MILITARY RANKS OF EARTH. BUT YOU ARE OF TWO WORLDS, CAR-ELL DANVERS, AND YOU HAVE NEVER FOUGHT FOR OURS.
AS ACTING COMMANDER OF THE KREE FORCES--WITH THE EMPEROR'S APPROVAL, OF COURSE...
...YOU ARE OFFERED A PLACE IN THE KREE ACCUSER CORPS.
WHAT SAY YOU?
FOR THIS? YOU GOT IT.
AGAINST THE COTATI?
I SAY WE NEED ALL THE POWER WE CAN GET.
TANALTH WAS RIGHT.

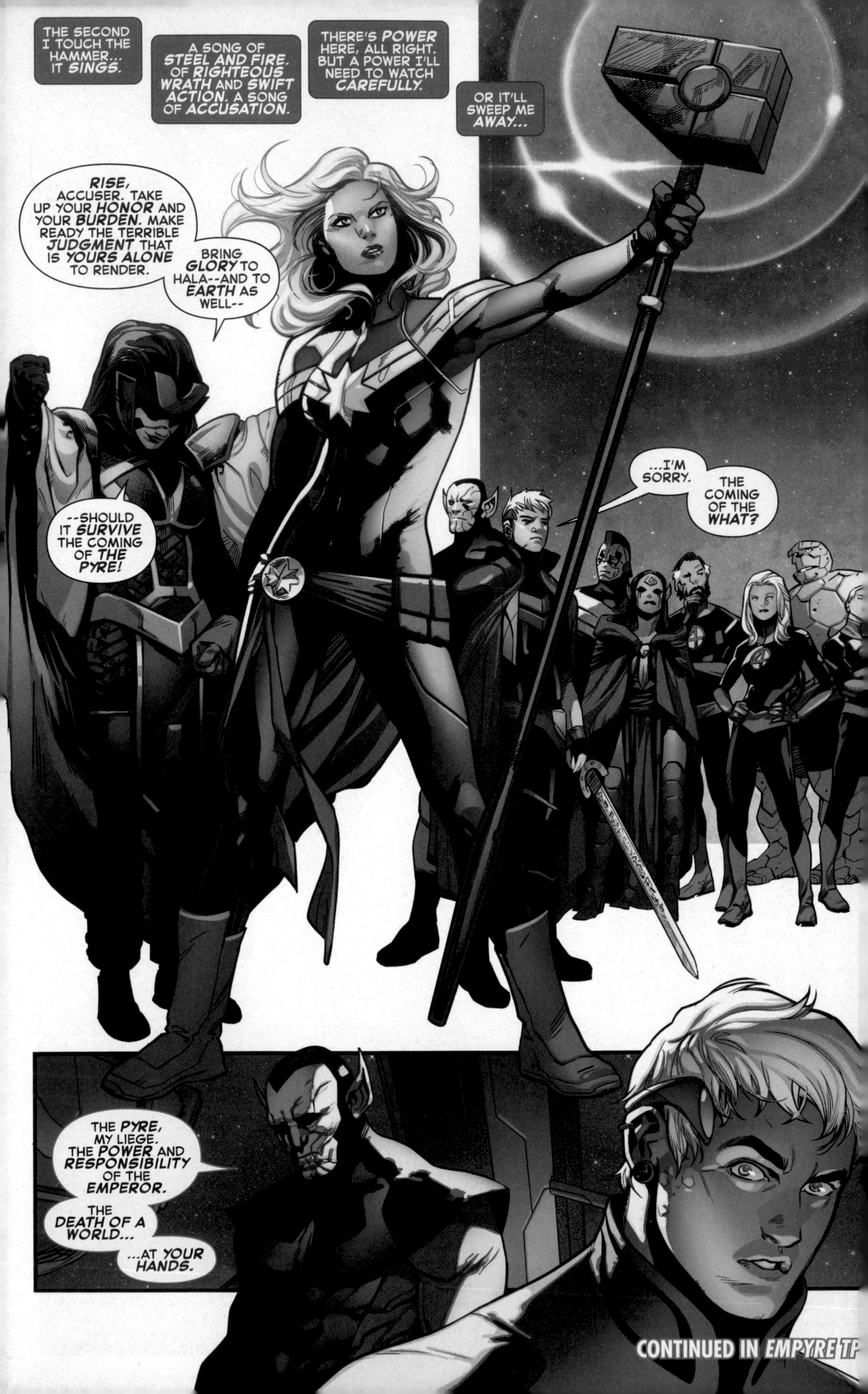
THE SECOND I TOUCH THE HAMMER... IT SINGS.
A SONG OF STEEL AND FIRE. OF RIGHTEOUS WRATH AND SWIFT ACTION. A SONG OF ACCUSATION.
THERE'S POWER HERE, ALL RIGHT. BUT A POWER I'LL NEED TO WATCH CAREFULLY.
OR IT'LL SWEEP ME AWAY...
RISE, ACCUSER. TAKE UP YOUR HONOR AND YOUR BURDEN. MAKE READY THE TERRIBLE JUDGMENT THAT IS YOURS ALONE TO RENDER.
BRING GLORY TO HALA--AND TO EARTH AS WELL--
--SHOULD IT SURVIVE THE COMING OF THE PYRE!
...I'M SORRY.
THE COMING OF THE WHAT?
THE PYRE, MY LIEGE. THE POWER AND RESPONSIBILITY OF THE EMPEROR.
THE DEATH OF A WORLD...
...AT YOUR HANDS.
CONTINUED IN EMPYRE TP

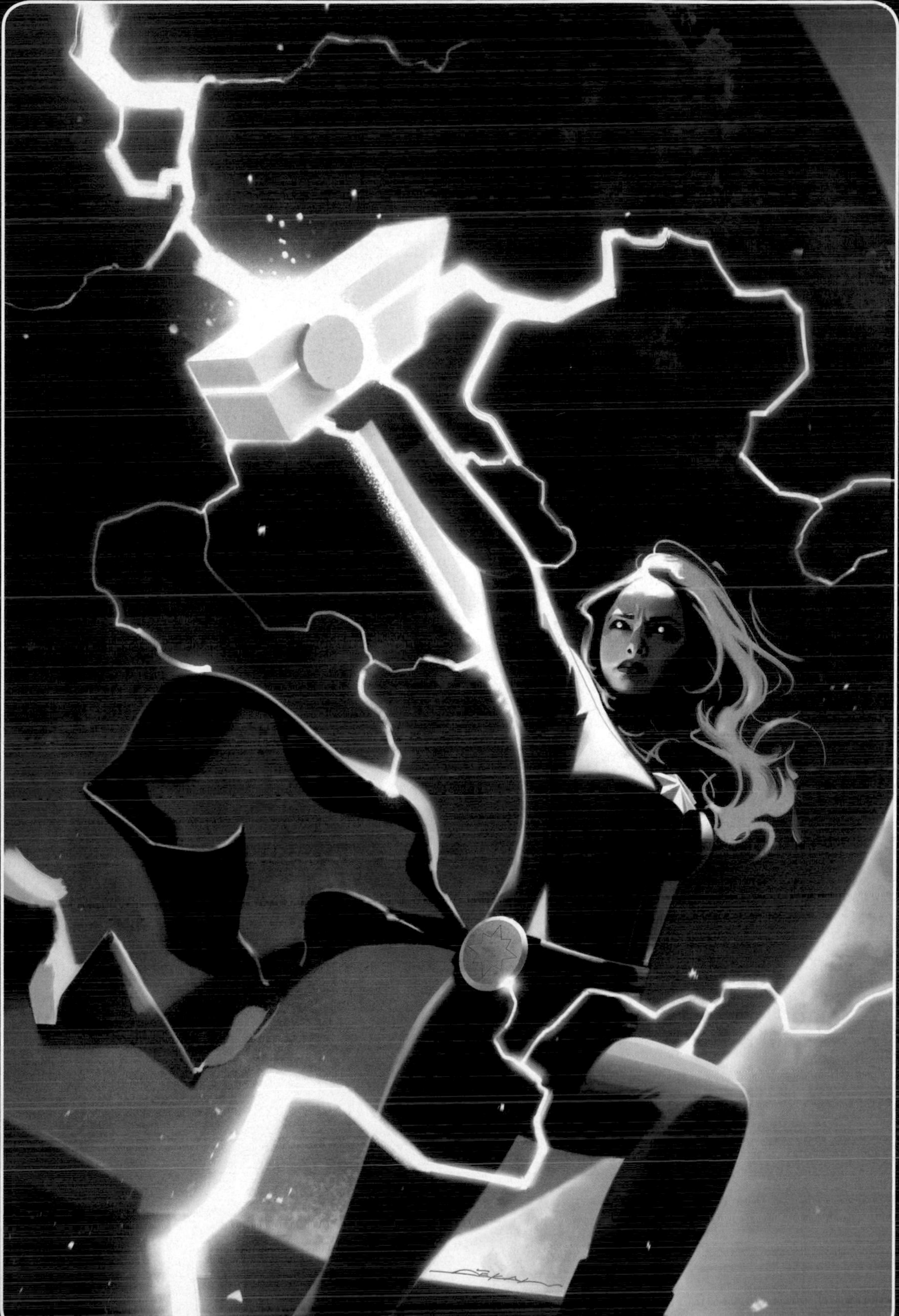

JEFF DEKAL
20 VARIANT

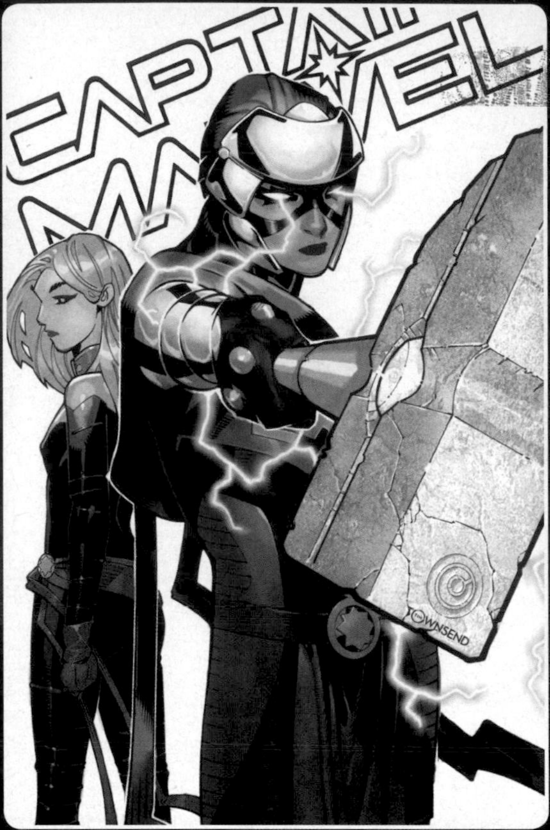
TOWNSEND

CHRIS BACHALO & TIM TOWNSEND
21 VARIANT

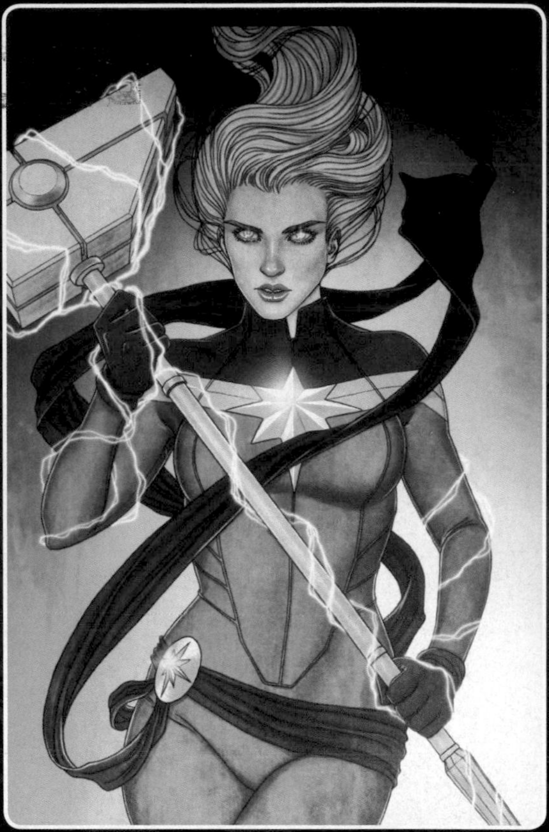

JENNY FRISON
21 VARIANT

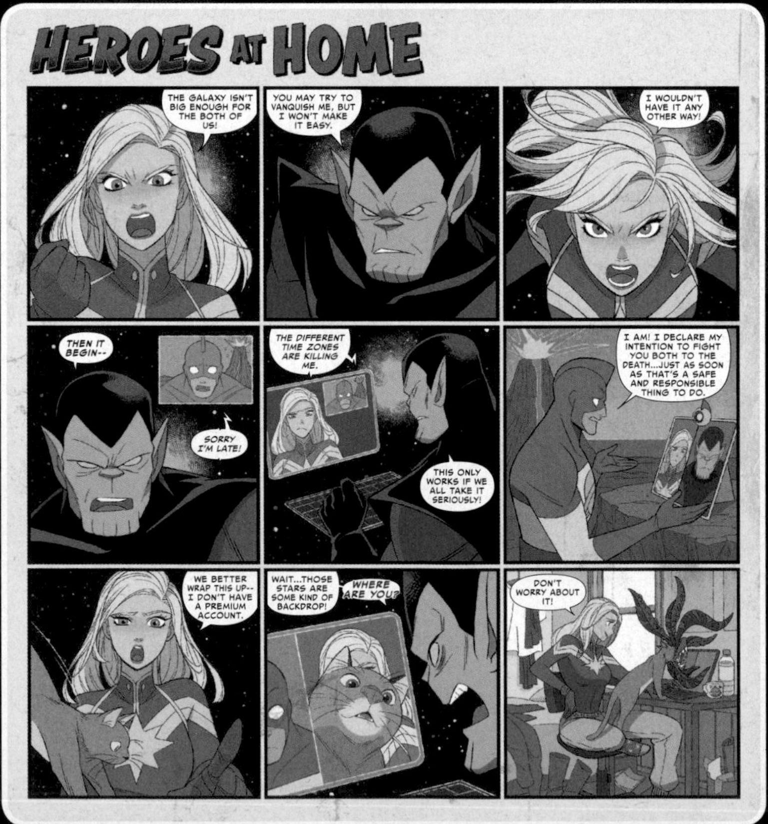
HEROES AT HOME
THE GALAXY ISN'T BIG ENOUGH FOR THE BOTH OF US!
YOU MAY TRY TO VANQUISH ME, BUT I WON'T MAKE IT EASY.
I WOULDN'T HAVE IT ANY OTHER WAY!
THEN IT BEGIN--
SORRY I'M LATE!
THE DIFFERENT TIME ZONES ARE KILLING ME.
THIS ONLY WORKS IF WE ALL TAKE IT SERIOUSLY!
I AM! I DECLARE MY INTENTION TO FIGHT YOU BOTH TO THE DEATH...JUST AS SOON AS THAT'S A SAFE AND RESPONSIBLE THING TO DO.
WE BETTER WRAP THIS UP-- I DON'T HAVE A PREMIUM ACCOUNT.
WAIT...THOSE STARS ARE SOME KIND OF BACKDROP!
WHERE ARE YOU?
DON'T WORRY ABOUT IT!

GURIHIRU & ZEB WELLS
21 HEROES AT HOME VARIANT